The New Science
of Retailing

The New Science of Retailing

How Analytics Are Transforming the
Supply Chain and Improving Performance

Marshall Fisher
Ananth Raman

Harvard Business Press
Boston, Massachusetts

No part of this publication may be reproduced, stored in or introduced into a retrieval system, or transmitted, in any form, or by any means (electronic, mechanical, photo-copying, recording, or otherwise), without the prior permission of the publisher. Requests for permission should be directed to permissions@hbsp.harvard.edu, or mailed to Permissions, Harvard Business School Publishing, 60 Harvard Way, Boston, Massachusetts 02163.

Library of Congress Cataloging-in-Publication Data

Fisher, Marshall L.
The new science of retailing : a how analytics are transforming the supply chain and improving performance / Marshall Fisher and Ananth Raman.
    p. cm.
ISBN 978-1-4221-1057-7 (hardcover : alk. paper)
1. Retail trade—Management. 2. Business logistics. I. Raman, Ananth. II. Title.
HD38.5.F57 2010
658.8'7—dc22

                              2009045240

The paper used in this publication meets the requirements of the American National Standard for Permanence of Paper for Publications and Documents in Libraries and Archives Z39.48-1992.

Contents

Acknowledgments   vii

Introduction   1

1. Retail Valuation   9

   How Investors Value Product Availability and Inventory Management

2. Assortment Planning   29

   Mining Sales Data to Discover "Home Run" Products You Are Missing

3. Product Life Cycle Planning   61

   How to Reinvent Forecasting, Inventory Optimization, and Markdown Pricing

4. Flexible Supply Chains   105

   How to Design for Greater Agility End to End

5. Goal Alignment   131

   Reducing Perverse Incentive Misalignment

6. Store-Level Execution   151

   Increasing Sales Through Better Availability of Products and Store Associates

7. Technological Risk   181
   How Retailers Should Assess and Manage
   Emerging Technologies

8. Companywide Implementation   199
   Managerial Issues Affecting Implementation

   Conclusion   215
   The Way Forward

Appendix   223
Notes   229
Index   241
About the Authors   251

Acknowledgments

We are fortunate to have worked with and learned from numerous academics and retail executives as we conducted research and developed the manuscript for this book.

We owe an enormous debt of gratitude to Walter Salmon, Stanley Roth, Sr. Professor of Retailing (emeritus) at Harvard Business School. We approached Walter in 1996 with the idea that in the computer age the scientific component of retail decision making would grow, and asked whether this phenomenon might create research opportunities. He provided encouragement, wise counsel, and crucial access to numerous retailers. He has continued to be a wonderful mentor, for which we are deeply appreciative.

We also extend thanks to three senior retail executives who have provided extensive guidance over the years and who reviewed and provided helpful feedback on an initial draft of this book: Robert DiRomualdo, Paul Gaffney, and Herbert Kleinberger.

We have greatly benefited from numerous doctoral students whom we have individually or jointly advised and collaborated with on retail operations research. The truth is, we learned far more from them than they did from us. Over the years, we have worked with Gerard Cachon (currently at Wharton), Nicole DeHoratius (University of Portland), Vishal Gaur (Cornell), Saravanan Kesavan (University of North Carolina), Gurhan Kok (Duke), Santiago Kraiselburd (MIT Zaragosa Logistics Center), Jayanth Krishnan (International Monetary Fund), Richard Lai (Wharton), Kumar Rajaram (UCLA), Zeynep Ton (Harvard Business School), Ramnath Vaidyanathan (McGill), and

Noel Watson (MIT Zaragosa Logistics Center). We are confident that our current doctoral students Andres Catalan, Nathan Craig, and Bill Schmidt and our students' students will continue the proud tradition established by these individuals, each of whom has worked countless hours over many years, sharpening the intellectual arguments relating to a particular area of the "new science of retailing." This book is in many ways a necklace strung together from the intellectual beads that these students created over time.

Our doctoral students' work has been very effectively complemented by the work and experience of our MBA students. We are fortunate to have taught for a number of years courses in retail operations and supply chain management that allowed us to bring some of our doctoral students' research into the classroom. Our MBA students acted as a test market for and helped refine many of these ideas and materials. Thankfully, a number of these students have stayed in touch even after they had graduated from our classes and joined the "real world." Many tried some of our ideas, and if these ideas did not work exactly as we had envisaged, they let us know and provided us with an opportunity to improve our thinking. We especially wish to mention several students who worked with us on projects, spoke in our classes, and/or provided extensive feedback on draft chapters: Tamar Bruckel, Robert Gsanger, Mandee Heller, Tamara King, Lilian Kuo, Daniel Marous, Colin McGranahan, Denis Minev, Rob Price, Joanne Stoner, Chris Utgaard, and Colin Welch.

We have benefited greatly from the Consortium for Operational Excellence in Retailing (COER), an industry-academic collaboration that included several dozen retailers and about a dozen schools. Each year more than fifty participating retail executives come to our annual COER conference to critique and sharpen our research. Many COER retailers have also opened up their firms for us to study, willingly sharing intimate details and data that allowed us to write case studies and papers. To each past and current participant in COER and our annual conferences, we would like to say: Thank you! This book and the underlying research could not have happened without your support.

After graduating from Harvard Business School in 1997, Anna Sheen McClelland became the executive director of COER. Her visible contributions included coauthoring a *Harvard Business Review* article and multiple case studies with the two of us. However, her real contributions were behind the scenes. Not only did she keep us organized and on schedule, she used her prior work experience with retailers like The Gap and J. Crew to keep us grounded in reality. This work would not be what it is without Anna's involvement.

We have benefited greatly from interactions with other faculty, who have collaborated with us on projects, spoken at our COER conferences, provided advice on our research, or feedback on draft chapters of this book. These include Erin Armendinger, David Bell (HBS), David Bell (Wharton), Eric Bradlow, Dennis Campbell, Felipe Caro, Daniel Corsten, Nick Dedeke, Karen Donohue, Jan Fransoo, Frances Frei, Jérémie Gallien, Stephen Graves, Jan Hammond, William Hardgrave, Stephen Hoch, Arnd Huchzermeier, Chris Ittner, Katariina Kemppainen, Stephen Kobrin, Abba Kreiger, Rajiv Lal, V. G. Narayanan, Serguei Netessine, Andre Perold, Sanjay Sarma, Roy Shapiro, Jay Swaminathan, Anita Tucker, and Giulio Zotteri.

We have learned much from interactions with hundreds of retail executives. It is not feasible to list all of them, but we wanted to name a few who have provided extensive advice, allowed us access to their companies, spoken in our classes, or actively participated in COER: Chris Alcorn, Tim Andreae, Ved Arya, Ernesto Avendaño, Jay Baker, David Berman, Arrigo Berni, Kishore Biyani, Greg Block, John Bloomfield, Timothy Brokaw, Pamela Cloud, William Cody, Rick Cohen, Michael Cramer, Steve Davis, Miguel Diaz, David Dobrin, Gordon Eiland, William Emerson, Rol Fessenden, Jerome Fisher, Marc Fisher, Kevin Freeland, George Frongillo, Gary Gleckner, James Halpin, Ari Haseotes, Richard Hayne, Rick Helfenbein, Tim Hopkins, Frank Jansen, David Johnston, Matt Kaness, Steve Kaufman, Jan Louagie, Robert Marshall, Catherine Martin, Steve Mastrogiacomo, Rebecca Matthias, Constantine Moros, Chris Moye, Yoko Ohara, John Reinertsen, Gene Rosadino, Katja Ruth, Bernie Sapienza, Bart Scheffer, B. J. Scheihing, Gerald Schleiffer, Leonard Schlesinger, Mark Schwartz, Glen Senk, Paul Shandlay, Sanjiv Sidhu, Amar Singh, Jeff Steinhorn, Thomas Stemberg, Andres Stockert, Jack Swem, Jules Takagishi, Hidezo Terai, Brian Tilzer, Charles Turlinski, Julian Van Erlach, Robert van Lunteren, Steve Walker, Michael Weiss, Freeman Zausner, and Michael Zisman.

Acknowledgments

The research would not have been possible without the financial support of Harvard Business School and The Wharton School, both of which generously supported us, our doctoral students, our research assistants, and our various research activities. The Alfred P. Sloan Foundation provided substantial financial support early in the project. A portion of the store execution research described in chapter 6 was supported by grants from Procter & Gamble and the ECR International Commerce Institute. Colin Peacock, director, Shrink & Store Operations Improvement at Procter & Gamble, and Andrew Buteux, formerly with P&G and now a partner with The Partnering Group, were wonderful mentors to us in this research. Retailers that provided financial support include Albert Heijn; Borders; Bulgari; H. E. Butt Grocery Company; CompUSA; David's Bridal; Giant Eagle; Iceland Frozen Foods; Nine West Group; Sears, Roebuck and Co.; Staples; Tiffany & Co.; and World Co. Ltd.

We were fortunate that, in addition to our academic research program, we also had a clinical practice. For more than a decade, we have had the pleasure of working on a number of consulting projects that culminated in the formation of a start-up company, 4R Systems, in early 2000. It has been fascinating to watch 4R "grow up" and stand on its own feet. The numerous people who have worked at and enriched 4R, as well as the investors and clients who had faith in the company's scientific approach, have contributed to our knowledge and this book. We especially wish to mention Jiri Nechleba, Steffano Alberti, Dave Leonard, and Wayne Hyatt, working at 4R; and Todd Miller, Walter Salmon, Tom Shepherd, Renny Smith, and Michael Zisman, who have served on 4R's board of directors.

We thank Tim Grey for his editorial assistance and Deborah English, Jacqueline Murphy, Kirsten Sandberg, Jennifer Waring, and Ania Wieckowski of Harvard Business School Press for their advice and guidance.

Clearly, none of this work would have been possible or even worthwhile without our families. We owe a special and deep debt to our wives, Gerry and Padmaja, who put up with our long hours and competing interests.

Introduction

Two forces have combined over the last fifty years to cripple the retail sector's once remarkably customer-responsive system. Consolidation has led to chains of hundreds, even thousands, of stores where merchandisers can rarely observe customers and glean the firsthand insights on their likes and dislikes that were available to the mom-and-pop operations that once populated Main Streets and city centers. On top of this, global sourcing has created supply chains that stretch across oceans and time zones. These chains save money, connecting stores to the cheapest suppliers, but those gains come at the expense of longer lead times—often half a year for products sourced in Asia. Having to wait so long precludes nimble reactions to customer demand. It often forces retailers to make single purchases for their entire seasons and hope that they have bought what will sell.

Buyers lack the clairvoyance to operate effectively within this system. They're human, after all. Since the two of us began consulting with retailers in the mid-1990s, we've heard executives lament poor performance by their buyers. Jerome Fisher, founder and former chairman of Nine West shoes, is someone who helped us enormously as we sought to understand the sometimes quirky world of fashion retailing.

His complaint was typical of what we heard: "Line up ten new shoes and ten buyers and ask them which one will be the hot shoe next season, and you get ten answers." Similarly, the president of a department store chain remarked, "No buyer I know can walk into a showroom, look at ten styles, and pick the winner." Finally, Michael Weiss, CEO of Express and former vice-chairman of Limited Brands, suggests that retail buying resembles baseball. "In baseball, if you consistently bat 300, you make the Hall of Fame. Buying is the same. Get it right 30 percent of the time, and you're a Hall of Famer."[1]

One of our earliest consulting clients was a seller of bargain-priced women's clothing. It sourced in Asia and had to buy most of its goods at the start of the season, based on little more than guesswork. Its customers tended to be poor, overweight, middle-aged women. But its buyers, as is typical in the fashion industry, were slim, affluent thirty-somethings. The buyers, who hailed from urban locales like New York and Los Angeles, had little chance to mingle with the customers in far-flung places like Corpus Christi, Texas, and Sheboygan, Wisconsin. Getting the buyers to understand the customers was so tough that, on a store visit, the executive vice president of merchandising turned to a group of buyers, pointed to a man unloading a truck at the back of the store, and said, "See that guy over there? His wife is your customer. Don't forget it."

Executives at a grocery chain likewise told us that their buyers were so much wealthier than their customers that the buyers had trouble making sensible purchasing decisions. The managers thus posted signs in the buying offices saying, "Remember, you're buying it to sell, not to use." They also required that their buyers live for one week a year on a typical customer's food budget. That way, the buyers could appreciate the trade-offs that customers faced daily.

Given stories like this, you won't be surprised to hear that a discrepancy has arisen today between what retailers stock and what their customers want. You've probably noticed it yourself when shopping. Have you ever visited a store and found piles of marked-down merchandise but not the one item you went to buy? That kind of frustration is the norm. Data from the National Retail Federation shows that retailers accumulate so much excess inventory, that, as shown in figure I-1, markdowns have increased from 8 percent in 1970 to nearly

FIGURE I-1

Markdowns have soared

Dept. store markdowns as a % of sales 1970–1997

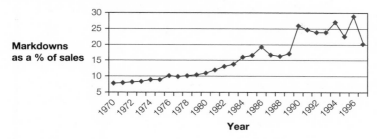

Note: After 1997 the NRF stopped reporting department store markdowns.
Source: Data from *National Retail Federation, Financial and Operating Results*.

30 percent in the 1990s. Despite this glut of merchandise, consumers aren't finding what they want. Of the 70 percent of respondents to Kurt Salmon Associates' (KSA's) Consumer Outlook Survey who said they'd entered a store with a clear idea of what they wished to buy, half of them left empty-handed because they couldn't find it. In-stock rate was listed as the biggest factor influencing store choice for respondents.

But the good news is that even small improvements in matching supply with demand can literally double a retailer's profit. Retailers start with high gross margins, but very little of that margin flows to the bottom line. That's because retailers have high fixed costs: outfitting, provisioning, and staffing a store is expensive, whether the location reaps $1 or $100 million in sales.

For example, during 2000 to 2006, publically traded jewelry retailers had average gross margins of 42 percent, but net profits of only 1 percent.[2] Suppose a jeweler can increase its in-stock rate from 90 percent to 93 percent through more accurate forecasts and better inventory management—a realistic goal—and thereby increase sales by 3 percent. The gross margin on those incremental sales equals 1.26 percent of revenue (0.42 × 3%). All of this incremental gross margin would probably drop to the bottom line. The additional sales thus would increase profits—currently 1 percent of revenue—by more than 100 percent.

Retail segments with smaller gross margins relative to sales would see a smaller—but still hefty—increase in profit from a 3 percent rise in in-stock rate. Improving the match between supply and demand has huge leverage because it costs no more to produce and transport goods that customers want than ones that they don't want. Yet the former sells at full price, and the latter, at perhaps fifty cents on the dollar. That can be the difference between bounty and bankruptcy.

You'd think that the consumer transaction data that nearly everyone in retailing collects would help to solve the problem of matching supply and demand. Technologies such as point-of-sale (POS) scanners, customer loyalty cards, and Web site cookies should enable retailers to understand their customers as well as the best mom-and-pop stores did.

Yet retailers have barely begun to mine the data that these technologies produce. Another of our clients, a vice president of merchandise technology at a department store chain, had a sign on her office wall that summarized the situation: "We are awash in data and starved for information."

Many retailers face this plight. They're drowning in numbers but lacking in insight. Witness our analysis of a clothier. We uncovered a surprising variety in the mix of sizes sold in its different stores. This was an obvious opportunity to improve purchasing and assortment selection. In the past, the chain had sent the same mix of sizes of all products to all of its stores. Thus some locations had many small sizes left over at the end of a season, while others had mostly large sizes left. When we reported our findings to the vice president of planning, he said, "Our buyers already have access to those patterns." He then dropped an eight-inch-thick computer printout on his desk. "It's all in my weekly size-selling report." The document gave a welter of sales data, broken down by size, style, color, and store.

With a little nudging, he acknowledged that the buyers had neither the time nor the inclination to pore over a thick computer printout. Even if they set aside the time occasionally, a single week's sales wouldn't give them enough information to detect patterns. A typical retailer might carry 10,000 SKUs at 500 stores, so a weekly report could contain 5 million numbers. Studying it with any diligence would outstrip anyone's manual effort; doing so requires algorithms incorporated in software, and such tools have been slow in coming to retailing.

4

On top of this, retail goods change frequently, and many folks in the retailing industry don't understand how to extrapolate sales projections from the sales histories of products that they no longer carry, particularly trendy ones. The sign on the office wall of a vice president of planning captures this conundrum: "History's a mystery; trend's your friend." Put differently, conventional wisdom says that sales data on current styles is useful in guiding buying but the history of prior ones is worthless.

Yet history can inform decision making when mined appropriately. While products turn over frequently, the parameters of consumer demand can endure for years, and sales histories can help you understand and estimate them. Among these stable parameters are seasonality, size mix, the types of products that sell best at given stores, price elasticity, and category growth trends.

Even using current sales to guide buying decisions vexes many retailers. You can't just buy more of what's selling well. For one thing, most products sell at a slow rate, so it's hard to spot trends. In a study of thirty-two retailers, we found that an average SKU sold about one unit per month per store.[3] Yes, there was variation; groceries were faster, and jewelry, slower. But for most categories, you can't forecast from store-SKU sales data, because the sales rate is so slow. To detect patterns, you must aggregate the data by grouping similar stores and SKUs.

Also, you can't just examine raw sales. You need to know the conditions under which those sales occurred. All retailers have a few important causal factors that influence sales. Price and product availability always matter. Weather and competitive activity often do, too—needless to say, retail sales dropped in New Orleans after Hurricane Katrina. To do a forecast, you must understand how each of these factors influenced your past sales, and you must make educated assumptions about how they'll affect future ones.

Retailers today find themselves teetering on a knife-edge ridge in slick-soled shoes. They have lost their old way of understanding their customers—through regular one-on-one interactions—but have not found a reliable new one. In this book, we offer an approach to understanding customers and planning inventory that's just as reliable as the hard-won wisdom of the best old-school retailers. And we share techniques that we've developed to assist forward-thinking retailers in facing their biggest challenge today: the transition from hunch-driven to data-driven buying. Make that transition, and you'll turn your inventory faster and mark down fewer goods. Put simply, you'll make more money.

Retailers trying to make this transition can draw inspiration from a similar movement that began in the late 1970s on Wall Street, when several forces converged to transform money management from art to science. At the time, powerful new software and hardware permitted the capture and storage of reams of data on security trades. Mathematical models enabled the analysis of that data so that it could guide investment decisions. And a new breed of employee—the so-called quants or rocket scientists—arrived, abandoning careers in academia, science, and engineering to join investment banks, brokerages, and hedge funds.

With the financial crisis of 2008 and early 2009, Wall Street has come in for some deserved derision. Certainly, some of the quants, along with legions of other staffers in investment banks and hedge funds, promised more than they could deliver. But the methods remain valid and powerful, even if egos inhibited their sensible use. Information technology and smart analysis can't abolish risk, nor can they guarantee success. But used properly, they can help you sort through scads of information and make well-informed projections. Think of them as a microscope to a biologist: they don't replace judgment, experience, or even common sense, but they can help you see more clearly.

It may seem a stretch to draw an analogy between Wall Street and Wal-Mart, but consider the similarities of the jobs of a money manager and a retail category manager. Both buy stocks—one of companies, the other of products—that they seek to resell at a profit. Both face the risk that they might sell their stocks at a loss, and both must react quickly to market signals.

We hope that the insights and stories that we share in this book will help anyone who works in retailing. But please understand that not every method will work in every company. Just as products have a life cycle, so do retailers. Rocket science approaches work best at particular points in a retailer's life.

Introduction

As in any life, one of the most significant events in retailing is birth. Retailers match products with people, and a change in products, people's habits, or the technology for matching them affords the opportunity for a new type of retailer to be born. CompUSA began as an attempt to exploit a new product: the personal computer. Destination Maternity, with a 50 percent share of the maternity apparel market, started because more pregnant women were working at professional careers and couldn't find appropriate clothes. And Amazon.com aimed to exploit a new technology for matching people with products: the Internet.

A business adage says that out of chaos comes revenue; out of order comes profit. Success requires balancing the chaotic process of attracting customers to raise revenue with the order needed to derive profits from the resulting gush of sales. As every businessperson knows, without the discipline provided by systems, you can *grow* broke.

In their early years, most retailers focus on proving that their concept works and tweaking store designs. They're more worried about basic execution than cutting-edge analysis. Once they refine their concept and store layout, they move to open stores as quickly as possible. They learn to live with the chaos that goes with revenue generation, and rocket science retailing is probably less useful to them at this time than it will be later in their lives. At some point, usually at about fifty stores, they start to worry about profitability and must inject order into the hurly-burly of their operations. Here, rocket science practices can make the difference between success and failure. They can, for example, help to determine which products to carry and how best to price them.

At this crossroads, a firm strives to add discipline without destroying the creativity that generates excitement and draws customers. Too little order translates to lost profits; too much means lost customers. The goal of rocket science retailing is to harness the best analytical techniques without disrupting the creativity that excites customers. Achieving this ideal combination of creativity and cunning requires a new way of thinking. In this book, we'll show you how to implement these ways of thinking at your company. We aim to make you smarter. We'll leave it up to you to preserve your creativity and excitement.

Chapter 1 sets the stage for our discussion, showing the links between intelligent inventory management and stock market valuation at retailers. As you'll see, Wall Street rewards companies that excel at managing their inventory, paying more for their stocks than those of competitors.

In chapter 2, we examine current practice in assortment planning and describe our experiences in helping two retailers—a convenience store chain and a tire seller—strengthen their assortment planning. In chapter 3, we provide tools to help you decide how much inventory of each product to carry in each of your stores at any point. We also show you a more profitable way of managing markdowns.

Chapter 4 describes how to create a supply chain that is flexible enough to respond to demand signals, so you can identify and exploit today's winning products rather than chasing yesterday's. Chapter 5 lays out an approach for better aligning incentives within your company and supply chain. New ways of doing business disrupt people's routines and make their usual ways of operating and thinking obsolete. Too often, corporate innovators defeat themselves by introducing new ideas, like rocket science retailing, without also introducing incentives for their adoption.

Chapter 6 addresses store-level execution, helping you to identify the reasons that determine whether a potential customer shops with you or a competitor. Retailers must know what matters to their customers. Offering Nordstrom-quality customer service won't help you if what your customers really want is Target-level prices.

Chapter 7 explores the ways in which information technology enables rocket science approaches, with a focus on radio frequency identification, or RFID. Accurate information is the lifeblood of rocket science retailing. You can't make good decisions if you don't have good data. Finally, chapter 8 starts with the premise that rocket science retailing requires more than just formulas. You also must have the right organizational structure and an implementation plan. You can't just flail about, assuming that a new software package and a few quants will deliver salvation. You have to know exactly what you want to achieve in your particular context and how you intend to get there.

CHAPTER ONE

Retail Valuation

How Investors Value Product Availability and Inventory Management

Retailers beware! David Berman is watching you. Berman, general partner of Berman Capital Management in New York, invests in retail stocks, often after investigating a retailer's inventory levels.[1] He's a member of an emerging group of rocket science investors who believe that operational data, such as inventory levels, foretell future increases or decreases in sales, earnings, and share price. Publicly traded retailers must understand how investors like Berman operate in order to effectively communicate with them. This chapter offers guidelines on how you can do so. Moreover, adopting the investor's perspective can help you benchmark your firm's performance along various dimensions against other retailers, and also identify how you can better forecast your firm's sales using past macroeconomic and financial data.

To understand Berman's approach, consider his experience with Saucony, a shoemaker based near Boston, which, though not primarily a retailer, illustrates Berman's investment approach well. In 2003, Berman rated it a strong buy when he noticed that, though sales were flattish, inventories had declined about 20 percent year over year. The stock looked riskier than average. It was thinly traded, and managers were reluctant to share information. But to Berman, a falling inventory level foretold a future rise in gross margin. He started buying shares at $14 in late 2003 due primarily to the leaner inventories. A year later, the stock had doubled. During this period, sales rose, as did inventories, and of course, the gross margin expanded significantly, just as Berman had predicted. Saucony's earnings per share increased from $0.85 in 2002 to $1.29 in 2004.

Then in late 2004 Berman decided to unload his shares. This decision, which came shortly after management asked him to ring the NASDAQ bell with them, was based on his inventory analysis. But this time, the numbers told a troubling tale. Inventories were growing at the same pace as sales. To make matters worse, managers were ignoring his calls. Sure enough, in March 2005, before Berman had been able to unwind his illiquid position, Saucony announced that it would miss earnings estimates. The stock dropped 20 percent.

A similar sort of analysis led him in 2003 to dump his shares of Bombay, a home accessories and furniture retailer. That November, the company announced that revenue had risen a healthy 19 percent. But as Berman combed through its financials, he noticed that inventories had increased 50 percent year over year. Then executives acknowledged early November sales weakness. That day, the stock fell 20 percent, to $10. Even that correction didn't satisfy Berman.

"Going into Q4 it was clear they would *have* to miss numbers again unless the consumer saved them, which would be a shocker," he said. About two weeks later, the company issued guidance, saying that it expected earnings to fall, and the stock slipped another 20 percent. Remarkably, just four weeks later, after the Christmas selling season, managers lowered their guidance yet again, and the stock declined another 20 percent. "It was so sweet to see the classic inventory/ earnings relationship at work so quickly," Berman recalls. In just one and a half months, the stock declined 50 percent primarily because of inventory mismanagement and weakening sales.

This chapter examines the relationship between retailers' stock market valuation and inventory management capabilities. We start by discussing inventory *from an investor's perspective*. That is, we analyze a firm's inventory levels and capabilities based on the information available to an investor, which is often just a subset of the data available within the firm. Then we zero in on the ever-popular inventory-turns metric, explaining how you should modify it to better understand your inventory levels and to arm yourself to communicate more effectively with sharp-eyed investors like Berman. Even if your company isn't publicly held, understanding Wall Street's perspective will help you hone your operations and communications. Financial metrics are the road map to any business. Operating without fully understanding them is like driving in a foreign country without a map or GPS.

How Does Berman Use Inventory Information to Predict Stock Price?

We'll use a numerical example to show how a deep understanding of inventory helped Berman make the smart stock calls we've just described, and to lay out how a sophisticated investor such as David Berman might assess your firm.

Scenario 1: Impact of Same-Store Sales Growth

Consider two apparel retailers, A and B, whose projected performance is summarized in table 1-1. Both have projected gross margins of 40 percent of sales and selling, general, and administrative (SG&A) expenses of $180 million per year. Both of their sales are expected to hit $500 million in the first year. The only difference is their growth rate. Firm A is stable, neither growing nor declining, while firm B is growing at 3 percent per year. Neither firm is adding stores in the next few years.

To evaluate the two firms, a professional investor would use a discounted cash flow model (albeit a much more complicated one than the one we will describe). In such a model, a firm's value equals the present value of its future cash flows. Table 1-2 shows such a model for

TABLE 1-1

Scenario 1

Financial metric	Retailer A	Retailer B
Sales	$500 million	$500 million
Gross margin	40%	40%
Net margin (current year)	4% ($20 Mn)	4% ($20 Mn)
Sales growth (1 year)	0%	3%
Comp. store sales growth (1 year)	0%	3%

TABLE 1-2

Sample cash flow projections

Firm A   Gross margin %   40%

FIRM A			
Year	1	2	25
Sales	500	500	500
GM	200	200	200
SG&A	180	180	180
Net margin	20	20	20
Cash flow	20	20	20

firm A. For simplicity's sake, we ignore taxes, depreciation, and capital expenses. We project cash flows for twenty-five years and assume that at the end of that time, the terminal value of each firm and its inventory is zero. Finally, we assume that the discount rate is 10 percent per year.

This discounted cash flow analysis values retailer A at $182 million. Retailer B, on the other hand, is valued at $625 million, or more than three times as much. Its higher growth rate has such a big impact on cash flow because the gross margin from the additional sales falls to the company's bottom line. In year 2, for example, firm B has sales of

$515 million, a gross margin of $206 million, and cash flow of $26 million. This example underscores why analysts pay such close attention to a retailer's projected growth.

Scenario 2: The Impact of Higher but Steady Inventory Levels

Now, to understand how inventory factors into Wall Street's valuation of your firm or its competitors, let's complicate the scenario. Assume that, in addition to the data above, we discover that retailer A operates with 182.5 days of inventory, while retailer B operates with 365 days' worth.

Retailer A's inventory level does not affect its cash flow or valuation; the company is stable, so its inventory is also stable. But retailer B's higher inventory load, when combined with its growth, does hurt its cash flow compared with scenario 1. As the company grows, it has to devote part of its cash flow to funding the additional inventory needed for that growth. In the second year, for example, its inventory grows from $300 million to $309 million, and its cash flow drops by $9 million, amounting to only $17 million (as opposed to $26 million in the prior example). This time, retailer B's valuation is only $578 million.

Scenario 3: Impact of Inventory Growth Rate

Now let's add another wrinkle of just the sort that catches David Berman's attention. In this scenario, retailer B's inventory is growing at 6 percent per year. In other words, it's rising faster than the firm's sales are growing.

Plug those numbers into our discounted cash flow model, and future cash flows change substantially. In the second year, for example, inventory increases to $318 million (from $300 million in year 1), and cash flow is only $8 million (down from $26 million in scenario 1 and $17 million in scenario 2). The sharp reduction in cash flow cuts firm B's valuation to $430 million.

Scenario 4: Impact of Inventory Write-offs

If you have too much inventory, as retailer B appears to, you'll eventually have to write off some of it. So let's add into our valuation a $10 million annual write-off for obsolete inventory. Not surprisingly, our discounted cash flow model now values retailer B at $339 million.

The logic underpinning the scenarios described above also limns the views of David Berman. The relationship between inventory levels and a firm's valuation, he says, "is astoundingly powerful, but surprisingly few understand why." Berman points out that rising inventory levels are often a function of the retailer's failing to take markdowns in a disciplined way. He argues that the game of failing to mark down obsolete inventory cannot be played indefinitely. Ultimately, the "music has to stop," he says. In other words, for Berman, rising inventory levels can predict future earnings declines.

Berman likewise argues that sales growth achieved through inventory increases isn't as sustainable as growth powered by greater consumer acceptance of a brand. Consider a retailer that has historically suffered from stockouts due to insufficient inventory. When it adds inventory to its stores, sales should rise. But Wall Street analysts, who typically pay close attention to "same-store sales growth," often fail to distinguish between these two types of growth and thus overvalue retailers that inflate their sales by adding inventory. Undoubtedly, the market corrects the overvaluation when future sales growth fails to meet Wall Street's optimistic projections.

The relationship between inventory and sales can be understood from Berman's analysis of The Home Depot. In 2001 and 2002 Home Depot's new CEO, Bob Nardelli, seemed to struggle in managing the transition from a cash flow GE-type philosophy to a retailer Home Depot–type philosophy.[2] In his *DeeBee Report* dated June 10, 2003, Berman stated, "Bob Nardelli learned the power of inventory the hard way. In focusing on cash flow improvement, he dramatically lowered inventories—and yes, increased cash balances—only to see a huge decline in same store sales, and in its stock price (the stock went from around $40 to $22). And so, under immense pressure, Nardelli reversed course and focused intensely on increasing inventories. Since

Q2 of last year, inventories had been building until they were up 25 percent year over year. And yes, same store sales did improve, as did the stock price."[3] Recognizing this as potentially a short fix, Berman continued: "Now the cynical would view this increase in sales with skepticism, noting that it wasn't of 'high quality' as it was due, in part, to the massive inventory build. It is, however, pleasing to note that Home Depot simply got inventories back to 'normal,' in that it now has turns similar to [its] competitors."[4] The stock, following the same-store sales and earnings increases, which in essence followed the inventories increase, rose from $22 at the start of 2003 to $36 by the end of 2003. When asked about this "fix," Berman responded, "It will be more challenging for Nardelli to increase same store sales and margins going forward because his increasing inventories and therefore same store sales is arguably a one-time benefit and is essentially what caused the 'fix.'" Berman concluded by saying, "As such the stock ought not to climb as rapidly as it did during that 2002 to 2004 inventory growth period."[5]

Recent research by Saravanan Kesavan, one of our doctoral students and currently a professor at the University of North Carolina's Kenan-Flagler Business School, supports Berman's assertion that inventory can be used to drive sales and that Wall Street understates the relationship between inventory and sales.[6] On average across all segments, a 1 percent increase in inventory is found to cause roughly a 0.224 percent increase in sales. Moreover, the impact on sales of a 1 percent increase in inventory differs substantially among different segments. Furniture retailers witness only a 0.188 percent increase in sales, while apparel and accessory retailers witness a 0.322 percent increase in sales for a 1 percent increase in inventory. Moreover, the analysis reveals that Wall Street investment analysts' forecasts fail to incorporate sufficiently the effect of inventory and price changes on sales and earnings. We find that analysts, when forecasting sales, overestimate sales for retailers whose past inventory has been inflated and prices have been lowered. On average, the analysts' bias amounts to roughly 5 percent of sales. A similar pattern applies to earnings as well. Analysts overestimate future earnings for retailers whose inventories were inflated in previous years, while they underestimate future earnings for retailers whose inventory was low in previous years.

How—in Practice—Do Inventory Levels Affect a Retailer's Valuation?

How closely are inventory levels tracked in analyst reports? If you work for a publicly traded retailer, you know that analysts often ignore inventory. Page through their reports, and you'll seldom see the word mentioned—unless a company has landed in trouble.

A scan of roughly seventy-five analyst reports for electronics retailer Best Buy, for example, shows that the words *inventory* or *inventories* were mentioned at a rate of 0.15 times per page. In contrast, *sale, sales,* and *revenue* were mentioned at a rate of 1.83 times per page (or roughly twelve times as often). Inventory gets a little more attention at retailers that are prone to markdowns and discounts, particularly specialty apparel retailers and department stores with substantial apparel and footwear sales. When examining outfits like Abercrombie & Fitch, analysts will use informal techniques such as store visits to get a sense of the likelihood of future markdowns. One report on the firm, for example, mentioned "a few back tables and racks of clearance tees and tops marked down at 20–40 percent."

But when a company stumbles, inventory springs to the front of analysts' minds, leapfrogging from ignored to obsessed over, without ever passing carefully observed. Witness Jos. A. Bank, a men's clothier. In 2004 and 2005, its inventory turns steadily dropped even as sales and gross margin increased; in other words, inventory was growing faster than sales. Soon, the company's inventory level—at roughly 350 days—was roughly double that of competitors like Men's Wearhouse. Then on June 7, 2006—after close of stock market trading—the company announced earnings that fell far short of Wall Street's expectations of $0.46 a share. Sales had risen 18 percent, but "discounting and rising expenses clipped margins," the company said.[7] And despite that discounting, the company's inventory had continued to swell.

Suddenly, analysts began to scrutinize Jos. A. Bank's inventory levels. A typical report, this one issued on September 8, 2006, read as follows: "On the positive side . . . [i]nventory increased only 12 percent year over year, well below the 20.8% sales growth. This is a significant reduction over 1Q06 inventory growth of 27%, and 38% inventory growth at the end of 4Q05." Qualitative observations often accompanied the quantitative analysis. "The company carries a higher level of inventory than many of [its] competitors," one analyst wrote. "Because the company has a lower level of fashion risk, in that most of the product offering is very classically styled and has a longer shelf life, we expect [it] to carry more inventory than other more fashion sensitive retailers. We also note that the company is building inventory in preparation of new store openings."

An analysis of roughly two hundred analyst reports, from mid-2005 through December 2007, for Bank reveals that *inventory* or *inventories* were now mentioned at the rate of 0.55 times per page, while *sale*, *sales*, or *revenues* were mentioned 2.28 times per page (or roughly 4 times as often). Meanwhile, when assessing Men's Wearhouse, analyst reports mentioned these terms far fewer times, in fact *inventory* and *inventories* were mentioned roughly 0.24 times per page.

Inventory Turns: A Commonly Used Benchmark for Evaluating a Retailer's Inventory Level

How can we assess whether a firm has too much or too little inventory? How should we compare inventory levels across "similar" retailers? Across "dissimilar" retailers? For a single retailer over time?

As a retailer, you might carry inventory for many different reasons. Maybe you're trying to leverage scale economies in purchasing and transportation or buffering against demand and supply uncertainty. Or perhaps you're trying to stimulate demand through "display inventory." Regardless of the reason, you're aware of the challenge you face—you're trying to balance on the razor's edge between too little and too much. Err on one side, and you risk bankruptcy. Err on the other, and you miss out on sales and potentially lose customers to your competitors.

But despite the centrality of inventory to your or any retailer's operations, you'd think that analysts who follow the sector would've developed sophisticated models that pinpoint exactly how much inventory a retailer should have. In reality, they have a notoriously difficult time determining whether a retailer has the "right" amount of inventory. To make this judgment, they need to know not only the retailer's inventory level but also its service level (that is, the level of product availability that it aims for).[8] Higher service levels usually require more inventory. If service level could be observed externally, an analyst could get a sense for whether a retailer was using its additional inventory to offer better availability to consumers or whether it was simply covering up for inefficiency. What if, for example, a substantial portion of the inventory on a retailer's balance sheet were obsolete? This portion would not enhance the service level. What's more, service level isn't reported in public financial statements (and only rarely tracked even internally). In other words, the analyst cannot see the *mix* of inventory at the retailer and thus cannot identify whether the retailer is on or below the "inventory-service frontier."

In an attempt to sidestep these problems, analysts and even retail executives often use *inventory turns* as shorthand for the appropriate level of inventory at a retailer.[9] That's unfortunate because this metric, while useful, has shortcomings. Turns, after all, can vary substantially from one retail segment to the next. They can vary across similar firms and even over time for a single retailer. Supermarket chains like Kroger Company, for example, achieve roughly fourteen inventory turns per year, while apparel sellers like Gap (NYSE: GPS) achieve only around seven. Comparing turns for these companies makes little sense given the considerable differences in their business models.

Likewise, retailers within the same segment can show substantial differences in turns. Electronics retailer RadioShack turns its inventory less than thrice per year, while Best Buy manages more than seven turns a year. Best Buy's closest competitor, Circuit City, achieved just above five inventory turns per year (when it was a healthy retailer).

Finally, inventory turns can vary substantially for a single retailer over time. From 1985 through 2000, Gap's annual inventory turns varied between 3.6 and 6.3, Best Buy's bounced between 3.8 and 9.1, and Wal-Mart's zigzagged between 4.9 and 7.2.

What explains all of this variation in inventory turns? Is the variation in turns correlated with other variables such as gross margin or investment in noninventory assets that can be obtained from public financial data? If we could identify these variables, could we derive an alternate metric for inventory productivity that "controlled" for the variation?

Explaining the Variation in Inventory Turns

Can we use the large amount of public financial data available for retail firms to quantify the relationship between inventory turns and other metrics? Would the relationship also provide an alternate metric for evaluating inventory productivity?[10]

Adjusted inventory turns—a metric that we developed with Vishal Gaur, one of our former doctoral students and currently a professor at the Johnson School at Cornell University—compensates for the problems with the traditional turns. It better measures inventory productivity by accounting for variation in other variables that affect inventory productivity.[11] To understand why, you have to walk through the logic—and a little bit of math—behind it as well as the factors that influence it.

Let's begin with gross margin.[12] Here, we'll use *markup*, defined as the gross margin divided by cost of sales, instead of the more common form where gross margin is represented as a percentage of sales. As a rule, a retailer should carry more inventory when its markup is higher. That way, it can cover unforeseen surges in demand; a higher markup implies greater costs associated with sales lost due to insufficient inventory.[13] In other words, we would expect gross margin (or markup) and inventory turns to be negatively correlated—that is, when markup rises, turns fall.

Retailers with high markups are termed *earns retailers* and often have low inventory turns. In 2005, for example, RadioShack Corporation had markup of roughly 84 percent (or gross margins of roughly 46 percent of sales) and 2.8 inventory turns a year. In contrast, those with low markups and high inventory turns, such as Costco Wholesale Corporation, are termed *turns retailers*. For the year ending September 3, 2006, Costco had markup of roughly 14 percent (or gross margins of 12.5 percent) and 11.5 inventory turns a year.

Capital intensity—the amount of noninventory investment that a company makes—operates in the opposite way: the more a company invests in noninventory assets, such as warehouses and information technology, the higher its turns should be. And firms often justify investments in information technology based on the technology's ability to enable faster inventory turns. To really understand the influence of capital intensity on turns, you need a precise picture of a retailer's various investments. Unfortunately, these investments are almost never broken out in a retailer's public financial statements. We'll therefore use an alternate measure of capital intensity, the fraction of a retailer's total assets that is represented by its noninventory assets, for the purposes of our calculations.[14]

A third driver of inventory turns is *sales surprise*, which is the ratio of actual sales to sales forecast in a particular year.[15] If sales are higher than had been forecast previously, sales surprise would be greater than 1. All else remaining equal, a retailer would see higher inventory turns when sales surprise is higher.

Analyzing the Data to Quantify the Relationships

Public financial data provides us with a context in which to try to quantify the relationship between these three factors and inventory turns. To do our calculations, we collected data for all public retailers in the United States for the years 1985 through 2000. (Details of the data set and the analysis can be found in Vishal Gaur, Marshall Fisher, and Ananth Raman's "An Econometric Analysis of Inventory Turnover Performance in Retail Services.")

Before we explain what we found, let's take a moment to consider why an old-fashioned analysis of the relationship between our three variables and turns could mislead.

Consider figure 1-1, which shows the time trends in average inventory turns for public retailers for the period of our analysis. For it, we've calculated average inventory turns in two ways: (1) the higher line shows the average inventory turns for all retailers, while (2) the lower one shows average cost of goods sold divided by average inventory level for all retailers. According to either one, you'd conclude that there are no time trends in inventory turns for these retailers during this period. And if you did, you'd be dead wrong.

A simple example shows why this kind of analysis misleads.[16] Consider two firms whose inventory turns vary over time, as shown in figure 1-2. Clearly, they're demonstrating downward sloping trends over time. Yet taking a simple average of the two firms' inventory turns would

FIGURE 1-1

Retail inventory turn data suggests no increase in turns from 1985 to 2000

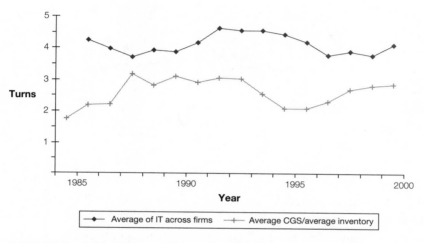

- Data: 311 firms in 10 retail segments for the years 1985–2000.
- Two ways to compute aggregate inventory turnover: (1) as the average of inventory turns (IT) across all firms in that year; or (2) as the average of cost of goods sold (CGS) across all firms in that year divided by the average of inventory across all firms in that year.

FIGURE 1-2

Firm C's and firm D's inventory levels are decreasing over time

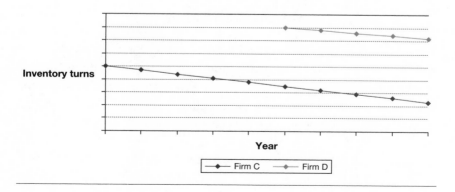

FIGURE 1-3

But average inventory for the two firms shows no decrease over time

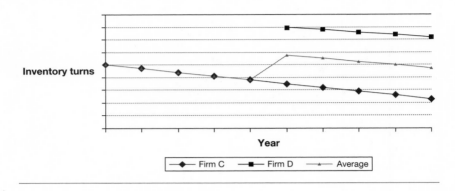

yield the line in figure 1-3, which shows small fluctuations up and down but no change in inventory over the 10 years (notice that the inventory turns in years 1 and 10 are roughly the same). In other words, the changing mix of firms makes it hard to gauge true inventory progress.

To address this problem, our analysis does not draw conclusions based on the performance difference across firms. Stated a tad technically, we allow for a firm "fixed effect" and draw conclusions on the relationships between inventory turns and other variables, such as gross margins based on intrafirm variation in inventory turns. In other words, we fit separate lines for firms C and D but require the two firms to have the same slope.

Findings from the Data

Get ready, because this is where the math gets a little tougher. We'll use what's called a *pooled model* (that ignores the differences among various retailing segments) to compensate for the problems outlined above. If the computation looks a little scary, the conclusions aren't. So bear with us.

According to the pooled model:

$$\log IT_{it} = F_i + c_t - 0.2431 \log MU_{it} + 0.2502 \log CI_{it} + 0.143 \log SS_{it} + e_{it}$$

where,

IT_{it} = inventory turnover for firm i in year t
MU_{it} = markup for firm i in year t
SS_{it} = sales surprise for firm i in year t
e_{it} = residual in the equation for firm i in year t
log = of a quantity denotes the logarithm to the base 10 for the appropriate quantity
F_i = fixed effect for firm i
c_t = fixed effect for year t

In words, the logarithm of inventory turns for a firm is a function of the markup (MU), capital intensity (CI), and sales surprise (SS) in a particular year. In this equation, a 10 percent increase in markup would translate into a 2.3 percent reduction in inventory turns, a 10 percent increase in capital intensity translates into a 2.4 percent increase in inventory turns, and a 10 percent increase in sales surprise translates to a 1.4 percent increase in inventory turns. This equation explains 67 percent of the variation in inventory turns *within* a firm, and *98 percent of the entire variation* in the data set.

Managerial Implications from the Analysis: Time Trends and Benchmarks

During the period of 1985 through 2000, inventory turns and markup declined quite clearly, while capital intensity increased. But a more interesting trend—at least in our minds—is the pattern observed in c_t, which is a year fixed effect. It shows changes in inventory turns after controlling for variation in markup, capital intensity, sales surprise, and firm differences (as measured by the firm fixed effect F_i). Thus c_t can be viewed as a metric of "average" inventory productivity for a given year. Figure 1-4 shows the trend over time. Notice that c_t has declined almost steadily, suggesting that inventory productivity has declined over time. This decline does not necessarily imply that retailers' ability to manage inventory has fallen. Other factors—such as a more competitive retail environment or changes in

FIGURE 1-4

Time trend in inventory productivity estimated from yearwise fixed effects

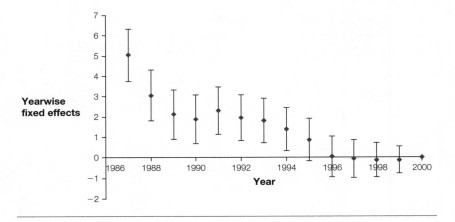

consumer taste—can affect inventory productivity as well. We aren't sure what caused the steady decline in inventory productivity during this period.

Regardless, controlling for variation in markup, capital intensity, and sales surprise yields our benchmark for inventory productivity— adjusted inventory turns. Inventory turns and adjusted inventory turns can offer divergent insights. Consider the example of Ruddick Corporation. Ruddick owns and operates Harris Teeter, a chain of supermarkets in seven southeastern states, and also manufactures and distributes thread and technical textiles. Note in figure 1-5 that Ruddick's inventory turns showed a very small decrease from 1985 through 2000 even as capital intensity rose. But notice, too, that markup was rising concurrently; consequently, adjusted inventory turns were rising during this period. While we have not studied Ruddick in great detail, our understanding is that Ruddick developed a strong private label program during this period. This program required Ruddick to carry a little more inventory but afforded the company greater markups.

FIGURE 1-5

Comparison across years within a firm: Ruddick Corporation

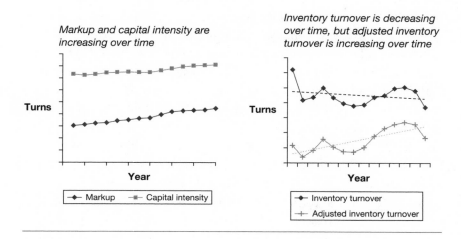

Markup and capital intensity are increasing over time

Inventory turnover is decreasing over time, but adjusted inventory turnover is increasing over time

Turns

Turns

Year

Year

—◆— Markup   —■— Capital intensity

—◆— Inventory turnover
—+— Adjusted inventory turnover

Plotting the Future: A Resurgence in the Importance of Inventory Turns

If our computations seem obscure, understand that these are exactly the sorts of analyses that sophisticated investors like David Berman are using. They're dissecting your inventory turns—or those of your publicly traded competitors—even if you're not.

The increasing importance of inventory to retail valuation can be gauged from the conversation one of us had with a Wal-Mart executive recently. He noted that inventory "is now woven into the performance metric at every level of the organization." When pressed to explain the reasons for this, he said, "Our shareholders care more about inventory now than they did in the past." If a supply chain innovator like Wal-Mart is concerned, imagine the scrutiny that less efficient operators might face from shareholders.

On top of this, professional investors like Berman hire people to visit individual stores and collect data on pricing, markdowns, and freshness of inventory. A leading investment house sends a bunch of its staffers to visit about fifty stores every month to assess inventory and discount levels for a comparable basket of products at each store.

Finally, academics are developing tools like adjusted inventory turns that will help investors extract information from public financial data. Two streams of work seem especially promising to us.

In one study, Gaur validated adjusted inventory turns (AIT) by comparing the performance of a portfolio of stocks compiled using AIT with one compiled using plain-old inventory turns (IT).[17] Gaur ranked retailers by AIT and IT and then created the portfolios by investing in the top-ranked retailers and selling short the bottom-ranked ones. He updated the ranks and portfolios each year and evaluated the portfolios' performance after a number of years. The AIT-based portfolio easily beat the market, while the IT-based portfolio did not.

A caveat applies to these results: Gaur did not validate AIT-based portfolios as an investment strategy to achieve above-market returns. As is typical in research, he assumed that accurate financial data was available immediately after the end of each year in commercial databases like Compustat. That assumption is generally not valid in the real world. Before investment managers can roll out strategies based on AIT (or IT), they'll have to develop ways to quickly collect the necessary information from earnings announcements and corporate filings. As the situation stands today, it can be weeks and even months before the data appears in a user-friendly form in databases such as Compustat. Creating such processes can be challenging and expensive; the studies so far have not factored in those costs.

A second stream of academic work links retail sales to the return on aggregate indexes, such as the S&P 500 index, and identifies segments where the wealth effect is most pronounced.[18] We use the term *wealth effect* to describe the phenomenon in economics that has studied the effect of income and wealth on consumption. Not surprisingly, perhaps, scholars have found that consumption increases or decreases with wealth—the recent paper identifies segments that are more substantially affected by this phenomenon. For example, sales of "discretionary items" (such as TVs) seem more susceptible to the wealth effect than nondiscretionary items like food. Moreover, within each segment, sales of high-margin retailers are more susceptible to the wealth effect. The study identifies implications for forecasting and finds that forecast quality can be improved by combining sales forecasts from experts with information from broader market indexes.

Implications Going Forward for Retail Managers

Investors—led by a new breed of fund managers—are paying very careful attention to retailers' inventory levels. And as in many other fields of business, greater data availability and superior technology have enabled investors to glean deeper insights about firms' management capabilities.

Should you, as a retail manager, change your practices in the face of investors' closer scrutiny? Absolutely. To fail to do so would be foolish. We suggest three steps.

1. Watch your inventory numbers carefully, and if you're publicly traded, be aware that eagle-eyed investors are watching them just as closely. That doesn't mean that you should never let your inventory level increase or allow your inventory turns to slow. In fact, as we'll argue throughout this book, retailers often have compelling reasons to carry more inventory. But when that happens, you must offer a compelling explanation to your investors. Ideally, that explanation should come before the increase in inventory does.

2. Many retail executives with whom we have spoken acknowledge that their firms sometimes use inventory and gross margins to manage sales and profit levels. As one of our friends said with knowing smirk, "My firm never does this, but my friends at other companies say they do." Understand that the opportunity to play these sorts of games with inventory is eroding as investors become savvier.

3. Most important, invest substantially in your ability to plan and control your inventory level. For years, retail executives have complained to us that investors do not care about inventory. Those days are gone. Led by investors like Berman, Wall Street is paying ever-closer attention to inventory management. Isn't it time retailers did so, too?

CHAPTER TWO

Assortment Planning

Mining Sales Data to Discover "Home Run" Products You Are Missing

A retailer's assortment—the set of products carried in each of its stores—defines the company for consumers. L.L.Bean may sell far more wool blankets than cross-country skis but, by stocking the skis, it announces that it specializes in outdoor recreation, not just rustic house goods.

In choosing an assortment, retailers must take into account strategic issues like whether products align with their brands: L.L.Bean isn't going to start stocking silk negligees.

But retailers must also ponder nitty-gritty operational puzzles. Best Buy, for its part, might have to choose only twenty digital cameras, among the thousands available. On top of that, it might not carry all of those twenty in each of its stores.

The rhythm of assortment planning varies across the three major retailing segments. A grocer can frequently tweak its offerings, even varying them within a single day. Albert Heijn, a Dutch supermarket chain, offers a different assortment to breakfast-time shoppers than it does to those who arrive right before dinner. Shoe and apparel peddlers, in contrast, plan around the seasons, usually spring and fall. Hard-goods retailers hew to annual cycles corresponding to their fiscal years. Pianos don't lend themselves to being shuttled on and off the showroom floor.

Assortment planning happens at two levels. At the *strategic level*, you address the amount of resources, including shelf space and purchase dollars, to allocate to each category. This kind of planning often resembles capital budgeting, especially for retailers that plan assortments annually. At the *operational level*, you drill down to the SKUs that you'll carry in each category. In both sorts of planning, you consider whether and how much to *localize* your assortment. Options here range from having a single assortment for the entire chain to unique assortments for each store.

Current Practice

In this chapter, we examine current practice in each of these categories and then describe our experiences helping two retailers strengthen their assortment planning.[1] By giving greater care to picking their assortments, they were able to boost their sales. We suspect that you'll see the same sorts of gains by taking greater care with yours.

Strategic Planning: Thinking Big

Assortment planning begins with setting goals for each department and product category for unit sales, market share, revenue, and profit.[2] You'll increase resources, including store space and purchase dollars, earmarked for some product categories, while decreasing them for others to reflect product, competitive, and fashion trends.

A forecast of future sales helps to decide which categories to expand and which to contract. Figure 2-1 shows Best Buy's sales of digital and film cameras for 1995 to 2002. A logical forecast for 2003 would be a decrease in the sales of traditional cameras and an increase in sales for digitals, compared with sales in 2002.

FIGURE 2-1

Historical sales of film and digital cameras

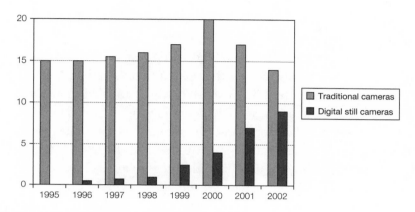

This figure is an illustrative example and the values are approximate.

Source: Kevin Freeland, chief operating officer, Advance Auto Parts, and former senior vice president for inventory management, Best Buy.

But figure 2-1 also shows the limitation of this approach. A forecast of 2001 film camera sales based on an extrapolation of historical sales would have erred high. A smarter forecast would have factored in intelligence from trade shows, conversations with vendors, observations of competitor moves, and reviews of new technology. With this information, a retailer identifies potential changes in sales for a product or category that might not be apparent from a straightforward extrapolation of sales history. In the case of cameras, these sorts of observations would've led you to predict the fast rise in the sales of digitals.

The method we'll describe relies on recent sales history to identify profitable assortment changes and therefore is most appropriate for product segments where demand patterns change slowly. Many product segments, particularly in grocery and hard lines, satisfy this requirement, but some, such as fashion apparel, do not. Urban Outfitters' CEO Glen Senk's remark that "In fashion apparel, there is nothing as boring as last season's hot seller," clearly illustrates that for fashion products, history can lead one in exactly the wrong direction. But even in the volatile world of fashion apparel, attributes can help. Urban Outfitters has developed an impressive approach to dynamically adjusting their assortment within a season by having their buyers focus on current sales and identify which product attributes are trending upwards or downwards.

Borders, the bookseller, has an even more advanced approach to strategic assortment planning. Two brothers, Tom and Louis Borders, founded the company. Tom majored in English at the University of Michigan, which explains why they based their chain in Ann Arbor. Louis studied computer science at MIT, which enabled their chain to develop sophisticated information technology in its early days.

Borders segments its books into about nine thousand categories and allows each store to carry a different number of titles in each category.[3] To choose the number of titles in each category for each store, it relies on a measure called *relative sales per title* (RST), which equals the sales in a category in a store over a specified period, divided by the number of titles carried in the category over the same period. If RST is high for a store category in a recent period, then Borders increases the number of titles in that category. If RST is low, it reduces them. It might, for example, divide the one thousand categories in a store into upper, middle, and lower thirds of RST values and then increase the number of titles carried in the upper third by 10 percent and reduce the lower third by 10 percent. (Borders' process also takes seasonality into account, but that is outside the scope of this chapter.)

The philosophy behind Borders' approach makes sense—put resources where they can earn the greatest return. Borders' approach is on the right track, but we can do even better by understanding that as you analyze your company's assortment, what matters is the *marginal return on incremental resources*, not the average return of resources already deployed.

Figure 2-2 shows revenue versus SKU count for two hypothetical product categories. The SKUs in each category are ranked by dollar sales rate. Then the revenue is plotted as SKUs are added, one by one, in rank order. Note that the first category has higher average sales per SKU, but just a few high sellers cause this; the weakest SKUs in the category barely sell and add little revenue. By contrast, the second category has lower average sales per SKU, but all of its SKUs are equally productive. It would therefore make sense to reduce the SKU count for category 1 and increase it for category 2. You can delete half the SKUs

FIGURE 2-2

Enhancing the Borders approach by considering the marginally performing SKU in each category

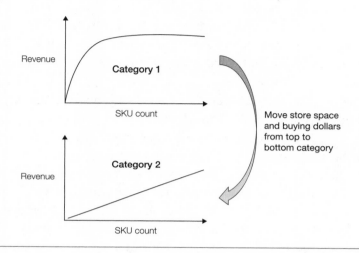

in category 1 with little loss of revenue. If you then use the resources freed to add a comparable number of SKUs to category 2, their sales rate will probably resemble that of the SKUs currently in the category.

As you apply these insights in your company, you should evaluate categories by *their marginal productivity*—that is, you should target categories where the worst-performing SKUs have relatively low sales rates, and delete them to free space to add SKUs to categories where the worst performers have relatively high sales rates, indicating potential for growth.

Operational Planning: Getting Specific

Once a retailer decides how many SKUs to carry in a category, it faces the operational problem of picking particular ones. In flat panel TVs, for example, Best Buy might stock 82 different models. The number of potential SKUs, of course, is much larger, comprising eight diagonal widths, five screen types, seven resolution levels, and nine major vendors, for a total of 2,520 (that is, of $8 \times 5 \times 7 \times 9$). Company buyers select the specific SKUs, and they incorporate many factors into this decision, including ensuring that Best Buy offers products from a variety of vendors. That way, the chain can benefit from competition when negotiating on price, and its customers have more choices.

One challenge in assortment planning is including new products; buyers will have to consider many goods for which Best Buy has no sales experience. The lack of sales histories for these thwarts analytic planning. A buyer will have little, if any, data to use in making decisions.

Be aware that assortment decisions aren't only about maximizing the profit on every single SKU. Though that's the focus of this chapter, you might also select a SKU to help sell other goods. An obvious example would be a loss leader that attracts shoppers to your store. And low-priced offerings are not the only way of enticing customers. A broad array in a category, including high-end aspirational goods, can signal that your store is the best place to buy all of the products in that category. Bike shops, for example, will often sell custom-built frames by makers like Seven and Independent Fabrication, even though the vast majority of their sales come from off-the-rack offerings like Trek and Cannondale. The custom frames give shops cachet with bike aficionados, even if many of those customers choose not to pony up that much money for a bike.

Carrying a premium-priced offering can increase the sales of other pricey products by making them look like relative bargains. In a Publix supermarket, one of us noticed a bottle of wine selling for $264—a lofty price anywhere, much less in a grocery store. The natural question for the wine manager was how much of that wine he sold. His response: "None, but we sell a lot of this $67 bottle next to it *because* we carry the $264 bottle."

Another reason to carry slow-moving SKUs is to please your best customers. Jim Halpin, former president of BJ's, tells a story that illustrates this point.[4] Soon after he became president of BJ's, he got a sales report and noticed a dessert pie SKU at the bottom of the list: BJ's was selling a whopping three a week. So he deleted the SKU. That was a no-brainer, he thought—until he got an angry call a few days later from one of his best customers asking why he'd stopped carrying his dessert pie. Those three a month mattered to this customer, and this customer mattered to BJ's.

Grocery chains, which can obtain data on customers' baskets of purchases through loyalty cards, are ideally positioned to protect themselves from this pitfall. Before they delete a SKU, they can assess the average size of the basket of goods purchased by customers who typically bought that SKU. If they notice that caviar buyers tend to purchase $500 worth of groceries every time they visit, they should keep the slow-selling fish eggs.

All Retailing Is Local

Traditionally, a retailer would use the same assortment in all of its stores, except perhaps for eliminating less important SKUs in smaller outlets. Recently, some firms have made great efforts to localize their assortments.[5] They'll group their stores into clusters with similar demographics or sales mixes and then apply their chain-level assortment planning process to each cluster.

Though it sounds promising—after all, what's better than catering to your customers?—problems arise with this approach. It's a ton of work. Manual planning must be done not just once for the chain but for each cluster. And despite all of the toil, localization may not lift sales. One home-fabrics retailer implemented the approach for a category that it thought would benefit, and achieved an 18 percent sales increase. Pleased with the results, it tried a second category, but saw no rise. That ended its enthusiasm for localization.

Another challenge is figuring out the right number of clusters to form and picking one of the many ways of forming them.

Politics complicates localization, just as it complicates many things. If you choose to localize, you also have to decide *who gets to decide*. That is, you have to figure out how to divide decision-making authority between your headquarters and stores. The most common approach is for headquarters personnel to dictate a single common assortment to be carried by all stores. But a few retailers—Bed Bath & Beyond is one—allow their store managers considerable authority in deciding which SKUs to carry. Usually, the corporate office mandates a portion of the SKUs, and store managers choose the rest for their locations from an approved list of options. Differing offerings in each store end up, in theory, tuned to the tastes of that location's customers. Delegating a portion of the assortment decision to stores is decentralized localization, but it's also possible to make all assortment decisions centrally and still localize the assortment. The Borders approach to assortment planning described previously is an excellent example of localized assortments created centrally.

Real Experiences in Assortment Planning and Localization

By now, you probably have come to understand that SKU assortments resemble the weather: they can bollix even the best-laid plans. But as with the weather, a forecast, even an imperfect one, helps.

In this section, we'll describe a method (developed in collaboration with one of our doctoral students, Ramnath Vaidyanathan, now a professor in McGill University's business school) for making such a forecast of store-SKU demand, even for SKUs for which you have no experience. As examples, we'll use the snack cake assortment of a regional convenience chain and the tire assortment of a national tire retailer.[6] Our approach mostly left alone the overarching strategic planning process at both retailers. We just injected analytics and information technology to help the two retailers pick better items.

The best retail buyers consider their products as packages of attributes. A buyer for a home-fabrics seller, for example, will see bed sheets in terms of size, color, fabric type, and thread count. She'll try to carry a set of SKUs that includes all possible values of these attributes but will overweight the ones that customers seem to most want. If she sees that twin sheets are selling better than queens, she'll carry both but stock more twins.

Not everyone, of course, has the experience or talent to make these sorts of judgments. What we do with our analytic approach is to translate a talented buyer's way of thinking into a formulaic approach that anyone can use.

Like the talented buyer, we define each SKU as a collection of attributes. We then use prior sales to forecast market share in a store for each attribute value and use this information to forecast demand for any potential SKU. This approach lets you forecast the demand for SKUs that you haven't sold before. If you're in the home-fabrics business, you may never have sold a set of pink twin sateen 400-thread-count sheets, but you would have surely sold twin sheets and sateen sheets and 400-thread-count sheets and probably even pink sheets. You can use their sales history to estimate the percentage of customers who will buy sheets that combine all of the attributes. You simply multiply the percentage of demand for pink and the percentage of demand for twin and the percentage of demand for sateen and the percentage of demand for 400 thread count.

This approach can be applied at any level from chain to cluster to individual store. It lets you do lots of what-if analyses to answer questions like how much you'll gain by localizing your assortments.

Forecasting based on attributes lends itself to localization. Retailers typically think and talk in terms of attributes. Chat with them about what's selling and what's not, and you'll hear things like "We sell more black in Manhattan than in Madison, Wisconsin, more plus sizes in Iowa than in Florida, and more cotton in Canada than in Los Angeles."

Understand that using attributes as the basis for forecasts isn't perfect. It entails approximation because it assumes that attribute demand patterns are independent of each other. In reality, customers who buy queen-size sheets may have a greater preference for 400-thread-count ones than those who buy twins, so using sales of all sizes to estimate demand for the 400-thread-count ones might cause you to overestimate the demand for 400-thread-count twins. Nonetheless, this simplifying assumption is extremely useful because it allows you to forecast the demand for a vast number of possible SKUs from a relatively small set of parameters. Your assumptions won't be perfect, but, as you'll see in our examples, they can be good.

We make other assumptions that you should be aware of. We assume that consumer preferences for attributes are stable over time or at least trend in a predictable way. That's certainly not true for some products, such as trendy apparel, where there's nothing staler than last season's hit. But in many categories, especially hard goods and food, customer preferences change gradually, so tracking customer preferences via sales history makes sense. We also assume that if a customer doesn't find her first choice, she may substitute a different product.

Tasty Techniques in the Snack Cake Aisle

Now let's turn to Little Debbie and her competitors in the snack cake aisle and use the example of planning an assortment for a convenience store chain to illustrate this approach. The primary input that we'll use is store-SKU sales over the last six months of 2005. Table 2-1 provides an example of the data for one store. This retailer carried thirty-nine out of the sixty-eight possible brand-size-flavor combinations (two

TABLE 2-1

July 1–December 31, 2005, snack cake sales in a convenience store[a]

	SINGLE SERVE		FAMILY SIZE		
PRICE	$1.29		$3.34		
Flavor	Yummy Cakes	Tiny Tina	Yummy Cakes	Tiny Tina	Revenue
Chocolate	7,246	3,100	472	456	$16,445.86
Cinnamon	3,182	1,487	551	385	$9,149.25
Butter	1,398	1,355		331	$4,656.91
Cheese	353	570		335	$2,309.57
Raspberry	3,100	1,471		398	$7,225.91
Vanilla	1,513	1,155		184	$4,056.28
Chocolate chip	2,034		185	139	$3,706.02
Fudge	2,926	563	274		$5,415.97
Butterscotch	3,009		325		$4,967.11
Peanut butter	4,780		380		$7,435.40
Honey	2,169	967			$4,045.44
Apple		224		60	$489.36
Cherry/cheese		1,596			$2,058.84
Vanilla/chocolate		2,162			$2,788.98
Oatmeal/raisin	4,049				$5,223.21
Coconut	1,827				$2,356.83
Buttercream			100		$334.00
Totals	37,586	14,650	2,287	2,288	$82,664.94
Sales shares	66%	26%	4%	4%	

a. The numbers in this table have been disguised to protect confidentiality.

brands × two sizes × seventeen flavors = sixty-eight combinations) at this location. We can't reveal the actual names of the two brands, so we'll call them Yummy Cakes and Tiny Tina.

These thirty-nine SKUs generated revenue of $82,665 during the six-month period. A crucial question is whether a different set of thirty-nine SKUs might generate more sales in the future. (Prices varied slightly across the different flavors and the two brands within a size, but for simplicity, we'll use the average prices for single serving and family size of $1.29 and $3.34.)

Not surprisingly, most retailers do better at identifying poorly performing SKUs and deleting them than at identifying promising new ones and adding them. As a result, many retailers follow a "gin rummy" strategy. They discard the worst-selling SKUs from their current hand of products and randomly draw from the deck of potential new offerings. They hope that, over time, they'll identify a productive assortment.

But what if you could have an accurate sales forecast for any assortment your store might offer? Instead of guessing which products might sell, you could then choose the exact assortment that would maximize revenue. That's what we'll show you how to do now.

Our challenge in working with the convenience store chain was to use the data in table 2-1 to estimate the demand for brand-size flavors not offered. We started by estimating the shares of the four brand-sizes. We could have just used the sales shares shown in table 2-1 to estimate demand shares of the four brand-sizes. But these sales shares had been influenced by the assortment offered and thus didn't represent true demand. The chain had previously offered Yummy Cakes in more single-serving flavors than it did Tiny Tina. That inflated the sales share of Yummy Cakes: in some instances, customers really wanted Tiny Tina in a particular flavor but had to settle for Yummy Cakes. We sidestepped this problem by focusing on the two flavors where the chain had offered all four brand-sizes—chocolate and cinnamon—and where sales thus represented true demand because no customers had been forced to substitute. Table 2-2 shows the calculation of demand shares for these two flavors. Notice that, as predicted, the demand share of Yummy Cakes is lower, and that of Tiny Tina is higher, than their sales shares in single serving. This shows the impact of the assortment on sales. Demand shares for family size also differ for the same reason.

TABLE 2-2

Calculating brand-size demand shares using the flavors where all four brand-sizes are offered

Flavor	SINGLE SERVE		FAMILY SIZE	
	Yummy Cakes	Tiny Tina	Yummy Cakes	Tiny Tina
Chocolate	7,246	3,100	472	456
Cinnamon	3,182	1,487	551	385
Total	10,428	4,587	1,023	841
Demand share	62%	27%	6%	5%

Next we used these brand-share estimates to estimate the demand for the SKUs not offered. How much, for example, would the store sell if it offered Yummy Cakes in family-size butter flavor? It's tempting to use the 6 percent and 5 percent shares for Yummy Cakes and Tiny Tina in family size, observe that Yummy Cakes sells 20 percent more than Tiny Tina, and reason that since the store sold 331 in Tiny Tina family-size butter, it might expect to sell about 397 of Yummy Cakes.

But this logic ignores product substitution. If customers don't find what they really want, they may buy another product instead. Thus the 331 units sold of Tiny Tina might have included customers who wanted Yummy Cakes but bought Tiny Tina when they couldn't find their first choice. Studies of convenience store customers have shown that they place a much higher weight on flavor than brand in their purchase decisions for snack cakes and that they are unlikely to jump between family size and single serving. Someone seeking a midmorning snack doesn't want to lug a box of Tastykakes or Hostess Ho Hos around in his backpack for the rest of the day. We assumed that the likelihood of substitution across flavors and sizes was zero, and focused on estimating the percentage of customers who substituted between brands within a size and flavor.

How can we estimate the likelihood of substitution between brands? Notice that for four of the flavors shown in table 2-1—butter, cheese, raspberry, and vanilla—the chain carried Tiny Tina in single and family sizes and Yummy Cakes in single size. In those flavors, it didn't offer any Yummy Cakes in the family size. With this information, you can estimate the fraction of customers who substituted Tiny Tina in family size for Yummy Cakes in that size. Table 2-3 shows the calculation.

Here's the logic behind table 2-3. The sales of Yummy Cakes and Tiny Tina in single serving represent true demand since the store offered both brands, and customers didn't have to substitute. These sales totaled 10,915 (6,364 + 4,551), and, as we calculated in table 2-2, they represented 89 percent of total demand for these four flavors. This means that the total demand for the four flavors was 12,264 (10,915 / 0.89). Thus the demand for Yummy Cakes and Tiny Tina in family size can be calculated as 6 percent and 5 percent of this total value, which are the values 736 and 613 shown in table 2-3. If 613 was the true demand for Tiny Tina in family size, then you could estimate that 635 (1,248 − 613) customers preferred Yummy Cakes *but substituted Tiny Tina* when their first choice wasn't available. This means that 86 percent (635 / 736) of the customers who wanted Yummy Cakes bought Tiny Tina instead. You thus can conclude that the likelihood of a customer substituting from Yummy Cakes to Tiny Tina in family size is 86 percent.

Here's another way to think about estimating the rate of substitution. You know from the share estimations that family size represents

TABLE 2-3

Calculation of the percentage of customers who will substitute from Yummy Cakes to Tiny Tina in family size

Flavor	SINGLE SERVE		FAMILY SIZE	
	Yummy Cakes	Tiny Tina	Yummy Cakes	Tiny Tina
Butter	1,398	1,355		331
Cheese	353	570		335
Raspberry	3,100	1,471		398
Vanilla	1,513	1,155		184
Total	6,364	4,551		1,248
Estimated demand	6,364	4,551	736	613
Substitution demand				635

Portion of customers who substitute from brand 1 to brand 2 in family size = 635 / 736 = 86%

TABLE 2-4

Estimating substitution percentage from Yummy Cakes to Tiny Tina in single serving

	SINGLE SERVE		FAMILY SIZE	
Flavor	**Yummy Cakes**	**Tiny Tina**	**Yummy Cakes**	**Tiny Tina**
Apple		224		60
Estimated demand	366	160	35	30
Substitution demand		64		30

Portion of customers who substitute from brand 1 to brand 2 in single serve = 64/366 = 17%

---

11 percent of demand. If everyone substituted from Yummy Cakes to Tiny Tina, then when Yummy Cakes was missing, family size would still represent 11 percent of sales. If no one substituted, then the 6 percent of sales to customers that prefer Yummy Cakes would be lost, and you'd only capture 94 percent of demand. The 5 percent of customers who buy Tiny Tina in family size would represent 5 / 94 = 5.3 percent of the total demand captured, and hence the share of family size would fall to 5.3 percent of sales. So family-size share when Yummy Cakes is missing will be between 5.3 percent and 11 percent of sales; closer to 5.3 percent indicates low substitution, while closer to 11 percent indicates high substitution. The share of family size is 1,248 units sold / 12,264 total units = 10.2 percent, very close to 11 percent and indicating a high level of substitution. In fact, 10.2 percent actual share / 11 percent maximum share = 93 percent, almost the same as the 86 percent substitution rate we calculated before, so the two viewpoints are similar.

Applying the same logic to the fudge flavor, you can estimate that the likelihood of substitution from Tiny Tina to Yummy Cakes in family size is 20 percent. Likewise, for chocolate chip, the likelihood of substituting from Tiny Tina to Yummy Cakes in single serving is 26 percent.

Estimating the substitution percentage from Yummy Cakes to Tiny Tina in single serving is trickier because there is no flavor in which Yummy Cakes single serving is the only missing brand-size. But table 2-4 shows how you can do this calculation, using sales data of apple-flavored cakes.

Thanks to the brand-size and substitution percentages for family size that you've already estimated, you know that the 60 units sold of Tiny Tina in family size correspond to 10.16 percent of total demand for apple (5 percent + 0.86 × 6 percent). You therefore can estimate total demand for apple as 591 (60 / 0.1016). You then compute the demand estimates shown in table 2-4 as brand-size shares multiplied by this total demand estimate. Once you know the estimated demand for Yummy Cakes and Tiny Tina in the single-serving size, you can compute the substitution demand for Tiny Tina and the substitution percentage from Yummy Cakes to Tiny Tina, as shown in table 2-4.

Table 2-5 summarizes the substitution frequencies we have calculated.

In our experience, most buyers guess that some customers will substitute if they can't find what they want, but many of these buyers lack a way to estimate these values and factor those estimates into their assortment decisions. Table 2-5 shows that substitution rates can vary a lot; customers who buy Yummy Cakes in family size are not very loyal: 86 percent of them switched to Tiny Tina. This made sense to the convenience chain's buyers when we presented our findings, as Yummy Cakes was strong in single serving but had only recently begun to offer family size. These sorts of differences in willingness to substitute have a big impact on assortment planning.

You can use the estimates of brand-size shares in table 2-2 and cross-brand substitution frequencies in table 2-5 to estimate the demand for all brand-size-flavors. Table 2-6 displays these estimates. For each

TABLE 2-5

Estimated substitution percentages

| | SINGLE SERVE | | | FAMILY SIZE | |
| | To | | | | To | |
From	Yummy Cakes	Tiny Tina	From	Yummy Cakes	Tiny Tina
Yummy Cakes		17%	**Yummy Cakes**		86%
Tiny Tina	26%		**Tiny Tina**	20%	

TABLE 2-6

Estimated demand for all brand-size-flavors

Flavor	SALES					Share of demand captured	ESTIMATED DEMAND					
	SINGLE SERVE		FAMILY SIZE				SINGLE SERVE		FAMILY SIZE			
	Yummy Cakes	Tiny Tina	Yummy Cakes	Tiny Tina	Total		Yummy Cakes	Tiny Tina	Yummy Cakes	Tiny Tina	Total demand	Total demand estimate
Chocolate	7,246	3,100	472	456	11,274	100%	7,246	3,100	472	456	11,274	11,274
Cinnamon	3,182	1,487	551	385	5,605	100%	3,182	1,487	551	385	5,605	5,605
Butter	1,398	1,355		331	3,084	99%	1,398	1,355	187	156	3,095	3,110
Cheese	353	570		335	1,258	99%	353	570	76	63	1,063	1,269
Raspberry	3,100	1,471		398	4,969	99%	3,100	1,471	301	251	5,122	5,011
Vanilla	1,513	1,155		184	2,852	99%	1,513	1,155	173	144	2,984	2,876
Chocolate chip	2,034		185	139	2,358	80%	1,827	796	185	139	2,947	2,947
Fudge	2,926	563	274		3,763	96%	2,926	563	235	196	3,920	3,920
Butterscotch	3,009		325		3,334	76%	2,719	1,184	263	219	4,386	4,386
Peanut butter	4,780		380		5,160	76%	4,208	1,833	407	339	6,788	6,788
Honey	2,169	967			3,136	89%	2,169	967	211	176	3,524	3,524
Apple		224		60	284	48%	369	161	36	30	595	595
Cherry/cheese		1,596			1,596	38%	2,636	1,148	255	213	4,251	4,251
Vanilla/chocolate		2,162			2,162	38%	3,571	1,555	346	288	5,759	5,759
Oatmeal/raisin	4,049				4,049	69%	3,637	1,584	352	293	5,866	5,866
Coconut	1,827				1,827	69%	1,641	715	159	132	2,647	2,647
Buttercream			100		100	7%	886	386	86	71	1,429	1,429
Totals	37,586	14,650	2,287	2,288	56,811	80%	43,381	20,028	4,294	3,552	71,255	71,257

flavor, you know total sales, given the assortment of brand-sizes offered in that flavor. You can also compute the fraction of potential demand captured, both from customers for whom a brand-size offered is their first choice and from customers for whom it is their second choice but who are willing to substitute. Witness the 7 percent share captured by buttercream. It results from the 6 percent of customers who made Tiny Tina family-size buttercream their first choice plus the 1 percent of customers who wanted Tiny Tina but substituted Yummy Cakes (20 percent of 5 percent equals 1 percent). You can then estimate total demand for a flavor, assuming the chain offered all four brand-sizes, as total sales divided by share captured. For buttercream, for example, the estimated total demand is 1,429 (100 / 0.07). You can then multiple total demand by brand-size shares to obtain estimates of SKU demand. The 62 percent share of Yummy Cakes in single serve, for example, implies a demand estimate for Yummy Cakes single-serving buttercream of 886 (.62 × 1,429).

Table 2-6 shows demand estimates for each brand-size. If the convenience store offered both brands in a flavor and size, we used sales as our demand estimate.[7] In this case, customers didn't need to substitute, so sales corresponded to actual demand. We computed other demand estimates as the shares times the estimated total demand for a particular flavor.

A key question in improving this assortment is which flavors customers want most. A traditional way of answering this is to look at sales rank. But the total demand estimate column in table 2-6 gives a different—and we'd argue, better—answer. Consider the flavor vanilla/chocolate. With total sales of 2,162, this flavor ranks twelfth, near the bottom, making it a candidate for deletion. But if you take our estimates into account, its total demand of 5,759 puts it in third place, near the top of the list.

Why such a big difference? Vanilla/chocolate is offered only in single serving, and is the least popular brand for single serve to boot, and this depresses its sales relative to other flavors. Despite this handicap, if you look closely, customers love this flavor. Its sales of 2,162 ranks second only to chocolate in Yummy Cakes single serving.

This is one more example that the assortment a retailer offers distorts sales away from true demand. If you want to discern true demand, you must tease out customer insights latent in sales data.[8]

Finding an Optimal Assortment—Let's Get Greedy

To use the demand estimates in table 2-6 to find an optimized assortment, you employ a technique called a *greedy rule*. For sake of concreteness, suppose you're seeking a revenue-maximizing assortment for this store, subject to the constraint that the assortment contain no more than thirty-nine SKUs. (You could just as easily apply this approach to the chain or a cluster of stores, and you can use it to maximize unit sales or dollar gross margin.) The greedy rule chooses thirty-nine SKUs sequentially, choosing as the first SKU the one that would maximize revenue if it were the only one in the assortment. Note that the revenue of a SKU is its primary demand revenue plus any revenue from substitution demand from other SKUs. Thus the first SKU that you choose might not have the highest demand; it might be many customers' second choice. You choose the second SKU to maximize the increase in revenue *given the first SKU that you picked*. You continue to pick SKUs that maximize the increase in revenue from their selection until you've selected thirty-nine of them.

Table 2-7 shows the resulting new assortment. We estimated that this assortment would capture $99,757 in revenue, a 21 percent increase over the current assortment revenue of $82,665. Note the other ways in which the assortment has changed. First of all, our assortment drops Yummy Cakes in family size in all flavors. Recall that 86 percent of the customers who preferred Yummy Cakes in family size were willing to switch to Tiny Tina. Thus the revenue lost by dropping Yummy Cakes is only 0.11 times its 6 percent share, or .66 percent. Our assortment also drops cheese and apple, the least popular flavors. The revenue lost is again small because few customers preferred these flavors. This frees room in the assortment to add additional brand-sizes in the more popular flavors, which generates the 20 percent sales lift.

Figure 2-3 shows the results of applying the greedy rule to the demand estimates for all of the stores of this chain. Figure 2-3 gives revenue as a function of SKU count for the two extremes of assortment localization: no localization, which corresponds to one assortment for the chain; and maximum localization, which corresponds to a unique assortment for each store. To get a single chain assortment, we applied

TABLE 2-7

Revised assortment—shaded cells are SKUs carried in the new assortment

Flavor	Single Serve		Family Size		Current	New
	Yummy Cakes	Tiny Tina	Yummy Cakes	Tiny Tina		
Chocolate	7,246	3,100	472	456	$16,446	$16,225
Peanut butter	4,780		380		$7,435	$10,096
Vanilla/chocolate		2,162			$2,789	$8,566
Cinnamon	3,182	1,487	551	385	$9,149	$8,892
Oatmeal/raisin	4,049				$5,223	$8,726
Raspberry	3,100	1,471		398	$7,226	$7,597
Butterscotch	3,009		325		$4,967	$6,523
Cherry/cheese		1,596			$2,059	$6,324
Honey	2,169	967			$4,045	$5,241
Butter	1,398	1,355		331	$4,657	$4,607
Vanilla	1,513	1,155		184	$4,056	$4,418
Fudge	2,926	563	274		$5,416	$5,294
Chocolate chip	2,034		185	139	$3,706	$3,619
Coconut	1,827				$2,357	$2,357
Buttercream			100		$334	$1,272
Cheese	353	570		335	$2,310	$-
Apple		224		60	$489	$-
Totals	37,586	14,650	2,287	2,288	$82,665	$99,757

the greedy rule to sequentially choose SKUs guided by the total revenue across all stores for a SKU choice.

These curves are a by-product of the greedy rule, which adds SKUs one by one, and every point on each curve is backed up by a specific assortment that is estimated to produce the revenue shown. The figure also shows a point that gives the revenue of the thirty-nine-SKU assortment currently used by the retailer. The revenue increase from reassorting at the chain level is 28 percent; maximum localization can give another 13 percent.

FIGURE 2-3

Reassorting is estimated to add 41% to revenue

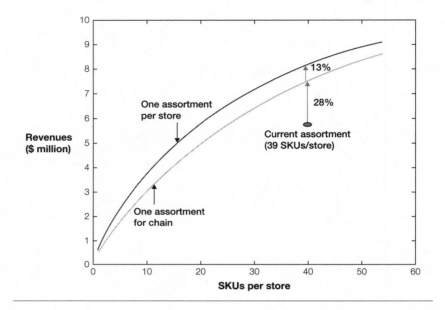

This retailer, like many, liked the revenue increase from localization but was reluctant to have a unique assortment for each store because of the high administrative costs. Its buyers asked about having five different assortments for the chain. To do that, you'd begin with the store-specific assortments and cluster these using the following approach, until you'd reduced the number of assortments to five. First, you'd choose two stores to combine. Your criterion for clustering them could be either least loss in revenue or greatest overlap between the two store-specific assortments. You'd then apply the greedy rule to this two-store cluster. You'd continue to pair up stores into clusters until you had exactly five assortments and every store had been assigned to one of these five assortments. The good news is that the localization gain from cutting back to just five assortments only dropped from 13 percent to 12.5 percent, so most of the gain was achieved with just five well-chosen assortments.

Tire Assortments—Where the Rubber Meets the Road

We also applied our approach to planning the assortment for a national tire retailer. When buying tires, people care about brand, mileage warranty, and size. This retailer offered several nationally known brands, including BFGoodrich, Goodyear, and Michelin, which we treated as one category called National. It also offered three house brands of decreasing quality, which we denote as House 1, House 2, and House 3, with House 1 being the best and costliest. Manufacturers provided a couple dozen distinct mileage warranties on their tires. Some of them varied only slightly, so the staff at the retailer believed that consumers viewed them as equivalents. For our analysis, we grouped the mileage warranties into three levels: high, medium, and low.

It doesn't make sense to sell an expensive tire with a low mileage warranty, or vice versa. The retailer therefore offered the following six brand-warranty combinations, which it believed to be logical pairings: National-High (NH), National-Medium (NM), House 1-High (H1H), House 2-High (H2H), House 2-Medium (H2M), and House 3-Low (H3L). The retailer could choose from 64 tire sizes, resulting in 384 (64 × 6) possible SKUs. It offered 122 of the 384 possibilities. That raised an obvious question: might any of the 262 tires *not* offered generate enough demand to warrant selling them?

As with many products, a customer might substitute another tire if she didn't find her first choice. The retailer didn't have sufficient data for us to estimate all possible substitution probabilities. We relied instead on management to tell us the most likely substitution patterns, and focused on those. Substitution across sizes didn't happen. Table 2-8 depicts the likelihood of substitution from a given brand-warranty level listed in a row to another listed over a column, as estimated by the vice president of the tire category. His analysis suggested the need to estimate three substitution frequencies: most likely, likely, and somewhat likely.

When creating a mathematical model of a problem, you face a choice between building a simple, tractable model with a few parameters and a more accurate, but complex, one with many parameters. Here, we could have used a complex model of substitution that

TABLE 2-8

Management's estimate of the most likely substitution patterns

From	NH	NM	To H1H	H2H	H2M
NH			S	S	
NM	L		S	S	
H1H	S			L	S
H2H			S		S
H2M				L	
H3L					M

M = most likely

L = likely

S = somewhat likely

A blank cell indicates no chance of substitution.

allowed for a different substitution frequency from any brand-warranty to any other brand-warranty, which would have led to thirty substitution parameters (six brand-warranties, each of which could substitute to five other brand-warranties). A more complex model often seems more appealing at first; after all, why wouldn't you want as much precision as possible? Unfortunately, that kind of complexity contradicts a statistical principle called *the law of large numbers* (also known as the law of averages), which says that you get a better estimate when you average a large number of values. Imagine, for example, that you wanted to predict the chances a coin would come up heads by flipping it a number of times. If you flipped it ten times, you might see six heads and estimate a 60 percent chance of heads. But this six is likely due to chance. If you flipped it one hundred times, and it was a fair coin, you'd likely see, say, forty-nine or fifty-one heads and estimate a likelihood of about 50 percent. Extend your experiment to a million flips, and you're likely to get a very tired wrist—and almost exactly 50 percent heads.

Now return to our example of modeling substitution. The more complex model had thirty substitution parameters; the simpler model, three. With a fixed amount of data, that's ten times more data per parameter in the simple model than in the more complex one, which is like flipping the coin one hundred times rather than ten. So the increased accuracy you get with more data per parameter often favors simplicity, especially if, as in this case, the retailer believes that substitution rates are similar between various options.

Table 2-9 shows sales data for a given store for a subset of sizes. We applied the analysis approach described above to this sales data for each store to estimate the six brand-warranty shares, sixty-four size shares, and the three substitution frequencies. Table 2-10 shows

TABLE 2-9

Input data for a store is sales during the last six months of 2004 by size-brand-warranty level for SKUs that were offered. A subset of sizes is shown.

Size	National-High	National-Medium	House 1-High	House 2-High	House 2-Medium	House 3-Low
P235/75R15	100				55	40
P215/70R15	282	21		334	203	
P175/80R13					5	20
P205/75R14					10	84
P205/65R15	72	64	20	272	570	
P225/60R16	56		97	285	763	
P215/60R16	10		16	70	76	
P195/70R14		7	33	157	377	
P205/70R15		10		272	524	
P185/65R14		39		225	568	
P225/70R15			8	100	73	
P185/70R14			8	95	223	
P195/65R15				152	298	
P215/65R15				144	221	
P205/75R15	8					200
P175/70R13						436
P185/60R14					101	
P195/60R14					115	

the average across all stores of the estimated brand-warranty demand shares and substitution probabilities. Figure 2-4 is based on store-specific estimates and shows that the House 3-Low share in a specific store is correlated with the income level in the store's zip code, which makes sense. (You should always seek confirmation for the conclusions of your analyses of sales history, and store demographic data is a wonderful place to start.)

TABLE 2-10

Estimation results

Brand-warranty	Sales share	Estimated demand share
National-High	1%	4%
National-Medium	1%	3%
House 1-High	3%	4%
House 2-High	26%	23%
House 2-Medium	45%	5%
House 3-Low	24%	61%

Substitution probabilities: somewhat likely = 2%, likely = 6%, most likely = 45%

FIGURE 2-4

Share of the low-price tire correlates with income

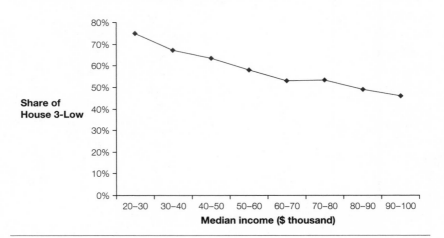

Table 2-10 also gives the sales shares for comparison with the demand-share estimates. Notice that the demand-share estimate for House 3-Low greatly exceeds the sales share. For House 2-Medium, it falls short of the sales share. This retailer offered House 3-Low in only nine of sixty-four sizes, so customers had few purchase opportunities. But as shown in table 2-11, when the retailer did offer House 3-Low, customers strongly preferred it over the next-highest price selection: House 2-Medium.

The retailer preferred to sell the higher-priced House 2-Medium, believing that its sales staff could persuade customers to trade up. The substitution estimate of 45 percent shows that many customers did trade up, and this explains the high sales share for House 2-Medium relative to its demand share. But the 55 percent of the 61 percent of customers preferring House 3-Low suggests that the retailer lost more than a third of demand due to the meager amount of House 3-Low in its assortment. It could have increased sales by adding House 3-Low in more sizes.

Figure 2-5 shows the results of our analysis. This retailer carried 105 SKUs per store in its current assortment. In the optimized assortment, it would replace 47 of these. The biggest contributor to the 36 percent increase in revenue would be carrying the House 3-Low tire-warranty combination in more sizes.

TABLE 2-11

In the nine sizes where they competed head-to-head, House 3-Low significantly outsold House 2-Medium

Size	House 2-Medium	House 3-Low
P205/75R14	2,419	134,183
P195/75R14	1,342	111,339
P235/75R15	1,852	102,749
P205/75R15	1,675	102,580
P185/75R14	1,846	88,348
P215/75R15	1,703	73,255
P225/75R15	2,659	50,664
P155/80R13	2,108	42,432
P175/80R13	2,432	16,486
Total	18,036	722,036

FIGURE 2-5

Reassorting is estimated to add 36 percent to revenue

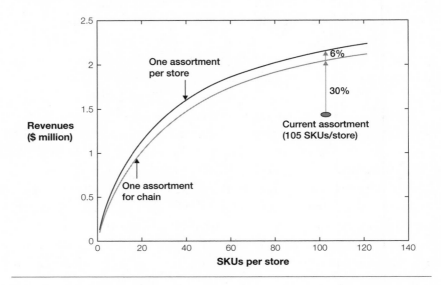

When Does Localization Pay?

We sought to understand why localization had a significantly lower impact on tires than snack cakes (6 percent versus 13 percent revenue impact). We first thought that the store-to-store variation in demand patterns for snack cakes was greater than for tires, but found that the variation was nearly equal for the two cases, and in fact slightly higher for tires. We then realized that the percentage of maximum demand captured by the single chain optimal assortment would also affect the benefits of localization. If a retailer carried such a broad assortment that the single chain assortment captured nearly all of the potential demand, then there would be very little improvement potential left for local- ization. The snack cakes assortment offers 40 percent of the potential SKUs, while the tire assortment offers 27 percent of potential SKUs, so it might seem that the snack cakes assortment is broader. However, as shown by the curves in figure 2-6 (which show cumulative percentage of maximum revenue captured by a given percentage of the SKUs in the

FIGURE 2-6

Cumulative revenue share versus percentage of SKUs

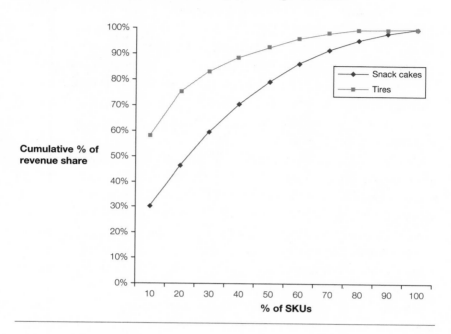

chain optimal assortment, where the SKUs have been sorted in decreasing order of contribution to revenue), the 27 percent of tire SKUs offered capture 82 percent of maximum revenue, whereas the 40 percent of snack cake SKUs offered capture just 68 percent of maximum potential revenue. Thus for tires, only 18 percent of maximum revenue is left to be captured by localization, whereas 32 percent is left to be captured by localization in the snack cakes case, nearly twice as much.

Thus the benefits of localization depend not only on the amount of demand variation between stores but on the percentage of demand captured by the single chain optimal assortment. This is an important principle for retailers to consider in choosing which categories to localize. The natural inclination is for a retailer to localize its most important categories, but we have seen cases where the retailer carried such a broad assortment in its most important categories that there was little to be gained from localization.

While localizing assortments by store added only 6 percent to revenue for the tire assortment, there were meaningful differences between stores. Table 2-12 shows demand estimates for two stores, in Nashville and New Brunswick, and gives median incomes for the zip codes in which these stores are located. New Brunswick customers, with 70 percent higher income than the Nashville customers, buy more of the most expensive national brand and less of the least expensive House 3 brand, and this is reflected in a higher demand share for National-High and a lower demand share for House 3-Low in the New Brunswick store.

These differences in demand estimates influence the store specific assortments for the two stores. The Nashville assortment contains twenty-one SKUs that are not carried in the New Brunswick store and, correspondingly, the New Brunswick store has twenty-one SKUs not carried in Nashville. Ten of the Nashville unique SKUs are the lowest-priced House 3-Low tires and another five are the next lowest-priced House 2-Medium. Conversely, twelve of the New Brunswick unique SKUs are the highest-priced National-High.

These SKU differences didn't arise because we explicitly considered customers' income levels. Our results stemmed purely from the demand data. Higher-priced tires ended up being carried in the wealthier zip code because higher incomes led to their purchase. And that, in turn,

TABLE 2-12

Demand shares and income for two stores

Brand	Warranty	ESTIMATED SHARES	
		Nashville	**New Brunswick**
National	High	2%	6%
National	Medium	1%	4%
House 1	High	3%	4%
House 2	High	28%	29%
House 2	Medium	6%	6%
House 3	Low	61%	51%
Median income		$45,377	$77,194

led to higher demand estimates for the costlier tires, which caused our revenue-maximizing greedy rule to choose more of those tires. Even so, the apparent causal relationship that emerged comports with common sense. It's a real-world check on the reasonableness of our results.

Implementation Produced a 6 Percent Revenue Increase

The retailer implemented a portion of these recommendations by adding eleven of the SKUs on our list of forty-seven and deleting eleven of the SKUs that we recommended dropping. We estimated these changes would increase revenue by 13 percent. In fact, the retailer got a revenue increase of 6 percent. The lower result stemmed from changes in demand patterns from the sales-history period to the implementation. Even so, a 6 percent improvement is large relative to what retailers typically achieve through enhancements to existing stores. In its annual report, for example, Canadian Tire reports achieving a 3 percent to 4 percent annual revenue increase in existing stores during 2005 through 2007 and is targeting the same increase through 2012.[9]

Conclusions

The process for assortment planning that we have presented comprises three steps: modeling, estimation, and optimization.

Modeling consists of choosing attributes, attribute values, and possible substitution paths. You'll typically encounter one of three types of attributes in your assortment planning; all three were represented in the examples considered in this chapter.

1. *Functional attributes* address whether and how a given product satisfies a consumer need. Examples include the sizes of tires, batteries, shoes, apparel, and sheets. There is no substitution across these attributes. Someone who needs a twin sheet won't buy a queen.

2. *Price* and *value* are typically seen in the good-better-best segmentation used by many retailers. Many consumers regard a

higher-thread-count sheet as a better product, and so it carries a higher price. In general, the closer the price of a product is to a customer's preferred price/value point, the more likely she is to accept it as a substitute.

3. *Taste* attributes include such things as flavor, color, and fabric type.

In defining attribute values, you should group values that differ only slightly and may be indistinguishable to the customer. We did this with the tires, grouping many distinct warranty levels into low, medium, and high. The same challenge arose with the snack cake package sizes. In reality, the manufacturers offered a large number of package sizes that varied only slightly. These thus could be grouped into single-serving and family sizes. A reason to group attribute values is that limited data undermines accurate estimation. Thus modeling requires some judgment, especially in choosing the right level of aggregation of attribute values. We have found a trial-and-error approach works well: make an initial choice and then revise, as needed, after seeing the results of your estimate.

The most important point about *estimation* is that the assortment currently offered affects sales, and you need to control for this in estimating demand shares. This was especially apparent in the tire example, where the House 3-Low tire had much higher potential demand than was reflected in the sales, because not much of it had been offered.

Typical ways of estimating demand for a new product assume that its sales will resemble the sales of a similar existing product. This works if a new product varies only negligibly from an existing offering, such as when this year's model replaces last year's. But in most cases, if a new product resembles an existing product that closely, you should question the value that the new offering brings to the assortment.

Our approach, in contrast, uses sales of the large number of existing products that have at least one attribute in common with the new product to estimate demand for the new product.

Thinking of a product as a collection of attributes is a familiar idea in marketing and is often used by manufacturers in estimating demand for potential new products. A variant of this approach is called *conjoint analysis* and consists of asking a panel of potential customers for the new product to make a series of pairwise comparisons of various product concepts. These comparisons enable the manufacturer to assess the utility of different attribute levels and then select an optimal basket of attributes. Conjoint analysis requires a considerable effort but makes sense for a retailer introducing a major new product intended to last for a long time, such as an electric car or a Blu-ray high-definition TV. It's probably too time consuming for evaluating the large number of new products that need to be considered in assortment planning. Even so, you can think of our process as "conjoint analysis on the cheap." When a customer shops in a store, he is making comparisons of products and expressing preferences, just as in conjoint analysis, and the approach described in this chapter mines those purchase decisions to find preferences for attributes.

In the two examples that we provided, the retailers had high in-stock rates. If instead a retailer had a high level of stockouts, you would need to account for this in analyzing the sales data. Understand that stockouts are both a blessing and a curse. If customers can't find their favorite products and frequently must substitute, then this distorts sales data and obscures true demand. But you can correct for this by calculating a sales rate during periods when a particular item is in stock and basing your analysis on sales rates rather than total sales.

If stockouts are high, then every day in every store, customers see a different assortment. In effect, the retailer is conducting a kind of ad hoc assortment planning experiment. Remember in the snack cake example where we were able to calculate the substitution rate by looking at "holes" in the assortment—that is, flavors where one or more brand-sizes were missing? Frequent stockouts create more holes and thus opportunities to estimate substitution frequencies.[10]

In our *optimization* analysis, we sought to maximize revenue—which was what the two retailers we helped cared about. But you could apply the same process to maximizing gross margin, unit sales, percentage margin, or really any metric of strategic importance. Also, sometimes the key decision isn't which products to carry but also how much of each one. In a grocery, for example, products can have multiple facings. You can modify the greedy rule to handle this case. When you are choosing the next SKU to add to the assortment, just expand the choices to also include adding another facing or product unit of a SKU already in the assortment. The revenue increase from adding another facing would come from a reduction in stockouts. This can be measured and used in comparison to the revenue increase in adding new SKUs.

The assortment that a retailer offers has an enormous impact on revenue. The revenue increases that we saw were 41 percent in the snack cake sales and 36 percent in the tire sales.

These increases sprang from a variety of factors, but the biggest in the cake example was recognizing, as is shown in table 2-6, that customers of Yummy Cakes in the family size were not loyal; 86 percent of them were willing to switch to Tiny Tina. Thus dropping Yummy Cakes in family size resulted in less than 1 percent in lost revenue and freed space for products that added much more revenue.

In the tire example, the biggest source of gain was discovering a product—the House 3 brand with a low mileage warranty—for which there was enormous latent demand. This is a common pitfall. A retailer assumes a particular product won't sell, and doesn't offer much of it. For that reason, the retailer then doesn't sell much of it, which seems to confirm the original assumption. When we have presented our findings to groups of retailers, many of them have told us of their own "sales surprise stories"—products that they thought had low sales potential but turned out to be blockbusters. Many of you are also sitting on hidden blockbusters: your current sales numbers can tell you what they are, but you have to take the time to tease them out. The aggressive application of the methods described here will help you to do that.

CHAPTER THREE

Product Life Cycle Planning

How to Reinvent Forecasting, Inventory Optimization, and Markdown Pricing

If you're a retailer, you're being hurt by your inventory. All retailers, at one time or another, end up carrying too much or too little. Too much, of course, leads to end-of-season surpluses that must be cleared with margin-killing markdowns. Too little causes stockouts and missed sales. That frustrates customers and can prompt them to shop elsewhere, sometimes forever.

How do you walk the tightrope between margin lost and sales forgone? The key lies in managing three ingredients that, together, enable product availability: an accurate forecast, a flexible supply chain, and, of course, an appropriate supply of inventory.

Any of these three factors, handled right, will suffice, ensuring that your customers get what they want when they want it. But too many retailers err on the side of carrying excessive inventory because of their inaccurate forecasts or slow, rigid supply chains. If they improved their forecasts and the flexibility of their supplies, they could please their customers without having to sink so much of their cash into goods that might not sell.

In this chapter, we'll provide you with tools to help you improve forecast accuracy and decide how much inventory of each product to carry in each of your stores at any point. We'll also advocate an unorthodox, but much more profitable, way of managing markdowns.

Retail products exhibit all the variation of human life. Many endure for decades, but some die young, and a few never make it out of prelaunch planning. Their lives can stretch from a few weeks, for a hit CD, to years, for a brand of flour peddled in a grocery store or a soap sold in the pharmacy. Unilever's Lifebuoy has existed for more than a hundred years. Many goods, ranging from cars to refrigerators, last only a year in stores because the industry operates on an annual new-product-planning cycle.

Figure 3-1 shows the events in the life of a product. These may be grouped into three phases: beginning-of-life launch, midlife replenishment, and end-of-life exit.

Long before a product reaches stores, a retailer will predict how well it will sell and use that estimate to determine an initial buy quantity. Retailers use a variety of approaches for forecasting sales. One is to identify a similar product from a prior season and use its sales as an estimate

FIGURE 3-1

Product life cycle planning

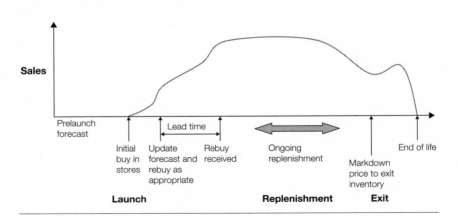

of the new item's prospects. This works well if the new product is just a variation of the old one. Other approaches include asking buyers to estimate the product's prospects or conducting a test by placing a small quantity of the product in a few stores and extrapolating from the sales.

Once sales of a new product stabilize, replenishment becomes the rule. Each week, the retailer ships units to stores based on what sold in the preceding week, bringing inventory up to a desired level. Eventually, either the end of the season arrives or sales slow, and the retailer decides to discontinue the product and sell off the remaining inventory through judicious markdowns.

You can split life cycle planning into three categories based on the ratio of length of life to replenishment lead time.

- If the lead time is greater than or equal to the life, then replenishment is impossible, and you're forced to make a single buy. That's known as the "one and done" mode of operation.

- At the other extreme, if product life is much longer than lead time—say, a life of a year and a lead time of four weeks—then the product goes on replenishment soon after launch.

- In the intermediate case, lead time is a little less than life cycle. Perhaps, the life is twenty-six weeks, and the lead time is twelve weeks. So you can order only a few replenishments. A variation is when you can make a single buy from a supplier but can allocate part of it to your distribution center and replenish stores from that supply.

Launch

We'll use a women's apparel catalog company to walk you through the key decisions faced in launching new products. We'll also describe a methodology for making those decisions that we developed while working with the cataloger.[1]

Our challenge was to decide how much to buy of each of an assortment of women's dresses and other clothing to be offered in a catalog that would last for twenty-six weeks. Because of long production lead times, the company needed to make orders several months before the catalog's mailing. If an item sold out during the twenty-six-week life of the catalog, it often could order more, giving customers the option of back-ordering. For simplicity in this explanation, we'll assume that customers couldn't back-order, so an order for a sold-out product became a lost sale. The firm sold any inventory remaining at the end of the catalog's life at a deep discount.

"We" Beats "Me": A New Way of Deliberating

A committee of four buyers decided how much of each item to purchase.[2] In making their decisions, the buyers studied drawings of each item, discussed target consumers, and considered the popularity of prior similar products.

In observing the committee's deliberations, we noticed that one of the buyers was more articulate and assertive than the others. Often, she swayed her colleagues, so the final decisions represented her preferences rather than the collective wisdom. The other buyers, though more reticent, didn't have less fashion sense, and we were concerned that the firm was losing 75 percent of the committee's wisdom. We therefore asked the buyers to vary their usual process. Each one would write down her forecast of each item's sales over the twenty-six-week life of the catalog, and we'd then compare them. Table 3-1 shows these individual forecasts for three of the items, together with the average and standard deviation of the forecasts.

TABLE 3-1

Forecast of four buyers for three products

	Anna	Laurie	Julie	Kim	Committee average	Committee standard deviation
Navy turtleneck	89	86	102	102	95	7
Red cardigan	51	100	152	39	86	45
Blue vest	30	91	183	76	95	56

The data in this table has been disguised.

Note the disparity between Julie's and Kim's forecasts for the red cardigan and between Anna's and Julie's for the blue vest. The usual groupthink process would have hidden these differences of opinion.

Given these dispersed forecasts, how much of each item should the cataloger have ordered? For now, assume that production lead times are so long that the company can't replenish during the season and must buy each item at the start of the season. One possible answer is to buy exactly what was the average forecast for each item—that is, 95 navy turtlenecks, 95 blue vests, and 86 red cardigans. That's what this company typically did.

Initial Forecasts: Groping in the Dark

Twenty-six weeks after the company mailed the catalog, we knew the total demand for each product and could evaluate how well this approach had worked. Table 3-2 shows actual demand and forecast error for the three items. Notice that forecast errors are generally high, but the forecast for the navy turtleneck, where the four buyers tended to agree, was reasonably accurate.

A common measure of forecast error, called *mean absolute deviation*, or MAD, equals the total absolute error as a percentage of total actual demand. For this example, MAD equals (10 + 47 + 66) / (85 + 132 + 29), or 50 percent. Notice that we measure error as the *absolute deviation* of the forecast from actual demand, so the errors of –10 and –66 drop their negative signs in the calculation.

TABLE 3-2

Forecast errors

	Committee average	Committee standard deviation	Actual demand	Error	Absolute deviation
Navy turtleneck	95	7	85	–10	10
Red cardigan	86	45	132	47	47
Blue vest	95	56	29	–66	66

Figure 3-2 shows actual versus forecast demand for all items, and figure 3-3 shows forecast error versus standard deviation for all items. Note that forecast errors are generally quite high, with a *mean absolute percentage error* (MAPE) of 55 percent, but tend to be lower when the four buyers' forecasts are closer to each other and the standard deviation is smaller. In fact, the items in the right half of figure 3-3, with standard deviation of more than 200, had nearly six times the forecast error as the items with standard deviation of less than 200. In our experience, high forecast error for new items is typical; we generally see the presales forecast errors on new items range from 50 percent to 100 percent.

Forecast Errors Cost Money

What's the cost of these errors? Because demand is hard to predict, we make mistakes, buying too little of some products and too much of others. Table 3-3 shows the per-unit cost of under- and overbuying the three items. If you buy too little, you lose the gross margin on sales that you could have made. Every missed sale of the red cardigan costs the per-unit gross margin of $83 (that is, $160 − $77). This $83 lost margin

FIGURE 3-2

Actual versus forecast demand for all items

Mean absolute percentage error is 55%

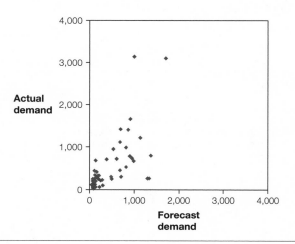

FIGURE 3-3

Forecast error versus committee standard deviation for all items

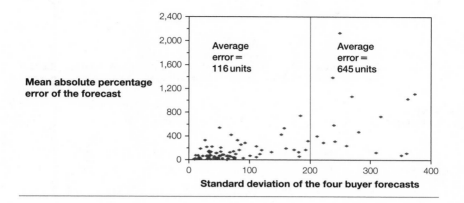

TABLE 3-3

The costs of under- and overbuying differ

	Cost	Normal price	Markdown price	Per-unit underbuy cost	Per-unit over-buy cost
Navy turtleneck	$40	$60	$18	$20	$22
Red cardigan	77	160	48	83	29
Blue vest	65	110	33	45	32

The data in this table has been disguised.

is called an *opportunity cost*; it doesn't appear on the income statement. Rather, it's the cost of *not* doing something. The per-unit underbuy cost for the three items is computed as the normal price minus cost.

Buying too much incurs a markdown. Every blue vest left over after twenty-six weeks costs the cataloger $32 (that is, $65 − $33). The per-unit overbuy cost for the three items is computed as cost minus the markdown price.

Table 3-4 displays a financial evaluation of four increasingly sophisticated strategies for buying the three items.

TABLE 3-4

Profitability of four increasingly sophisticated buying strategies

BUY THE FORECAST

	Buy qty	Actual demand	Sales	Gross margin on sales	Mark-down units	Loss on mark-downs	Net profit	Lost sales	Lost margin
Navy turtleneck	95	85	85	$1,700	10	$220	$1,480	0	$0
Red cardigan	86	132	86	7,138	0	0	7,138	46	3,818
Blue vest	95	29	29	1,305	66	2,112	−807	0	0
Totals			200	10,143	76	2,332	7,811	46	3,818

HEDGE: BUY THE FORECAST + 10%

	Buy qty	Actual demand	Sales	Gross margin on sales	Mark-down units	Loss on mark-downs	Net profit	Lost sales	Lost margin
Navy turtleneck	105	85	85	$1,700	20	$440	$1,260	0	$0
Red cardigan	95	132	95	7,885	0	0	7,885	37	3,071
Blue vest	105	29	29	1,305	76	2,432	−1,127	0	0
Totals			209	10,890	96	2,872	8,018	37	3,071

USE A PROBABILISTIC RISK ADJUSTED HEDGE

	Buy qty	Actual demand	Sales	Gross margin on sales	Mark-down units	Loss on mark-downs	Net profit	Lost sales	Lost margin
Navy turtleneck	89	85	85	$1,700	4	$88	$1,612	0	$0
Red cardigan	100	132	100	8,300	0	0	8,300	32	2,656
Blue vest	91	29	29	1,305	62	1,984	−679	0	0
Totals			214	11,305	66	2,072	9,233	32	2,656

TABLE 3-4

Profitability of four increasingly sophisticated buying strategies *(continued)*

RISK ADJUST USING A CONTINUOUS GAMMA DISTRIBUTION

	Buy qty	Actual demand	Sales	Gross margin on sales	Mark-down units	Loss on mark-downs	Net profit	Lost sales	Lost margin
Navy turtleneck	94	85	85	$1,700	9	$198	$1,502	0	$0
Red cardigan	109	132	109	9,047	0	0	9,047	23	1,909
Blue vest	96	29	29	1,305	67	2,144	−839	0	0
Totals			223	12,052	76	2,342	9,710	23	1,909

We will be describing these four strategies in the next few pages. The top tableau computes net profit, assuming that the retailer bought the committee members' average forecast. In this table, the sales value is the minimum of the buy quantity ("Buy qty" column) and actual demand; gross margin on sales is the per-unit underbuy cost from table 3-3 times sales; the markdown units value is the buy quantity minus sales; loss on markdowns is the per-unit overbuy cost from table 3-3 times markdown units; net profit is gross margin minus loss on markdowns; lost sales is actual demand minus sales; and lost margin is the per-unit underbuy cost times lost sales. The buy of blue vests vastly exceeded the demand of 29 units, so the retailer had 66 units left over, which cost it a total of $2,112 to liquidate. This loss exceeded the margin earned on the 29 units sold, so, overall, the firm lost money on this item.

While the $2,112 markdown loss looms large, an even bigger number is the $3,818 of *lost margin* on the red cardigan because the 86 units didn't come close to meeting the actual demand of 132 units. This is consistent with our experience: lost margin dwarfs the cost of ditching overstocks. Yet when we talk to managers about inventory problems, they usually grouse about some item that they thought would sell briskly but didn't, leaving a year's supply moldering in the warehouse. Mistakes like that are obvious and embarrassing.

69

The inventory sits there inviting recrimination. Eventually, the value of the goods has to be written down, which shows up on the income statement. That creates still more shame. If the mistake was big enough and the company is public, it can even lead to a decrease in stock price, when analysts and investors catch on. In contrast, an unsatisfied customer who didn't get what she wanted is invisible; the margin lost because of the missed sale doesn't appear on any financial record.

Cutting the Cost of Errors

You might guess that this retailer could have increased net profit by buying more than the forecast. The second tableau in table 3-4 shows that this supposition is correct. The tableau presents the same financial calculation described above, but this time the retailer simply buys 10 percent more than the committee members' average forecast.

Why did buying 10 percent more increase profit? The extra buy actually increases markdown units for the navy turtleneck and blue vest by a total of 20 units, and these extra markdowns cost an additional $540 in markdown losses. However, this loss is outweighed by the additional gross margin of $747 earned on the additional 9 sales of the red cardigan. Simply put, hedging high increases profit because the cost of underbuying is much higher than the cost of overbuying for the red cardigan.

Finding an Optimal Hedge

So hedging helps, but how much should you hedge? One way is to estimate the probability of different possible outcomes and then follow a strategy that works best on average. Assume, for example, that each of the four catalog buyers is equally likely to be right, and thus assign a probability of 0.25 to each of their forecasts. Following this approach for the navy turtleneck, you'd assume there was a 25 percent chance of orders of 86 units, 25 percent of 89, and 50 percent of 102, since both Julie and Kim predicted 102 for this item.

If you bought the committee average of 95 and demand were 86, you'd have overbought by 9 units, at a total cost of $198 (9 units × $22). If demand were 89, you'd have overbought by 6 units, at a cost of $132. And if demand were 102, you'd have underbought by 7 units, at a cost of $140 (7 units × $20). Your probability-weighted cost in this case therefore is (0.25 × $198) + (0.25 × $132) + (0.5 × $140), or $152.50. This probability-weighted cost is called the *expected cost*. The next step is to find the expected cost for all other buys and choose the one that does best on average.

Table 3-5 shows the expected cost for many different quantities. The purchase with the lowest expected cost is 89 and is highlighted in

TABLE 3-5

Finding an optimal buy for the blue turtleneck, assuming probabilistic demand

	If demand = 86		If demand = 89		If demand = 102		
Buy quantity	Lost margin	Mark-down cost	Lost margin	Mark-down cost	Lost margin	Mark-down cost	Probability weighted total cost
80	120	0	180	0	440	0	295.0
81	100	0	160	0	420	0	275.0
82	80	0	140	0	400	0	255.0
83	60	0	120	0	380	0	235.0
84	40	0	100	0	360	0	215.0
85	20	0	80	0	340	0	195.0
86	0	0	60	0	320	0	175.0
87	0	22	40	0	300	0	165.5
88	0	44	20	0	280	0	156.0
89	0	66	0	0	260	0	146.5
90	0	88	0	22	240	0	147.5
91	0	110	0	44	220	0	148.5
92	0	132	0	66	200	0	149.5
93	0	154	0	88	180	0	150.5
94	0	176	0	110	160	0	151.5
95	0	198	0	132	140	0	152.5
96	0	220	0	154	120	0	153.5
97	0	242	0	176	100	0	154.5
98	0	264	0	198	80	0	155.5
99	0	286	0	220	60	0	156.5
100	0	308	0	242	40	0	157.5

the table. The same analysis applied to the other two items shows that buying 100 red cardigans and 91 blue vests minimizes the expected cost of lost margin and markdowns.

The third tableau of table 3-4 displays financial results for these purchases. Notice that taking into account the high cost of lost margin relative to the cost of markdowns on the red cardigan has led to buying more of that item, while the reverse logic has led to buying fewer navy turtlenecks. Overall, net profit has shot up.

A Fancy (and Useful) Formula—The Gamma Distribution

One valid objection to this approach is that we've only allowed for four possible values for demand (corresponding to the four buyer forecasts), while actual demand can vary continuously from zero upward. We can fix this problem using various formulas statisticians have created to represent the probabilities of real-life phenomena. One well-known example is the famous bell-shaped normal distribution. However, the bell curve doesn't work well for uncertain demand because it assigns a positive probability to negative values, and negative demand is impossible.

The *Gamma distribution* is less well known but frequently used for modeling uncertain demand. It resembles the normal distribution but allows only positive values. Figure 3-4 is the Gamma distribution with a mean of 95 and a standard deviation of 7, which would be appropriate

FIGURE 3-4

Gamma probability distribution for the navy turtleneck

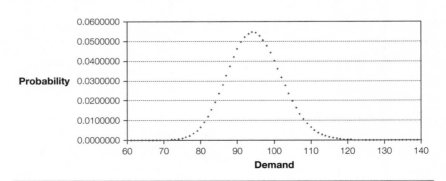

for the navy turtleneck, since these are the values of the average and the standard deviation in table 3-2. Figure 3-5 gives the Gamma distribution with a mean of 95 and a standard deviation of 56, which would be appropriate for the blue vest, given the values in table 3-2. Note that the shape of a Gamma distribution can vary considerably, depending on the value of the mean and the standard deviation. The Gamma for the navy turtleneck looks very much like a standard normal, whereas the Gamma for the blue vest is significantly skewed to the left.

You can find an optimal buy quantity with these probability distributions using exactly the same approach as before, except that now, instead of evaluating four demand scenarios, you evaluate hundreds. Conceptually, the approach is exactly the same. For each possible quantity, you compute the markdown and lost-margin cost for every possible demand value. You then multiply these costs by their probabilities and sum all of the possible demands to compute an expected cost. That way, you find the buy with the lowest expected cost.

Table 3-6 gives numeric probabilities for the Gamma distribution for the navy turtleneck. The table gives a demand value, the probability of that demand value, and the probability (called the *cumulative probability*) that demand will be less than or equal to that value.

Previously, you had three demand values—86, 89, and 102—with probabilities 0.25, 0.25, and 0.5, respectively. Now you have fifty-two demand values, ranging from 70 to 121, with the probabilities given in

FIGURE 3-5

Gamma probability distribution for the blue vest

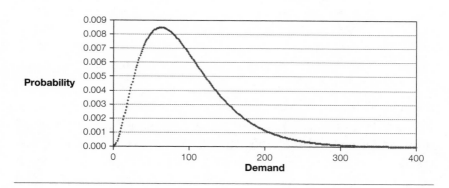

TABLE 3-6

Probability values for the navy turtleneck, using a Gamma distribution

Demand	Probability	Cumulative probability	Demand	Probability	Cumulative probability
70	0.000	0.000	96	0.053	0.604
71	0.000	0.000	97	0.051	0.654
72	0.000	0.001	98	0.048	0.702
73	0.000	0.001	99	0.044	0.746
74	0.001	0.002	100	0.040	0.787
75	0.001	0.003	101	0.036	0.823
76	0.002	0.004	102	0.032	0.854
77	0.002	0.006	103	0.028	0.882
78	0.003	0.010	104	0.023	0.905
79	0.005	0.015	105	0.020	0.925
80	0.007	0.021	106	0.016	0.941
81	0.009	0.030	107	0.013	0.955
82	0.012	0.042	108	0.011	0.965
83	0.015	0.058	109	0.008	0.974
84	0.019	0.077	110	0.007	0.981
85	0.023	0.100	111	0.005	0.986
86	0.028	0.128	112	0.004	0.990
87	0.033	0.161	113	0.003	0.993
88	0.038	0.199	114	0.002	0.995
89	0.042	0.241	115	0.002	0.996
90	0.046	0.287	116	0.001	0.997
91	0.049	0.336	117	0.001	0.998
92	0.052	0.388	118	0.001	0.999
93	0.054	0.442	119	0.000	0.999
94	0.055	0.497	120	0.000	0.999
95	0.054	0.551	121	0.000	1.000

the table. If you want to evaluate buying 95 units, you compute a cost for each demand value. For example, if demand is 70, you'll have 25 units left over, at a cost of $550 (that is, $22 × 25). If demand is 121, you'll fail to satisfy 26 units of demand, at a cost of $520 ($20 × 26). A similar calculation can be done for each possible demand value, and then multiplied by the probability of that value and summed to find the expected cost of buying 95, which is $123.04. Section A-1 in the appendix describes the details of this approach. Following this approach produces expected cost–minimizing buys of 94 for the navy turtleneck, 109 for the red cardigan, and 96 for the blue vest. The fourth tableau of table 3-4 gives a financial evaluation of these buys for the three items.

Fortunately, there is a simpler way to find optimal buy quantities with this approach, using a concept called *marginal profitability analysis*. Suppose you have justified buying at least 93 units of the navy turtleneck, and you're wondering whether to buy a 94th. If it sells, you'll earn a $20 margin. If it doesn't, you'll lose $22 when you have to mark it down at the end of the season. The probability that it won't sell is the probability that demand is less than or equal to 93, which, as you see, equals 0.442, the cumulative probability shown next to a demand value of 93 in table 3-6. The probability that it will sell is thus $1 - 0.442 = 0.558$. The expected net profit of the 94th unit is ($20 × 0.558) – ($22 × 0.442) = $1.44, and it is profitable to buy this unit. However, a 95th unit is not profitable because its expected net profit is negative. In this case, the equation is ($20 × 0.503) – ($22 × 0.497) = –0.87.

There is a formula that shortcuts this trial-and-error process for finding the point at which incremental profit shifts from positive to negative. It seems complicated, but it's really just a matter of plugging in values—as long as you've made good forecasts of demand.

Here's how it works. Let p denote the probability that the marginal unit sells, and then seek a buy quantity such that the net expected profit on the marginal unit is positive, but turns negative if we buy one more unit. The formula looks like this:

$$(\text{normal price} - \text{cost})p - (\text{cost} - \text{markdown price})(1 - p) = 0$$

Solving this equation for p gives you the following:

$$p = (\text{cost} - \text{markdown price}) / (\text{normal price} - \text{markdown price})$$

Plugging in numbers for the navy turtleneck gives a target sales probability for the marginal unit of $p = (40 - 18) / (60 - 18) = 0.524$. We see in the row for demand of 93 in table 3-6 that the cumulative probability that demand is less than or equal to 93 is 0.442, and hence a 94th unit has a 0.558 (that is, 1 – 0.442) chance of selling, which is greater than our target of 0.524. The net expected profit on the 94th unit therefore would be positive. Similarly, the probability demand that is less than or equal to 94 is 0.497, so a 95th unit would have a 0.503 chance of selling and a negative net expected profit. Thus 94 is the optimal buy quantity.

Using Early Sales to Improve Accuracy

This kind of analysis enables you to make smart gambles based on inaccurate forecasts, but it also cries out for better forecasts if yours are shaky. In trying to help the catalog company, we searched for ways to improve its forecasts. To this end, we examined past catalogs and sales cycles and found that its apparel sold at predictable rates throughout the season. Sales chugged along in the first week, rose quickly in the second, and tailed off as the end of the season approached. Table 3-7 shows the average sales rates that we computed. We used table 3-7 to update

TABLE 3-7

Distribution of sales by week

Week	% of total sales by weekend	Week	% of total sales by weekend
1	2%	14	55%
2	11%	15	59%
3	15%	16	62%
4	18%	17	65%
5	21%	18	69%
6	25%	19	73%
7	29%	20	77%
8	33%	21	81%
9	37%	22	85%
10	40%	23	88%
11	43%	24	92%
12	47%	25	96%
13	51%	26	100%

forecasts during the season by extrapolating early sales based on what fraction of the total we estimate they constitute. For example, suppose an item had sold 11 units by the end of the second week. Then we'd forecast total sales of 100 for the twenty-six-week season, reasoning that these 11 sales represented 11 percent of total-season sales.

These midseason corrections proved to be remarkably accurate. While we've used three items to illustrate our approach, the category we were planning actually had twenty-seven items, and figure 3-6 shows forecast results for all twenty-seven items. The left panel of figure 3-6 shows the original preseason forecasts, based on the assessment of the four buyers, while the right panel shows forecasts for the same items created by extrapolating the first two weeks of sales. Clearly, *obtaining even a small amount of initial sales data can have a dramatic impact on forecast accuracy*.

We have since applied this approach in a variety of companies and found the picture shown in figure 3-6 to be remarkably consistent. Before product launch, without current sales data, forecasts typically have an error rate of 50 percent to 100 percent, but just a few weeks after launch, updated forecasts based on initial sales have an error rate of only 10 percent to 20 percent.

FIGURE 3-6

A little sales data dramatically improves forecast accuracy

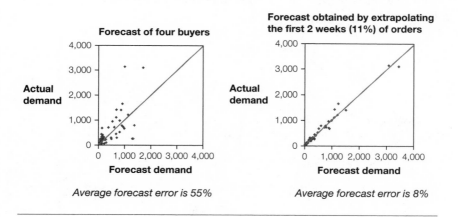

Forecast of four buyers

Average forecast error is 55%

Forecast obtained by extrapolating the first 2 weeks (11%) of orders

Average forecast error is 8%

Wouldn't it be ideal if you could buy using the forecasts in the right panel? You can, at least partially. For simplicity's sake, our examples have so far assumed that the lead time was so long that it allowed only a single buy at the start of the season. But a typical lead time for the replenishment of an existing item is twelve weeks. This means you could reorder at the end of the second week based on the accurate forecasts shown above, and the additional product would arrive at the end of the fourteenth week of the season, with twelve weeks left to sell it.

This suggests a strategy of "buy a little, sell a little, update your forecast, and buy more, if needed." How much should you buy initially? Enough that you probably won't sell out in the initial fourteen-week period, but not so much that you'll have excess inventory that you'll have to dump at a loss at the end of the season. To gauge the probability of selling out in the first fourteen weeks, you need a probability distribution of demand over this period. Fortunately, you can derive this from the distribution that you already have of total-season demand. Notice from table 3-7 that 55 percent of total predicted season sales should have occurred by the end of week 14. Thus the probability that demand in the first fourteen weeks will be less than or equal to X equals the probability that total-season demand is less than or equal to X / 0.55. Figure 3-7 shows the probability distributions for the navy turtleneck derived using this approach, and table 3-8 gives the exact probabilities for different demand values.[3]

FIGURE 3-7

14-week and 26-week probability distributions for the navy turtleneck

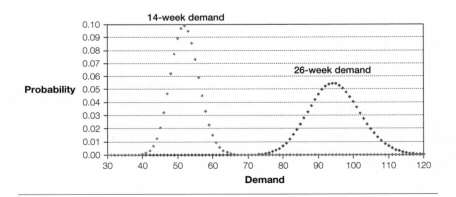

TABLE 3-8

Probabilities for first 14 weeks and for 26-week season for the navy turtleneck

Demand	Season probability	14-week probability	Season cumulative probability	14-week cumulative probability
30	0.000000	0.000000	0.000000	0.000000
31	0.000000	0.000000	0.000000	0.000000
32	0.000000	0.000000	0.000000	0.000000
33	0.000000	0.000000	0.000000	0.000000
34	0.000000	0.000000	0.000000	0.000000
35	0.000000	0.000001	0.000000	0.000002
36	0.000000	0.000006	0.000000	0.000008
37	0.000000	0.000023	0.000000	0.000031
38	0.000000	0.000077	0.000000	0.000108
39	0.000000	0.000231	0.000000	0.000338
40	0.000000	0.000622	0.000000	0.000960
41	0.000000	0.001511	0.000000	0.002472
42	0.000000	0.003332	0.000000	0.005804
43	0.000000	0.006692	0.000000	0.012495
44	0.000000	0.012294	0.000000	0.024789
45	0.000000	0.020743	0.000000	0.045532
46	0.000000	0.032262	0.000000	0.077793
47	0.000000	0.046414	0.000000	0.124208
48	0.000000	0.061969	0.000000	0.186176
49	0.000000	0.077013	0.000000	0.263190
50	0.000000	0.089346	0.000000	0.352535
51	0.000000	0.097022	0.000000	0.449557
52	0.000000	0.098868	0.000000	0.548425
53	0.000000	0.094770	0.000000	0.643195
54	0.000000	0.085646	0.000000	0.728841
55	0.000000	0.073128	0.000000	0.801968
56	0.000000	0.059113	0.000000	0.861082
57	0.000000	0.045326	0.000000	0.906408
58	0.000000	0.033027	0.000000	0.939435
59	0.000000	0.022908	0.000000	0.962343
60	0.000000	0.015150	0.000000	0.977493

TABLE 3-8

Probabilities for first 14 weeks and for 26-week season for the navy turtleneck (continued)

Demand	Season probability	14-week probability	Season cumulative probability	14-week cumulative probability
61	0.000000	0.009569	0.000000	0.987062
62	0.000000	0.005780	0.000000	0.992841
63	0.000000	0.003344	0.000001	0.996185
64	0.000001	0.001855	0.000002	0.998041
65	0.000002	0.000989	0.000004	0.999029
66	0.000005	0.000506	0.000009	0.999536
67	0.000010	0.000250	0.000019	0.999785
68	0.000020	0.000119	0.000039	0.999904
69	0.000039	0.000054	0.000077	0.999959
70	0.000072	0.000024	0.000149	0.999983
71	0.000130	0.000010	0.000279	0.999993
72	0.000227	0.000004	0.000506	0.999997
73	0.000385	0.000002	0.000891	0.999999
74	0.000631	0.000001	0.001522	1.000000
75	0.001005	0.000000	0.002528	1.000000

When we examine figure 3-7, an initial buy of about 70 makes sense. It's unlikely that demand in the first fourteen weeks will exceed 70, but it's also unlikely that demand over twenty-six weeks will be less than 70, and you'll be forced to markdown a portion of the purchase at the end of the season.

We can take a more accurate approach to the task of determining an initial buy by using a marginal expected profitability calculation similar to what we did previously when we were making only a single buy for the season. This analysis will lead to an initial buy of 69, very close to the 70 we guessed to be right by looking at the graph. And the beauty of this approach is that the calculations can be automated within Microsoft Excel, saving the manual effort of guesstimating from a graph.

The reasoning is essentially a cost-benefit analysis on the marginal, 69th unit we buy. The benefit of this unit is that if demand exceeds 68, we will sell it, and it reduces by 1 our lost sales. The probability of demand exceeding 68 is 1 minus the probability demand is less than or equal to 68, or, using the "14-week cumulative probability" column for row 68 in table 3-8, 1 – 0.999904 = 0.000096.

The probability that we need to markdown this 69th unit is the probability that twenty-six-week demand is less than or equal to 68, which can be read from the "Season cumulative probability" column for row 68 in table 3-8 to be 0.000039. Using the margin of $20 for this item and the per-unit markdown cost of $22, we can compute the expected net profitability of the 69th unit to be (20 × 0.000096) – (22 × 0.000039) = .00106. Since this is greater than 0, the 69th unit is profit justified. It's easy to confirm that a 70th unit has negative expected net profitability and hence is not profit justified. The same analysis for the other two products shows that 71 is an optimal initial buy for the red cardigan and 68 is an optimal initial buy for the blue vest.

Once sales begin, you update your forecast and make a second buy if needed. How big should the second buy be? Table 3-9 shows sales in the first two weeks for the three items, an updated twenty-six-week forecast obtained by dividing the first two weeks' sales by 0.11 (that is, the 11 percent discussed above), and a forecast for the first fourteen weeks obtained by multiplying the twenty-six-week forecast by 0.55 (that is, the 55 percent discussed above). These calculations produce fractional values, which we have rounded to the nearest integer in table 3-9. The updated twenty-six-week forecast still has a margin of

TABLE 3-9

Determining the second buy

	Initial buy quantity	Sales in first 2 weeks	Updated 26-week forecast	Forecast sales for weeks 1–14	Forecast lost sales for weeks 1–14	Second buy quantity
Navy turtleneck	69	9	82	45	0	13
Red cardigan	71	15	136	75	4	61
Blue vest	68	2	18	10	0	0

error, which you would take into account in determining a second buy, just as you would have with the initial buy. But this margin of error is much smaller, so for simplicity, assume that the updated forecast is perfectly accurate.

You clearly don't want to buy more of the blue vest. You're forecasting total-season sales of roughly 18, and you've already bought 68. The second buy for the navy turtleneck is set to the total-season forecast minus what you've already bought, or 13 (that is, 82 – 69), which avoids lost sales.

The second purchase for the red cardigan is trickier. You could follow the same approach that you used for the navy turtleneck and set the second buy to 65 (that is, 136 – 71). But this ignores the fact that forecast sales of 75 units for the first fourteen weeks exceeds the initial buy of 71, so you would have sold out during the first fourteen weeks and lost 4 units of demand. Thus a better second-period buy is 136 minus the 71 units already bought and sold and also minus the 4 units of lost demand, for 61 units of expected demand in weeks 15 through 26.

The first tableau of table 3-10 provides a financial summary of results for this sequence of two buys. Notice that going from one buy to two has dramatically improved net profit, from $9,710 in the best one-buy scenario shown in table 3-4 to $12,653 in the two-buy scenario.

Profits Take Flight

The twelve-week replenishment lead time in this example assumes that a Chinese factory made the product and shipped it by boat to the United States, which takes about a month. An alternative would be to ship the replenishment order by air, raising shipping cost by $1 per unit, but reducing lead time to eight weeks. The second tableau of table 3-10 shows revised initial and second buys as well as financial results for this approach. The second buy quantity was determined using the approach described above. Net profit has increased by $384, to $13,037. This increase is offset by the $102 cost of airfreight for 102 replenishment units at a cost of $1 per unit. Still, the arrangement yields a profit.

TABLE 3-10

Profit under the two-buy scenario

PROFIT UNDER THE TWO-BUY SCENARIO WITH A 12-WEEK LEAD TIME

	Actual demand weeks 1–14	Actual demand weeks 15–26	Initial buy qty	2nd buy qty	Lost sales in weeks 1–14	Lost sales in weeks 15–26	Sales	Gross margin on sales	Mark-down units	Loss on mark-downs	Net profit	Lost sales	Lost margin
Navy turtleneck	41	44	69	13	0	3	82	1,640	0	0	1,640	3	60
Red cardigan	70	62	71	61	0	0	132	10,956	0	0	10,956	0	0
Blue vest	17	12	68	0	0	0	29	1,305	39	1,248	57	0	0
Totals								13,901	39	1,248	12,653	3	60

PROFIT UNDER THE TWO-BUY SCENARIO WITH AN 8-WEEK LEAD TIME

	Actual demand weeks 1–10	Actual demand weeks 11–26	Initial buy qty	2nd buy qty	Lost sales in weeks 1–10	Lost sales in weeks 11–26	Sales	Gross margin on sales	Mark-down units	Loss on mark-downs	Net profit	Lost sales	Lost margin
Navy turtleneck	31	54	58	24	0	3	82	1,640	0	0	1,640	3	60
Red cardigan	50	82	58	74	0	0	132	10,956	0	0	10,956	0	0
Blue vest	10	19	56	0	0	0	29	1,305	27	864	441	0	0
Totals			172	102				13,901	31	980	13,037	3	60

Putting It All Together

We have used the catalog buying example to describe many different strategies for buying, including just buying what we forecast, hedging the buy by a somewhat arbitrary 10 percent, optimally hedging using a discrete and a continuous Gamma approach, and reacting to early sales with twelve- and eight-week lead times. Tables 3-4 and 3-10 show the steady increase in profit as we increased the sophistication of the buying strategy. Note that the big increase in profit comes from reacting to early sales, something we have found to be true in general.

Figure 3-8 shows the results of the methodology described here when applied to all twenty-seven items in the category. We estimated that taking a sharper pencil to the buying decisions that factored in risk increased margin by an amount that equaled 3.5 percent of what the base case revenues would have been under the current policy of simply buying what was forecast and then chasing the winners. We were also able to simulate what would happen with a shorter lead time; and, remarkably, cutting lead time from the current twelve weeks to nine weeks, as might be done with airfreight, adds 4 percent of revenue to margin dollars. This is because with a nine-week lead time, we can buy less initially, which reduces markdowns, and then jump on winners

FIGURE 3-8

Profit increase when this approach is applied to all items

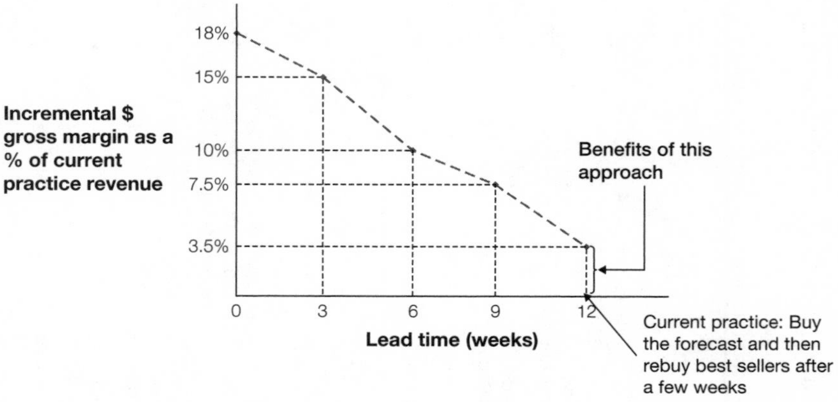

88

sooner, which avoids lost sales due to stockouts. Chapter 4 provides a recipe for reducing lead time and achieving overall supply chain flexibility.

Other Examples for Improving the Accuracy of Launch Forecasts

Reference Product from a Prior Season

The most common approach to initial demand forecasting is to identify a similar product, sold previously, and extrapolate from that product's prior sales. In using past sales, be sure to correct for sales lost due to stockouts and for the impact of other sales drivers that are not going to be repeated, such as promotions, or holidays like Easter and Thanksgiving, whose timing varies year to year.

The strength of this kind of forecasting is that it is easy to understand and do. The weakness is we humans. We're fallible, and we have to execute it. Choosing a reference product and adjusting its sales to factor out one-time events requires judgment. Thus this approach works best when the new product closely resembles one you sold before.

Using Test Sales

Test sales cost more, in time and money, but also yield more reliable results. With this method, you place small batches of the new product in a few stores and measure how well they sell. If the tests disappoint, you might even cancel the product. A variation of this approach is to introduce a new product in a few stores and then gradually roll it out to more stores as it proves itself. Here, you might use test sales to gauge which types of stores a product will sell best in.

As an example, consider a fall product like a wool sweater, sold September through December. Its lead time from order to placement in stores is four months. April would thus be a reasonable month in which to test it. On the basis of these sales, you'd place an order for delivery into stores at the start of September.

A challenge would be tempting customers to buy a product in April designed to be worn in the fall. You might sidestep the problem by testing during August. Assuming the manufacturer is in Asia, you'd ask that it ship the test goods via air, rather than boat, so they'd arrive in time for the test. If the product sold well, you'd order more at the end of August for arrival at the start of December to support Christmas sales.

Key questions in designing tests are picking stores to test in, including the right number, and predicting chain sales from the tests. We had a chance to ponder these issues in depth while working with a value-priced apparel seller that extensively tested products but doubted the accuracy of its forecasts.[4]

This outfit believed in the old quip "Will it play in Peoria?" For years, the conventional wisdom in consumer packaged-goods testing was that Peoria worked well as a test market because of its averageness. The city, in central Illinois, is about a three-hour drive from Chicago and is located near the country's geographic center. Retailers regarded it as average in terms of age, income, and family size. This particular retailer's philosophy was, "If one Peoria is good, then twenty-five are perfect." It would test products in twenty-five stores chosen to be as close as possible to chainwide averages on sales and other metrics. To predict chain-season sales, it simply multiplied the test sales, accounting for the total number of stores in the chain, and weeks in the season. If it sold 80 units in three weeks in twenty-five stores, its forecast for a twenty-four-week season in two hundred fifty stores would be $80 \times 8 \times 10 = 6,400$. The factor of 8 scaled from three weeks to twenty-four, and the factor of 10 scaled the twenty-five stores to two hundred fifty stores. Trouble is, this approach ignores the effects of seasonality. A twenty-four-week season might have a higher (or lower) weekly sales rate than a three-week test.

To evaluate the retailer's approach, we matched actual sales in a recent fall season for knit tops with our reconstruction of the retailer's forecasts. (The original forecasts were no longer available.) The left panel of figure 3-9 shows our results, with each dot corresponding to a style/color combination. The horizontal axis shows the forecast, and the vertical axis shows actual demand. As you can see, the retailer's doubts about the accuracy of its tests were well founded. That didn't surprise us. It had more than one thousand stores and much diversity in its customers. Just within the Philadelphia region, it had urban, sub-urban, and rural locations, and the demographics of shoppers at each kind of location differed. We suggested trying to capture that diversity in the test sample and proposed clustering stores into similar groups. To conduct a test in ten stores, for example, we recommended identify-ing ten clusters of similar stores and choosing a test store from each.

We considered clustering on geography and demographics but con-cluded that what we should cluster on was taste, which was reflected in the mix of products that customers buy. We formed clusters based on the product mix that stores had sold in a prior season, following the process described in section A-2 in the appendix.

The right panel of figure 3-9 shows forecast versus actual results using this technique. Notice that the forecasts are much more accurate. Table 3-11 summarizes extensive testing of this approach at the apparel retailer and at three other retailers and shows that it cuts forecast error approximately in half compared with traditional testing.

A common alternative is clustering based on attributes such as store size, location, or climate. This approach is rife with problems. Location data is typically broken out by zip code, but many people don't shop where they live. Likewise, it's not clear which store attributes are the

FIGURE 3-9

Scientific testing produces more accurate forecasts with fewer test stores

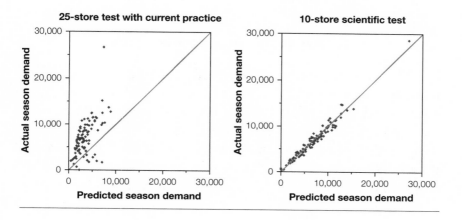

TABLE 3-11

Results for four retailers

Retailer	New test process forecast error, 10 test stores	Traditional test forecast error, 10 test stores
Women's apparel	12.9%	41.9%
Shoe retailer 1	17.6%	27.9%
Shoe retailer 2	12.7%	22.7%
Home fabrics	17%	43%

right ones to use, and choosing the wrong ones can do more harm than good. Many retailers, for example, cluster based on region or store size, but we found that differences in sales mix were essentially uncorrelated with location and store sales volume and instead correlated with ethnicity and average temperature at the store location.

Store clusters have applications beyond testing. Retailers frequently use them to guide in planning, buying, and allocating merchandise. Cluster analysis enables a retailer to cater to differences in consumer taste stemming from factors such as gender, age, ethnicity, wealth, and climate. In this respect, clustering resembles segmentation in marketing. In the previous chapter, we described another approach to sales-based clustering, motivated by retailers' efforts to localize assortments. We have found that both approaches produce very similar clusters, and, for convenience, we would recommend using one set of clusters for both purposes.

Updating the Forecast Based on Early Sales

In 1998, a leading shoe seller contacted us, saying that it wanted to improve its forecasts within a season based on early sales. Shoes have a spring and a fall season, each six months long. The spring season starts in early January and extends through June. This retailer didn't sell a lot of shoes in January and February, but it did sell some, so using those sales to forecast the rest of the season made sense to us, and we proposed doing that. The retailer had reservations, pointing out that early buyers are more fashion-forward than later ones and thus not good predictors. We pressed on, arguing that a simple forecast would at least be a start. We tabulated total sandal sales by week for the 1997 season and noticed that 10.7 percent of total-season sales occurred in the first eight weeks of the season, so we created a 1998 total-season forecast by dividing sales in the first eight weeks by 0.107. We applied this model to history and found that it had an average forecast error of 34 percent.

Pondering the results, we thought, "Ouch, they were right. Simple extrapolation of early sales didn't work. A 34 percent forecast error stinks." We then talked with managers and discovered something. Often, the retailer had run out of inventory for style/color combinations that sold worse than forecast. In contrast, for those that sold better than forecast, the shoe seller had taken significant price markdowns relatively early in the season. We therefore tweaked our forecast to incorporate the impact of price and inventory on sales. This significantly improved forecast accuracy, as shown in figures 3-10 and 3-11. For a step-by-step explanation of how you can make the same sort of calculation, see section A-3 in the appendix.

FIGURE 3-10

Taking price and inventory into account cut forecast error to 16%

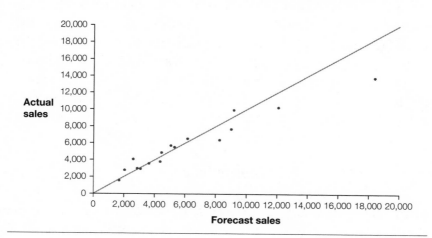

FIGURE 3-11

Weekly forecast versus actual for one sandal

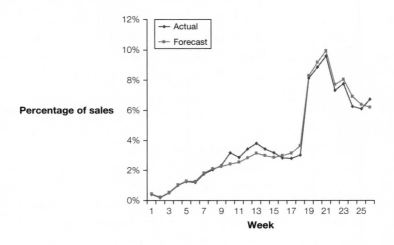

At the end of February 1999, we used this formula to obtain a forecast of sandal sales for the 1999 spring season. Our results predicted that one style would be a runaway hit; our forecast based on early sales was much higher than the retailer's expectations. It had placed orders for twelve thousand pairs and wasn't planning to order more. But our analysis indicated that the retailer should order another eight thousand pairs and that this would increase its margin by nearly $200,000. So, as an experiment, it placed the order. The results are shown in table 3-12. Despite the fact that not all of the additional shoes arrived in time—supply can be just as uncertain as demand—our forecast proved to be accurate. The shoe seller increased its gross margin from $359,627 to $522,309.

Replenishment

Many retail products have a life cycle of a year or more. Sometime during the launch phase, the retailer decides whether the product is a "keeper." If it is, it becomes part of the regular lineup and goes on

TABLE 3-12

Application of this approach to one sandal

	Original plan	Optimized plan based on our analysis	Actual results
Unit receipts	12,469	20,410	18,575
Unit sales	9,882	14,875	14,579
Gross margin $	$385,497	$580,274	$562,269
End-of-season inventory units	2,587	5,535	3,996
Inventory purge cost	$25,870	$55,350	$39,960
Maintained margin $	$359,627	$524,924	$522,309

replenishment. Most retailers have millions of store/SKU combinations on replenishment. For these, they collect sales data continuously and ship additional quantities to stores periodically to restock. They establish a target maximum inventory level, called an *order point*, for a given product and regularly ship enough to each store to replace what has sold. It's important to adjust the target inventory week to week as the sales rate changes due to seasonality and shifting popularity of the product.

Sometimes, a store sells out of a product before new stock arrives. The higher the order point, the lower the chance of selling out, but a higher order point also implies more inventory and greater carrying costs. A key question is, "What's the right trade-off between carrying costs and the cost of lost sales due to stockouts?"

Here's a test of your retailing intuition. Suppose you tracked a group of items over time, and their in-stock rate was 95 percent. (The in-stock rate for a SKU is the percentage of stores in a week that *didn't* run out of that product before replenishment arrived.) Is that good or bad? Most people believe, correctly, that they can't answer this question without more information. They want to know such facts as the products' gross margins, the cost of carrying inventory, the likelihood a customer will buy a substitute product if they encounter a stockout, and how well competitors do at keeping merchandise in stock.

It's also important to realize that a 5 percent stockout rate can result in much greater lost sales. Table 3-13 shows an example of six products where the in-stock rate averages to 95 percent, and therefore the stockout rate is 5 percent. But because most of the stockouts are concentrated in the fastest-selling, highest-priced item, the lost-sales rate is 24 percent.

Many retailers report higher stockout rates on fast movers than on slow ones, and they often fixate on in-stock rate as a performance metric rather than *sales-capture rate*. Because it takes less inventory to maintain in-stock for a slow mover than a hot seller, they often end up increasing their in-stock rate by providing worse in-stock performance on their most popular products, to the detriment of their sales-capture rate.

Kevin Freeland, former senior vice president for inventory management of Best Buy, saw this problem firsthand when he visited one of that chain's stores.[5] He discovered that the store had sold out of three best-selling personal computers. At the time, PCs and peripherals contributed to more than a third of Best Buy's annual sales.

Freeland remarked to the staffer showing him around, "This is terrible. We're losing all these sales." The assistant zeroed in on the slow

TABLE 3-13

Lost revenue can be much greater than the stockout rate indicates

Item	In-stock rate	Demand units per week	Price	Potential revenue	Average lost revenue per week
A	0.99	0.25	$10	$2.50	$0.03
B	0.99	0.5	9	4.50	0.05
C	0.99	1	5	5.00	0.05
D	0.99	0.4	15	6.00	0.06
E	0.99	0.9	10	9.00	0.09
F	0.75	10	100	1,000.00	250.00
Totals				1,027.00	250.27

Average in-stock rate = 95%

Lost revenue = $250.27 / $1,027.00 = 24%

sellers, pointing out that because the store had plenty of inventory for those, its numbers looked good. Freeland promptly changed Best Buy's service metric from in-stock rate to sales-capture rate.

Customers can respond in a variety of ways when they encounter a stockout, and how they respond determines the impact on your sales. In the best case, the stockout has no impact because the customer either returns after you've restocked or purchases a substitute. Another possibility, of course, is that you lose the sale because the customer either decides she can do without the item or buys it elsewhere. A third possibility is that you lose the sales on an entire basket of goods the customer planned to buy. And the fourth—and worst—possibility is that a customer, usually after encountering repeated stockouts, abandons your company and shops elsewhere.

Now that you've considered the behavior of this imaginary customer, ponder this question: what happens to your sales if your in-stock rate rises by 1 percent? Do sales rise by 1 percent, too? Or do they rise less than that or more? The answer, it turns out, depends on the relative percentage of times that you lose none, one, or more than one sale on that stockout. Our studies, in which we regressed sales against the in-stock rate for a large number of stores over several years, have found cases where the sales lift from a 1 percent in-stock improvement exceeded 1 percent because a stockout frequently caused the loss of a basket of potential purchases.

Profit Optimizing Replenishment Inventory

With this background, let's consider how to choose an optimal order point for a single item in a single store based on two costs: the cost of carrying inventory and the lost margin due to stockouts when we don't have inventory. Assume that the customer doesn't ever buy only that one item, but her other purchases are unaffected. Sure, that's unrealistic, but it will help illustrate the core concepts of inventory optimization.

We can find an optimal order point by using the marginal expected profitability approach we described for the catalog buying example. In that example, we imagined that we increased the buy quantity unit by unit and did an expected profitability calculation on each incremental unit. In the catalog example, the expected profit of an incremental unit was the probability it sold times the gross margin minus the probability it didn't sell times the markdown cost if it didn't sell.

In the replenishment case, an incremental unit of inventory injected by raising the reorder point by one only helps us in the weeks in which we would have stocked out without this unit. For example, if our in-stock rate at the current reorder point is 90 percent, then an incremental unit only helps us 10 percent of the time. For simplicity, assume we are making weekly replenishment shipments. Then an incremental unit provides value in only five weeks of the year, and in these weeks it increases sales by one unit. To obtain these five additional sales and the resulting gross margin, we need to carry the extra unit of inventory for one year. So, in general, the net expected profit from raising the order point by one is item gross margin times fifty-two weeks times (one minus the current in-stock rate) minus the cost of carrying an item for a year. We want to raise the order point to a level where the last unit we add is just marginally profitable, and we can find this point by solving the equation

$$\text{item gross margin} \times 52 \text{ weeks} \times (1 - \text{current in-stock rate}) -$$
$$\text{the cost of carrying an item for a year} = 0$$

to find that the optimal in-stock rate satisfies

$$\text{optimal in-stock rate} = (1 - \text{cost of carrying an item for one year} /$$
$$52 \times \text{item gross margin})$$

(Of course, if replenishment deliveries are made at a frequency other than weekly, we simply replace "52" in the formula above with the number of delivery cycles in a year.) Then the order point is set to the level where the probability of demand not exceeding that level in a week equals the optimal in-stock rate. This value can be found using a probability table of demand, such as the Gamma table we showed earlier in this chapter.

The formula provides a way to gauge whether you are carrying an economical level of inventory. If your in-stock rate is much higher than the formula would suggest, you're carrying too much, and vice versa. Of course, this formula is only approximate because of many real-world complications, such as the willingness of customers to substitute, but we have found it to be a good guide to see whether your inventory levels are in the right ballpark. Notice that a higher per-unit margin results in a higher in-stock rate, and a higher carrying cost results in a lower in-stock rate, which is intuitive.

An Implementation of These Ideas Had Major Impact

The two of us worked with 4R Systems, a software and consulting company, to develop a system for setting order points based on the concepts described here. That forced us to address many of the operating nuances of a real supply chain, such as seasonality, customer substitution, and varying lead times. Moreover, manufacturers ship most products in cases ranging from one unit to several dozen. This injects inventory into the system that serves as safety stock but also needs to be taken into account in setting order points. Likewise, you'll have to consider the minimum amount of inventory needed in your stores to create attractive displays.

Last but not least, we invested considerable effort in estimating the likely accuracy of forecasts. Forecast accuracy varied considerably by product, depending, for example, on sales velocity of the product and where the product was in its life cycle. The importance of estimating forecast accuracy was continually emphasized by 4R CEO Jiri Nechleba, who suggested that "admitting that one's forecasts have error, really uncertainty, is the first step towards making good decisions."

4R Systems deployed its system in December 2002 at a major retailer of products for the home, including bedding and small appliances. Every week the retailer electronically transferred sales and inventory data on more than 5 million store/SKU combinations. 4R processed this data to compute order points for all store/SKU combinations. It then sent its results to the retailer, which shipped enough product to stores to bring on-hand plus on-order inventory to the order point.

FIGURE 3-12

Results of an implementation

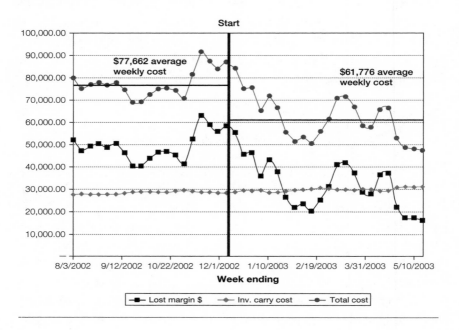

Figure 3-12 shows results for the first department in which the retailer used the 4R system. The line marked with diamonds shows inventory carrying cost, which equaled the inventory carrying cost rate multiplied by the dollar value of inventory on hand as shown on the department's weekly inventory report. The inventory report also showed which items were sold out in each store. To estimate lost sales and lost margin, we used the historical sales rate of each store/SKU combination that sold out, paired with an assessment of the fraction of customers who would not substitute another item when they encountered a stockout. The line marked with squares shows this weekly lost-margin cost. The total cost line marked with circles is the sum of these two costs.

We determined the impact by comparing average total cost over a number of weeks before and after implementation. Average weekly cost decreased from $77,662 to $61,776, implying an annual benefit of $826,072—that is, 52 weeks × ($77,662 – $61,776). This was one of thirty-four departments, and the total annual benefit calculated this way for all departments was about $20 million.

Exit

Eventually, a product reaches the end of its life. Maybe the season changes, a manufacturer phases out a model, or sales slow because of new competitors. Regardless, as a product's usefulness wanes, your goal changes from maintaining stock to selling off inventory as efficiently as possible.

The primary (and sometimes painful) tool for accomplishing this is a markdown. A typical product may be marked down several times in the store. If that doesn't clear the inventory, it may eventually be sold to a discounter, usually for pennies on the dollar. In addition to markdowns, consolidating remaining inventory in a smaller number of stores can help dispose of goods like apparel, where the sales rate tends to slow toward the end of a season because the assortment is broken—that is, many sizes and colors have sold out. Five hundred stores of broken inventory might constitute one hundred stores' worth of fully assorted inventory, so consolidation can accelerate sales. Transfers can also move product to stores where the climate allows for a longer sales season. You might, say, ship golf shirts from New England to Florida in the early fall, when New Englanders have begun to dig out their coats but Floridians are still seeing sunny, warm days.

Optimizing Markdowns

A crucial question in designing an exit is determining the depth and timing of markdowns to extract the greatest possible revenue. (You already own the goods, so product cost is a *sunk cost*, and maximizing revenue is equivalent to maximizing profit.) Doing this systematically involves three steps.

1. *Forecast*: estimate the sales lift that would result from a given markdown.

2. *Optimize*: Determine the depth and timing of markdowns to maximize revenue earned from the remaining inventory.

3. *Test*: Improve the accuracy of the estimates in step 1 through price tests in which you vary the price to determine the sales response to particular markdowns.

Figure 3-13 shows the sales lift experienced by several items that were marked down 20 percent, 50 percent, and 75 percent successively in a prior season. You can see that when these items were marked down by 50 percent, their sales rate increased by a factor of about 3. The curve shows the formula $e^{2.4\,\text{Markdown }\%}$, where $e = 2.7182$ is the base of the natural logarithm. This so-called exponential formula has been found to fit well how sales lift varies with depth of markdown, and in this case, 2.4 is the value in the exponent that best fits this data.[6]

The advantage of fitting a formula to the data is that next season you can use this formula as an estimate of the lift that would result from different markdown levels, assuming that you think customers will respond similarly. This enables optimization of markdowns.

We'll illustrate markdown optimization with an item for which you made a single buy of 3,300 units to cover demand for a sixteen-week season. The item is selling at 100 units per week, and for simplicity's sake, the example ignores seasonality. Without a markdown, you'd

FIGURE 3-13

Estimating sales lift factor versus markdown percentage

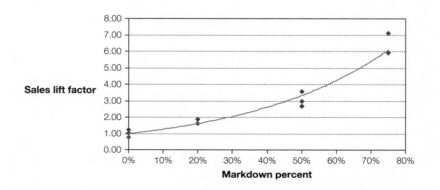

have 1,700 units left at the end of the season. Suppose you want to take a single markdown with either three weeks left in the season or ten weeks left. Which is the best time to markdown, and in each case, what level of markdown would maximize the revenue yield? To answer this question, we have compiled in table 3-14 the revenue that would result from different markdowns and for the two points in time at which a markdown could be taken, assuming that the revenue lift is given by the formula $e^{2.5 \text{ Markdown \%}}$, which you determined based on a

TABLE 3-14

Markdown optimization example

| Base sales rate | 100 units per week |
| Regular price | $60.00 |

			3 weeks left in season		10 weeks left in season	
Markdown	Sales lift factor	Sale price	Rest of season sales	Rest of season revenue	Rest of season sales	Rest of season revenue
5%	1.13	57.00	340	19,377	1,133	64,589
10%	1.28	54.00	385	20,801	1,284	69,337
15%	1.45	51.00	436	22,261	1,455	74,205
20%	1.65	48.00	495	23,742	1,649	79,139
25%	1.87	45.00	560	25,221	1,868	84,071
30%	2.12	42.00	635	26,674	2,117	88,914
35%	2.40	39.00	720	28,067	2,399	93,556
40%	2.72	36.00	815	29,357	2,700	97,200
45%	3.08	33.00	924	30,494	2,700	89,100
50%	3.49	30.00	1,047	31,413	2,700	81,000
55%	3.96	27.00	1,187	32,036	2,700	72,900
60%	4.48	24.00	1,345	32,268	2,700	64,800
65%	5.08	21.00	1,524	31,994	2,700	56,700
70%	5.75	18.00	1,726	31,075	2,700	48,600
75%	6.52	15.00	1,956	29,344	2,700	40,500
80%	7.39	12.00	2,000	24,000	2,700	32,400
85%	8.37	9.00	2,000	18,000	2,700	24,300
90%	9.49	6.00	2,000	12,000	2,700	16,200
95%	10.75	3.00	2,000	6,000	2,700	8,100

prior season's markdown. We assume that the lift factor is the same whether you take a markdown with three weeks or ten weeks left in the season, although, usually, earlier markdowns produce a bigger lift. Unit sales in the table is computed as the minimum of the remaining inventory and the base sales rate of 100 times the sales lift factor times the number of weeks left in the season.

You can see that for a markdown with three weeks left you'd achieve the maximum revenue of $32,268 by taking a markdown of 60 percent, and for a markdown with ten weeks left you would have achieved the maximum revenue of $97,200 with a markdown of 40 percent. Notice that these markdown levels do not sell all of the inventory. Retailers often consider markdowns a way to jettison *all* of their leftovers. But maximizing revenue makes more sense, assuming you can dispose of the leftovers at no cost by, say, donating them to charity.

Smart timing of a markdown matters as much as the magnitude. So which is better, a 60 percent markdown with three weeks remaining or a 40 percent markdown with ten weeks left? In the latter case, you'd receive $97,200 of revenue over ten weeks. In the former, you'd receive $32,268 during the three-week markdown period and $42,000 in the prior seven weeks (7 weeks × $60 × 100 units per week), for total revenue of $74,268. That's substantially less than you would've earned by taking a smaller markdown earlier.

Your buyers will be tempted to delay markdowns in the hopes that sales will increase, but usually they stunt your sales by doing this. A better rule is to take a markdown big enough to clear up the problem as soon as you realize that you bought too much. The consumer response to a small markdown in October will be much greater than to a larger markdown on December 26. In October, fall products are still in season and thus worth more.

Improving the Process with Price Testing

The shortcoming of the process described above is your ability to estimate consumer response to a markdown. Once again, a test can improve the accuracy of your estimates. We designed such a test for Zany Brainy, the toy retailer founded by David Schlesinger, to test alternative prices for three different toys.[7] This test was to set regular prices, but the same approach applies to markdowns.

We formed three matched panels of six stores chosen so that each store in a panel had a "twin" store in each of the other two panels that was as much like it as possible. We then identified low, medium, and high prices for each of the toys, as listed in table 3-15, and charged one of these prices in each of the three panels. We assigned the prices so that each panel had one toy each at the low, medium, and high prices. Table 3-16 shows sales at each of these prices over the six-week test period.

Product C surprised us. Its sales were much higher at the medium price than at the low or high ones. Here, we concluded that customers were using price as an indicator of quality. The product was an unbranded handheld two-way radio, so customers could not objectively evaluate the quality of its electronics. In contrast, product A was a branded product with known quality, while product B was an easy-to-assess wooden block set.

TABLE 3-15

Test prices and purchase costs

| | PRICES ($) | | | |
	Low	Medium	High	Purchase cost ($)
Product A	19.99	24.99	29.99	11
Product B	24.99	29.99	34.99	18
Product C	14.99	19.99	24.99	11

TABLE 3-16

Total unit sales for the three test products at each of the three price levels

| | TOTAL UNIT SALES | | |
	At low price	At medium price	At high price
Product A	7	4	3
Product B	33	26	14
Product C	47	74	36

For products A and B, we fit a demand curve and found optimal prices. Figure 3-14 shows the demand curve for product B. Figure 3-15 shows the optimal prices. We considered the 3 percent profit increase for product A to be significant.

FIGURE 3-14

Demand curve estimation for product B

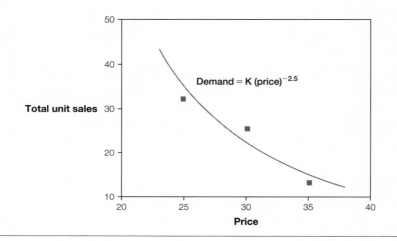

FIGURE 3-15

Finding optimal prices

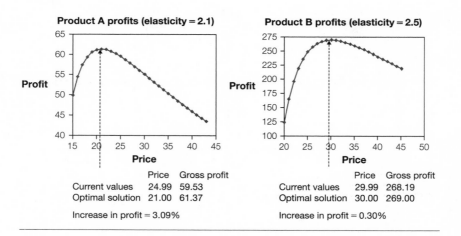

An easy way to improve estimation accuracy while avoiding the effort of a formal test is to take a relatively small markdown at the start of the markdown season and use this to estimate consumer response. This estimate will be highly accurate because it is made based on current information about the particular products. Then take a second optimal markdown based on your estimate.

Concluding Thoughts

Much of our focus in this chapter has been the launch of new products, because this is where forecasts are least accurate and inventory decisions most challenging. Here are the key principles to take away from our discussion.

Forecasting

- All forecasts are wrong, so you'll have too much of some products and too little of others. But even a little sales data dramatically improves the accuracy of new-product forecasts.

- The margin of error on a forecast matters as much as the forecast itself.

Inventory

- Buying what you forecast in the preseason does not produce the best results. Buy more than you forecast if the cost of too little exceeds the cost of too much, and vice versa. The size of your hedge depends on the margin of error on the forecast.

Supply Flexibility

- For short-lived products, lead times often exceed product life, so you'll be able to make only a single buy during the product's life. But going from one buy to two—a preseason purchase and an early-season one—can have a huge impact on reducing stock-outs and end-of-season markdowns.

- Shortening lead time still further, perhaps through replacing traditional shipping with airfreight, can improve performance.

CHAPTER FOUR

Flexible Supply Chains

How to Design for Greater Agility End to End

The logic for supply chain flexibility is compelling. Product sales are hard to predict—prelaunch forecasts of new products typically have a 50 percent to 100 percent error. So being able to respond quickly to satisfy this unexpected demand can have a huge impact on profitability. It also means that you can buy less initially, knowing you can chase winners. That, in turn, prevents margin-killing markdowns at the end of the season. Flexibility cures a merchant's two biggest headaches: having too little of the right products and too much of the wrong ones.

This chapter describes how to create a flexible supply chain. Many apparel and shoe retailers control their supply chains. Some grocers own factories to make private label goods. They can directly apply the ideas found here.

But what if you don't own any part of your supply chain? A big movement in retailing is greater coordination between retailers and suppliers. The grocery industry has formulated a concept called collaborative planning, forecasting, and replenishment (CPFR) that offers guidelines for cooperating to forecast demand and plan supply. Retailers in other industries can work with their suppliers to create the same sort of flexibility. We'll describe in this chapter how one retailer—Best Buy—did this with many of its suppliers, starting with Hewlett-Packard (HP).

A Mystery: Why Are There Such Big Differences in Lead Time Between Retailers?

In 1997, we began a study of thirty-two leading retailers to understand how they used data analytics to improve forecasting and supply chain flexibility.[1] Fourteen of the companies sold footwear and apparel or were department stores with heavy sales in footwear and apparel.

Table 4-1 shows their lead times, together with those of one other retailer we came to know after the study, Destination Maternity, a seller of maternity wear with a nearly 50 percent market share. Three of these retailers—Destination Maternity, World, and Zara—had such fast and efficient supply chains that, if necessary to avoid a stockout, they could replenish a hot-selling item within two to three weeks. By contrast, the other specialty retailers in the group had an average lead time of six months, and the department stores, a whopping eleven months.

We've studied World, Zara, and Destination Maternity to plumb their operations and understand how they've achieved such short lead times while other companies lagged. We have also pondered the equally interesting question of why many other retailers are so slow,

TABLE 4-1

Apparel retailer replenishment lead times

Retailer	Replenishment lead time
World. Kobe, Japan	2–3 weeks
Zara/Inditex. La Coruña, Spain	2–3 weeks
Destination Maternity. Philadelphia, PA, U.S.	2–3 weeks
U.S. specialty retailers	6 months
U.S. department stores	11 months

given that they all have access to the same equipment and processes as these three lightening fast retailers. In this chapter, we describe what we have learned.

Flexibility 101: Flexibility and Inflexibility at National Bicycle

The best way to understand the differences we observed in lead time between retailers is to study an inflexible supply chain to understand what makes it slow and compare it to a fast one to understand the enablers of speed. Fortunately, there's a company that operates both kinds, right next door to each other. National Bicycle, a subsidiary of the Japanese giant Matsushita Electric, produces Panasonic bicycles.[2] It's one of the three big Japanese bike makers.

National has several product lines, including kid's bikes, low-cost bikes marketed to students and others seeking cheap transportation, and sports bikes marketed to more affluent recreational riders. We'll focus on sports bikes, which can command high margins but also face inventory risk because of annual new-model introductions.

The Inflexible Mass Production Supply Chain

Figure 4-1 shows National's mass production supply chain. At the first step, long titanium or chromium molybdenum steel tubes enter a cutting machine and exit as short lengths that will constitute a

FIGURE 4-1

Mass production sports cycle supply chain

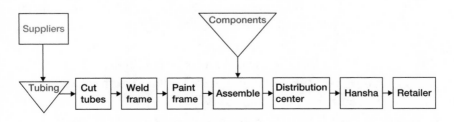

bicycle frame. These tubes are welded to form frames, which are then painted. Three parallel assembly lines, each attended by forty workers at separate stations, attach components like wheels, brakes, and gear shifters to the frames. After assembly, the bikes are boxed and sent to a distribution center on a conveyer. From the center, they're shipped to the warehouses of regional distributors called *hansha* and eventually to retailers.[3]

Each step in the process requires a time-consuming setup as National's workers switch from one model of bike to another. During welding, for example, the metal tubes are held in place by fixtures, which need to be adjusted for each different frame and size. Setup consumes thirty minutes for tube cutting, sixty minutes for welding, twenty-five minutes for painting, and five minutes for assembly, for a total of two hours. Because of the long prep times, the factory makes bikes in batches of fifty, one hundred, one hundred fifty, or more, depending on demand. National also uses batch production to enhance efficiency. Workers can complete bikes more rapidly as they do more of them and grow accustomed to each model.

The bike sales season begins in early spring. Retailers aim to have new models on display by March 1, so National begins planning its new line the preceding July. It builds samples and exhibits them in September and then finalizes designs in late November or early December. That gives it enough time to make bikes and ship them to retailers by March 1. Due to paperwork, it can easily take a week from the time a retailer places an order until it reaches the factory. If the bikes to fill the order are in inventory—the ten hansha, the factory, and retailers each carry about one month's worth of finished goods—they are shipped via truck from National to the hansha and then to the retailer. That takes seven to ten days.

If ordered bikes are not in stock, the time needed to produce more can drag out because of the minimum batch size of fifty bikes. Each bike requires an hour of direct labor. At one hour per bike plus a total of two hours for the setups, the time to produce a batch of fifty bikes is fifty-two hours. Add that to the order processing time of a week and a week to ten days for transport, and the lead time stretches to at least a month. The actual lead time can easily be even longer. A retailer typically orders several different bikes requiring several batches and thus several weeks to produce. Moreover, National has nine thousand retailers, so orders back up. And it won't produce a batch of fifty to satisfy an order for a single bike. It waits until other retailers have ordered enough of that model to justify another batch. This further stretches the lead time. A retailer can wait months for replenishment during the sales season, a delay that often results in stockouts and lost sales.

National works hard at projecting the popularity of each year's models. But random events and fickle consumers thwart accurate prediction, so each year popular models frequently sell out, while less popular models go unsold. When the season ends, everyone in the supply chain has bikes that have to be marked down. Thus National suffers from lost sales due to having too few of its best sellers and markdown losses due to too many duds.

Flexibility Arrives at National Bicycle

In 1987, in an effort to increase sales and reduce inventory risk on its sports bikes, National introduced the customization process depicted in figure 4-2. When customers visit Panasonic dealerships, they can still buy bikes from the stores' stock, and the mass production factory still supplies these bikes. But customers can also order custom-made

FIGURE 4-2

The Panasonic Order System (POS)

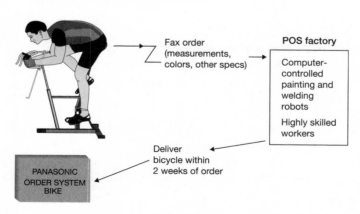

bikes from a greatly expanded selection of frame sizes, colors, and components—more than 2 million combinations in all. National offers seventy color patterns and eighteen frame sizes for its custom bikes, compared with one or two colors and two frame sizes for a typical stock bike. What's more, the retailer can tailor the fit of each custom bike by taking a series of measurements in his shop, using a special measuring stand developed by National. The stand—in effect, an adjustable bike without wheels—lets the customer try out the size and comfort of a proposed custom frame.

Once a customer has chosen his ideal bike, his order is sent to the factory (by fax in 1987, now over the Internet), and two weeks later he receives a bike custom built to his exact specifications.

By 1991, helped by this customization process, National had increased its share of the sports bike segment in Japan from 5 percent to 29 percent and was meeting a two-week delivery goal 99.99 percent of the time. Customers bought two-thirds of Panasonic road bikes and one-fifth of its mountain bikes via the custom process, and annual sales exceeded fourteen thousand bikes. National also received lots of media attention. Its process was one of the first examples of *mass customization*—that is, production of customized goods with nearly the efficiency of mass production. National built a new factory to make the custom bikes. It's housed in a small structure next to the company's larger mass production plant and uses computer-controlled welding robots together with highly skilled workers. Table 4-2 compares the performance of the old and the new factories.

TABLE 4-2

Comparison of POS and mass production factories

	Mass production	POS
Frame sizes	2	18
Color options	1–2	70
Batch size	50 or more	1
Lead time	Several months	2 weeks
Labor content	1 hour	2 hours
Control protocol	Push	Pull

Creating a Flexible Process

In our experience, flexibility requires four capabilities.

1. Efficient production of small quantities (This capability is crucial to taking advantage of a short lead time; a two-week lead time won't do you much good if your minimum batch size is a six-month supply.)

2. The ability to offer a wealth of product versions

3. Accommodation of variation in aggregate demand volume

4. A short lead time

Let's examine how National created each of these four capabilities

Efficient Production of Small Quantities

National achieved the ultimate in efficient small-quantity product: a lot size of one. In other words, each single bike is built individually. To enable single-lot production, National artfully blended technology and skilled workers to reduce the two-hour setup time in the mass production process to less than a minute. The longest setup time was the hour needed to adjust the equipment that held the tubes in place while welders connected them to create each frame. To reduce this time, National resurrected some old frame-building equipment that it had slated for the scrap heap. It then attached servomotors, controlled by a computer, to the old equipment.[4] After a worker cut tubes to the right length, he'd drop them into slots in a flexible device and scan a bar code that identified the bike. The servomotors would then adjust the fixtures to the appropriate dimensions for that frame, which was then welded by robots. This reduced setup time from an hour to a mere twenty seconds.

Robots also inspect frames for dimensional accuracy and apply base coats of paint. Craftsmen apply the finish painting manually, and a single worker assembles each bike, which eliminates the need for batch production that was required for the forty-worker assembly line used in the mass production factory.

Ability to Offer a Wealth of Product Versions

Once the setup time for a bike variant is reduced to less than a minute, it is feasible to offer an essentially unlimited variety of bikes. There was, however, one barrier to variety that needed to be overcome. In the mass production process, forty line workers contributed to the hour of work needed to build a bike, so each worker did (and needed to remember) 1.5 minutes of work. In contrast, workers in the custom factory must do the entire 120 minutes of work required for a single bike, and each bike that they assemble is unique. To make this situation workable, National employs its best workers in the custom factory and uses video terminals to provide instruction on the most complex tasks.

Accommodation of Variation in Aggregate Demand Volume

The demand for custom bikes fluctuates greatly over the year, with low demand in the winter and high demand in spring and summer. National accommodates this variation by setting factory capacity to the maximum weekly demand rate and then using the custom factory to make high-end made-to-stock bikes during the winter when demand for custom bikes is too low to fill factory capacity. Producing time-sensitive made-to-order products and less time-sensitive made-to-inventory products in the same factory allows the entire capacity of the factory to be devoted to the time-sensitive product if needed, while the less time-sensitive production can be scheduled when needed to keep the factory operating at high utilization. Of course, this requires that both types of products can be produced in the same factory, which was the case for National because the custom bikes were simply made-to-inventory bikes configured to a customer order. Hence an "order" to produce a lot of made-to-inventory bikes looked no different from an order from a customer.

Short Lead Time

Recall that lead time includes periods for (1) information processing (the time for order entry), (2) actual production, (3) batching, (4) waiting, and (5) transportation. Consider how each of these changed in the custom factory. Because the retailer transmits an order directly to the factory it eliminates all of the time lost in order processing and the handoffs from the retailer to the hansha, to the sales office, and finally to the factory. Once the factory receives the order, entering it takes just a day.

Actual production time is an hour longer in the custom factory because custom frames require more work. But thanks to its ability to handle batch sizes of one, the custom factory eliminates time wasted while waiting for a batch of orders to accrue. Yet it also has enough capacity to meet demand in the busiest week of the year, so it prevents orders from backing up. Delivery by truck takes only two days. If needed, National will resort to airfreight, even occasionally taxi, to deliver the bikes.

Though welding and assembly of a custom bike take only two hours, National set its delivery promise at two weeks to account for the fact that customers place about 30 percent of orders on Saturday and Sunday, when the factory doesn't operate. It takes the factory until midweek to work through the weekend's backlog. On top of that, parts shortages can delay assembly. National keeps inventory of all of the components required to build its bikes and has an average in-stock level of 99.4 percent. This sounds high, but a bike requires seventeen different components. While any given component is in stock 99.4 percent of the time, the chance that all seventeen are in stock at the same time is .994 raised to the power of seventeen, or 90.3 percent. Thus parts stockouts delay about 10 percent of the bikes. When this happens, National can usually get an emergency delivery of a component within a week and still fulfill its two-week promise. Failing this, it substitutes, with the customer's permission, more expensive parts than the ones that the customer ordered.

National considered setting a one-week lead time but settled on two, thinking that it was better to fulfill a two-week promise 99.95 percent of the time than to meet a one-week promise 90 percent of the time. National usually meets its promise of a two-week turnaround on orders with time to spare, but when it does miss its two-week guarantee, it refunds the customization fee.

The Supply Chain Decouple Point (aka the Push/Pull Boundary)

These capabilities allow the custom supply chain to operate under a control protocol called *pull*, in which the factory makes production decisions in response to customer orders or recent sales. By contrast, the mass production supply chain operates under *push* control, with National making decisions based on long-range demand forecasts and with production occurring long before sales.

In reality, even in pull supply chains, if you move far enough upstream, processes require push control. Consider furniture making. Building tables and sofas in response to customer orders makes sense, but no one would suggest growing trees in response to orders, or even harvesting and sawing them in response to orders. Likewise, in the auto industry, Toyota's famous just-in-time inventory controls exemplify the pull approach. But no one would suggest mining iron ore just in time to produce a car.

The point where a supply chain switches from push to pull is called the push/pull boundary or the *decouple point*, because at the boundary there is usually sufficient inventory to decouple the upstream push processes from the downstream pull processes. Where to position the decouple point is one of the most important supply chain decisions a company makes. Poor supply chain performance can often be traced to an ill-positioned decouple point.

Figure 4-3 shows the supply chain and the decouple point for National's custom factory. It's positioned right before tube cutting. National keeps inventory of uncut tubing and components and replenishes this inventory based on a forecast of demand; that is, it uses push control up to this point. The pull process starts with cutting the tubes for a specific frame and ends with delivery to the customer. National offers 14 bike models, each in 18 sizes, resulting in 252 versions (14 × 18). Each frame can be painted in one of 70 color patterns, resulting in 17,640 (252 × 70) possible painted frames. The addition of components results in over 2 million distinct configurations. Of course, with annual demand of about 14,000 units, National annually produces only a small fraction of these options, and probably no two of the 14,000 bikes will be the same.

FIGURE 4-3

The POS decouple point is upstream of the point of differentiation

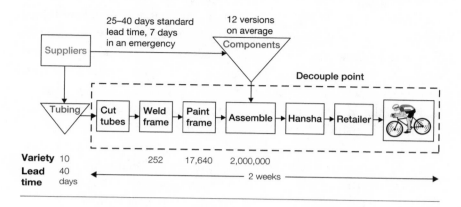

Its choice of decouple point works because National need only stock a small number of uncut tubes and components, and it can predict demand for them. What's more, it can perform all steps in the pull period within two weeks, a wait that customers accept because they get a much wider selection.

National Bicycle's experience illustrates the challenge of giving customers what they want when they want it. No single step in the process ensures success. Rather, a manufacturer must simultaneously design the product, with all of its needed variation, and the supply chain, especially the decouple point. To pick the right point, you want to have low variety upstream but high variety downstream. A wealth of choices makes the customer willing to wait for a made-to-order product, while efficient processes downstream from the decouple point ensure that they don't wait too long.

How Other Companies Decouple Their Supply Chains

Many companies have used the concept of supply chain decoupling to enable flexibility. The most famous example may be Dell. It cannot predict demand for specific computers, but it has the ability to assemble an ordered computer in three minutes from components whose demand it can predict. This allows it to employ push control, buffered by a modest amount of component inventory.

Similarly, Hitachi Global Storage Technologies found that demand at the SKU level was totally unpredictable, but that all SKUs were minor variations on a few generic base products, which are very predictable. So it builds the predictable base products to forecast, under push control, and then quickly modifies them as needed to fill customer orders.

Hewlett-Packard, in contrast, needs many printer model types to supply different countries' needs for, say, power supplies and local-language instruction manuals. It copes with this by stocking a generic printer and inserting, just before shipping, a country-specific localization kit, containing the needed power supply and manual.[5]

McDonald's has embraced efficient customization, too. In the mid-1990s, it found that it was tailoring 40 percent of its orders in response to customer requests like "No pickles, please." Because it made its sandwiches in advance, dealing with this simple request required considerable time and was making McDonald's "fast" food increasingly slow. The chain's solution was its "Made for You" process, in which restaurants precooked protein components such as hamburger patties and chicken to inventory and then assembled sandwiches in response to customer orders.[6] In essence, McDonald's decoupled the process at the component level, just as Dell does with its computers.

Finally, let's not ignore the role of product design in decoupling a supply chain. Sport Obermeyer, a designer and maker of skiwear, found that custom-dyed zippers created its longest lead times. Its designers had traditionally matched zipper and parka colors, but they decided that a black zipper looked fine in most cases. It provided an accent contrast color to the parka and dramatically reduced the lead time for sourcing this key component.[7]

The Cost of Flexibility—Does Mass Customization Pay?

Flexibility comes at a cost. When National introduced customization, building a bike required three hours of labor, compared with one hour for the traditional mass production process. Factory workers managed to reduce this to two hours via many small process improvements that they suggested. (The Japanese name for this sort of continuous process improvement is *kaizen*.) But the extra hour of labor per bike still adds 10,000 yen to each bike's cost. This is offset by a customization fee charged to customers—ranging from 7,000 to 15,000 yen, depending on the number of colors on the bike—that more than offsets the extra cost. Just as important, customization eliminates unsold inventory, which previously had to be marked down at the end of the season.

In the early 1900s, Henry Ford made an opposite change, converting from craft to mass production by introduction of an assembly line. He thus reduced the labor content of a car from 12.5 to 1.5 hours.[8] The 2- or 3-to-1 labor penalty for customization at National Bicycle is less than the more than 8-to-1 differential of craft versus mass in Ford's factory, presumably due to the use of flexible technology in the National Bicycle custom process. But basically, the physical characteristics of production haven't changed much since Ford's day. Mass production continues to have a significant productivity advantage over custom work. What has changed since Ford's day is consumer taste and pliability. Ford's clientele would accept, in the automaker's famous words, any color as long as it was black in exchange for a low-priced Model T. National Bicycle's customers, in contrast, are willing to pay a surcharge to get whichever color they fancy.[9]

Learning from Two Flexibility Champions: World and Zara

The discussion of National Bicycle has prepared us for a deeper look into two companies with which we began this chapter, World and Zara.[10] When we're done with them, you'll understand what they do to achieve flexibility.

World is headquartered in Kobe, Japan, called the country's "fashion capital" because of the many apparel firms located there. A group of managers who left another apparel company, called Empire, started it. They chose "World" for their name because it underscored their ambition to be bigger than Empire. When we visited in 1998, the company had sales of more than $2 billion and more than five thousand stores. Its mantra was, "We make what's selling rather than sell what we've made." It can replenish a hot seller in two weeks, and in six weeks, it can design, produce, and stock new styles similar to a big seller.

Zara is located half a world away in La Coruña, a coastal city in the northwest corner of Spain. Zara's founder, Amancio Ortega, began as an apparel maker in the 1960s and founded Zara, a retailer, in 1975 as a way to better understand the market for his wares. A decade later, he started Inditex, a parent company that sits atop Zara and several other retailers and suppliers that he'd also formed. Zara can replenish existing items in as little as two weeks and can design and produce new items in three weeks. It spends almost nothing on advertising and uses the savings to support the higher cost of producing in Spain, which enables the company to make what its customers want, not force on them what it has already made.

World's and Zara's supply chains are similar but not identical. Nearly all of World's stores are in Japan, so it can colocate production with demand. Zara's original stores were in Spain, but the company expanded into western Europe. It now sells in Europe, Latin America, the Middle East, and Asia. It replenishes all of its locations by air except for those in Mexico, which has more than 150 stores and its own distribution center.

Straightforward Steps to Flexibility

Many of the steps that World and Zara take to achieve their supply chain flexibility can be understood using the ideas developed in our analysis of National Bicycle. Both companies, for example, reserve production capacity far in advance and keep substantial inventory of undyed fabric. This is a logical decouple point because fabric production and factory capacity have long lead times, but demand for them is very predictable. To enable small-lot production, the companies employ skilled line workers, giving them flexibility to process smaller batches, and use efficient technologies such as laser cutting. Traditional fabric cutting requires a lot of labor, so manufacturers typically cut in layers of fifty or more sheets, which translates to a minimum batch size for a style and size of fifty or more. A computer-controlled laser can cut a single layer of fabric automatically, allowing a batch size of one and thus flexibility in responding to sales. Last, producing close to the market helps to reduce lead times, although the fact that Zara can quickly replenish its remote locations using airfreight shows that it's not essential.

Some More Subtle Keys to Flexibility: Information and Empowerment

But if all it takes to be a World or a Zara is a laser cutter and an airplane, why aren't more companies imitating them?

We had a chance to dig deeper when World's CEO, Hidezo Terai, came to New York for the opening of a World store in SoHo. There, we arranged for him to meet with a group of Nine West senior executives with whom we were working. By U.S. standards, Nine West was no slouch in supply chain speed, achieving an eight-week lead time from factories in Brazil. After the usual introductions and small talk, a Nine West executive asked Terai to explain how World managed its two-week lead time.

After the translator posed the question, Terai answered for several minutes in Japanese. When he finished, the translator said, "Empowerment!" We were perplexed. Something had been lost in translation.

The Nine West executives pressed the point, saying they were eager to learn more about World's human resource management, too, but for the moment wanted to focus on the supply chain. Terai elaborated and, this time, so did his translator. Terai believed that most supply chain decisions required coordination between functions. Suppose, he said, you want to make more of a hot seller but can't get the buttons used in the original design. Your search for a substitute requires interaction between your design, purchasing, and factory staffs. Suppose that communication between these departments gets channeled through the departmental vice presidents, with the CEO weighing in to referee disputes. The season will end by the time you make a decision. To make quick decisions, Terai had created cross-functional teams that included operating personnel from design, buying, and production. The teams could make a wide range of decisions on production and design without consulting their bosses.

Both World and Zara empower their people in this way, and both expect them to respond quickly to changes in the market. World has separate merchandising teams for more than forty brands, creating an ability to spot emerging trends. Zara follows a similar approach, with narrowly focused teams of designers and product managers. These teams oversee the design, sourcing, and production of, say, women's sportswear. They're responsible for both the initial collection and in-season responses.

World introduces new designs into a factory using a process intended to eliminate production problems that might cause delays. Using measurements and patterns sent electronically to the factory from the corporate headquarters, members of the design production team make a sample garment and formulate detailed instructions to be used by line workers in producing the garment. The production designers can make design changes if, in making the samples, they encounter difficulties that they think could cause delays in the factory. A common change is to increase the allowance for a seam.

Responding quickly to sales data requires knowing not just what sold, as revealed in point-of-sale (POS) data, but also what would have sold had it been offered. To find out what could have sold, Zara store associates query customers. If someone tries on a garment but doesn't buy it, they'll ask why. Maybe the collar on a blouse was too pointy or the stripes too wide. Whatever the reason, associates report their market intelligence every day to their managers, who funnel it to country managers and the product teams. Any retailer can get sales reports; that's in their POS data. What they don't have is the *nonsales* data that Zara's associates provide—they lack information on the customers who entered their stores but left empty-handed because they didn't find what they wanted.

While less aggressive than Zara in collecting nonsales data, World also gathers it via weekly handwritten reports from each store. It's also diligent in ensuring accurate store sales and inventory data and making this data immediately available. Each morning, design teams have access to online reports showing the previous day's sales by store SKU. World works hard to keep its store-SKU data accurate. In its distribution center, employees scan product bar codes when they're finished picking to ensure that they send the right goods to the stores. Salespeople log the merchandise into computers at the stores, thus backstopping the distribution center's accuracy. World also does monthly stock counts in each store using bar-code scanning and compares the results with its computer records. Its staffers routinely document an average store-SKU inventory error rate of less than 1 percent of the quantity stocked. Zara is less zealous in maintaining its data, believing that 95 percent accuracy is good enough, because it relies on its store associates to make visual stock inspections as part of the ordering process.

Interpreting and responding to market signals can be even trickier than accurately tracking store SKUs. Many factors, including unexpected supply disruptions, can distort sales, undercutting their ability to reflect true demand. Miguel Diaz, CFO of Zara, likes to tell a story that points to the energy that his company devotes to understanding sales' zigzags. Before meeting with one of his buyers, he pored over a thick sales report for the products that the buyer oversaw. Diaz found one, out of hundreds listed, with an aberrant pattern. Its sales had been strong but had suddenly fallen. So he tested the buyer by asking him to explain what had happened. Nonchalantly, the buyer reached over to a rack of clothes, pulled out an item, and said, "You mean this one. We've had a transportation problem with the supplier, and that has interrupted supply to the stores, but I'm working on getting another truck and should have the problem solved later today." The staff at Zara understands the adage about success being 10 percent inspiration and 90 percent perspiration.

The effort that World devotes to forecasting and inventory planning similarly contributes to its supply chain flexibility. It consciously plans for quick reactions to the vicissitudes of market demand. It begins each of its thirteen-week seasons by developing an aggregate sales forecast for each category and each store based on prior category and store sales. To forecast the sales of individual items, World adopted and enhanced the Obermeyer committee forecast process that we described in chapter 3.[11] Before each season, its staff creates a store mock-up in the basement of its Tokyo office building, with next season's line displayed as it would be in a store. Several dozen store associates who have the same characteristics as World's target customers then spend a day in the store test-shopping next season's line. They try on garments, check out how they look on each other, and rate each SKU on a seven-point scale. They also rate fabrics and colors. World combines the rankings with its aggregate forecasts to create an item-level forecast. The company, for example, knows that historically the top 10 percent ranked items account for 40 percent of sales. This fact can be used to create an item forecast from the aggregate forecast.

World buys and places in its stores half of the forecast demand for a style. On top of that, the factory and the fabric supplier each hold enough fabric to satisfy another 25 percent of demand. Thus the supply chain is primed to react to sales, with World, the factory, and the fabric supplier sharing the risk.

One thing distinguishes Zara and World. Zara produces in Spain to support sales across the globe, while World produces where its sells, in Japan. This suggests that while proximity to the market may be helpful to supply flexibility, it is not essential. What is important is a tight integration of design, merchandising, and production. Zara's planning *and* production facilities are in La Coruña. World's planning staff in Kobe is near to factories with which the company has close relationships. Both setups facilitate the integration of design, merchandising, and production.

Partnering with Suppliers: The Path to Flexibility If You Don't Own Your Supply Chain

If you don't own your supply chain, you can still apply the ideas of this chapter by working in partnership with your suppliers. Best Buy exemplifies this approach. Soon after Kevin Freeland joined the company as senior vice president of inventory management in the mid-1990s, he launched a vendor collaboration that proved instrumental to its late-'90s turnaround.[12] Around 1997, Best Buy approached Compaq, then its largest computer vendor, but Compaq declined to work with the firm. Similarly, its number two vendor, IBM, turned it down. But number three, Hewlett-Packard, readily agreed to work on improving the supply chain. They called their effort Project Gemini, because, like the Gemini twins of Greek mythology, they believed that they were joined in battle against Dell.

One indicator of the project's success is how Best Buy and HP fared relative to their competitors. When the project was launched, Circuit City dominated consumer electronics, and Best Buy was flirting with closure. Today, their positions are reversed. Similarly, HP was a distant third in its business to Compaq and IBM. Since then, HP has acquired Compaq, and IBM has exited the personal computer business. Project Gemini was so successful that Best Buy subsequently extended it to all major vendors.

One exercise that Freeland engaged in with suppliers was lead-time mapping. He would gather everyone with supply chain responsibilities from a particular vendor, together with their counterparts from Best

Buy, and have them write what they did on yellow sticky notes. He then drew a timeline on a whiteboard that began with the sourcing of the rawest of raw materials and stretched to the sale of the finished product in a Best Buy store. He'd next invite everyone to paste their stickies on the timeline where their activity happened.

Just through this simple process, he uncovered all sorts of inefficiencies. When he and his staff met with one of their Japanese computer vendors, for example, they found that Best Buy's people arrived Monday morning, looked at weekend sales, and sent an order to the vendor by noon. The vendor's personnel also arrived Monday morning, looked at orders received over the weekend, and set their weekly schedule, *also by noon*. And thus Best Buy's Monday orders would be put off for a week. In fact, Freeland and his team discovered delays like this all along the path from the factory to the store. At the end of the meeting, the most senior executive from the Japanese supplier present in the meeting handed Freeland his business card with a phone number written on the back. It turned out this was the fax number of the factory that made the products they had been discussing, and Freeland was asked to please fax directly to the factory the order they placed Monday at noon after reviewing weekend sales, thus taking many weeks of non-value-adding delay out of lead time.

Why Are Many Retailers So Inflexible?

The writer Leo Tolstoy observed in *Anna Karenina* that "happy families are all alike; every unhappy family is unhappy in its own way." Many ingredients create a happy family, and if all are present, bliss results. But if any are missing, misery rules. So it is, too, with flexible supply chains. Flexibility requires getting many things right. Miss one, and rigor mortis sets in.

Flexibility Is Hard to Value and Thus People Tend to Assume It Has Zero Value

As you design or tweak your supply chain, you have to make many decisions in which you weigh a slow and cheap alternative against a faster, more expensive one. Low costs are easy to see and measure, while flexibility enabled by speed isn't. Guess which factor usually gets the bigger weight? As a result, most supply chains are biased toward the slow and cheap. Even when one staffer or department wants to do the right thing, someone else will complain about the cost, forgetting that lost sales could dwarf the additional outlays.

Consider this tale from the senior vice president of merchandising for a major women's shoe retailer. She had a hot seller but was running out and wanted to buy another five thousand pairs. Her Hong Kong sourcing agent said it would take four months for the additional supply to arrive. By then, the season would have ended, and the chance to sell a fashion item like shoes would be gone. The vice president knew that actual production only took a week. If she had the shoes airfreighted, she could have them in stores within two weeks. She reasoned that if these shoes were hot for her, they were hot for other retailers too, and that the reason for the four-month lead time was that she had to wait in line behind other orders. Thinking it might move her to the front of the line, she told the agent to offer to pay the supplier $1 more per pair to fill her order within a week. Then she'd pony up for airfreight so she could receive the shoes in two weeks. This shoe sold for $80 and normally cost $30, so an additional $1 production cost and $4 for airfreight would only reduce the margin from $50 to $45.

The manufacturer agreed, and the vice president went to her CFO to get what she thought would be perfunctory approval. To her surprise, he rejected the deal, refusing to budge on the margin. This seems nonsensical—which is bigger, after all, $50 times 0 or $45 times 5,000? But it's too often how retailers think. They obsess over a few points of margin and refuse to pay for speed, which could reduce their margin percentage but would increase their total earnings.

The Trust Needed for Flexibility May Be Missing

Trust, or rather the lack of it, can erode supply chain flexibility just as quickly as rigid financial calculations do. Reacting quickly sometimes requires that your supply chain partners take risks on your behalf. If you seek short-term advantages at their expense, they won't be willing to put themselves out for you in the future.

An executive vice president of manufacturing for a women's sportswear apparel retailer, for example, told us of an initiative that he launched, with the encouragement of his company's buyers, to enable a better response to hot sellers. The company replaced its traditional point forecast of demand with high and low forecasts. The manufacturing department then made enough finished goods to meet the low forecast and bought enough extra fabric to cover the high forecast. The year that the vice president introduced this program, sales surged, and most of the extra fabric ended up as finished goods that the retailer sold. Not surprisingly, the buyers were thrilled.

The next season, sales slumped, leaving lots of extra fabric. When the manufacturing vice president asked the buyers to help cover the cost of the leftovers, the uniform response was, "No way! You bought it, not us." Needless to say, the vice president wasn't willing to do any speculative buying in the future.

This story clarifies the difficulty of World's program of having suppliers hold fabric. The suppliers wouldn't agree to it unless World strove to design new items that could absorb leftover fabric and helped its suppliers in other ways, such as ensuring a long-term relationship and significant sales.

A Virtuous Cycle: Reading and Reacting to Early Signals

An unwillingness to invest in accurate forecasting can lead to inflexibility, too. After all, to make what's selling, you have to not only know what's selling but also see it promptly. This kind of knowledge doesn't just come from the right software. You have to train your frontline staff to do their part in collecting solid sales data. Otherwise, you won't be able to distinguish between real trends and temporary blips.

To understand the importance of solid data in making these distinctions, consider our experience in working with American Pacific Enterprises (APE), a maker of quilts and comforters. We helped to create a market test for one of its products, which one of its leading retail accounts would conduct in its stores. Two of the test stores were in Chicago, where APE's CEO, Greg Block, happened to have had a long layover while traveling. He decided to visit the stores to see how the test was going. At the first store, when he introduced himself, the manager gushed about the new product. She'd displayed it prominently, and it was selling briskly. He left thrilled and headed to the next store. He was eager for another enthusiastic response. This time, the store manager looked perplexed and said that she didn't think she'd received his product. She checked the back room and found it in a corner, waiting to be logged in as received.

After this experience, we encouraged the retailer's supply chain vice president to display test merchandise uniformly. His wry response: "We can ask, but we can't control."

This story illustrates how hard it can be to get accurate feedback from the sales floor and shows why Zara puts so much energy into working with its sales staff to gather daily market intelligence.

What we've often seen with retailers is a vicious cycle: long lead times discourage making the effort to accurately read sales, and the inability to read sales becomes a reason for not bothering to reduce lead time. Thus *retailers fail to plan to react*. They buy exactly what they have forecast will sell, and any reaction is just a scramble to chase a hot seller. Smart reaction, in contrast, requires preparation, just like an audible play in football. That preparation includes all of the activities that we have covered in this chapter, such as prepositioning fabric and production capacity and buying less inventory up front because you know you'll be able to get more if you need it.

How Much Flexibility Do You Need?

Creating a flexible supply chain requires a big commitment of effort over a long time, so it's reasonable to ask whether the payoff is worth the cost and toil. In seeking an answer, consider the record of World and Zara.

When World was publically traded, its stock price appreciation significantly outperformed its Japanese competitors. Similarly, Zara's financial success over the last few years has been stellar. Figure 4-4 shows the stock price performance of Inditex, its parent, compared with Limited Brands and Gap Inc.

What's more, Zara recently reported gross margins of a remarkable 57 percent. Compare this with the typical specialty apparel retailer, where gross margins might start at 60 percent to 70 percent but, after

FIGURE 4-4

Stock price for comparison of Inditex with Limited Brands and Gap

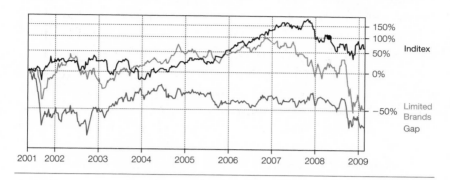

end-of-season markdowns, end up at 40 percent. The higher initial margin reflects the lower cost of sourcing from cheaper suppliers, but the severe margin erosion from markdowns happens because cheaper suppliers are farther away and slower. By contrast, Zara starts with a lower gross margin because of more expensive local production but marks down less merchandise and ends the season with a gross margin not much lower than its initial margin.

World and Zara show that flexibility works, but we don't think this constitutes a proof of the business case; too many factors affect a company's performance to chalk up success to any one ingredient. A more appropriate question for a particular retailer is, What is the right level of flexibility for your situation?

Balancing Accurate Forecasts, Flexibility, and Inventory

Retailers have three tactics at their disposal for matching supply with demand: accurate forecasting, supply flexibility, and inventory stockpiling.

Accurate forecasting, where it's possible, creates the most cost-effective supply chain. If you can forecast demand accurately far enough in advance, you can enable mass production under push control. A company rarely can do this for all of its products, but every firm has some aspects of its business that are predictable (usually total volume), some components that are common to a large number of products, and some products with strong, stable demand. This enables push planning. You might, for example, farm out production to low-cost countries like China, which are remote from the market.

There are many ways to increase forecast accuracy. Retailers, when they see how fickle consumers are, try to stick a little longer with established products or to emphasize basics over innovative offerings. Basics usually earn lower margins, but many retailers have created highly profitable businesses by selling them. These retailers can operate well with a less flexible supply chain, because basic merchandise tends to have more stable and predictable demand.

Retailers can also increase forecast accuracy through advertising that attempts to sell what they've made. Gap stands out as a company that has had success with basic product positioning and a "sell what we make" approach, which its executives call "standing for something."

Once the potential for accurate forecasting has been exhausted, supply flexibility comes next, using the techniques described in this chapter. Stockpiling inventory, because it's the most expensive tactic of the three, should be used only after you've pushed accurate forecasting and supply flexibility to their limits.

Unfortunately, for all too many retailers, stocking inventory is the beginning point for matching supply with demand, rather than the residual after working diligently on forecasting and flexibility. They combine a rigid supply chain with low forecast accuracy, and the only way they can maintain reasonable in-stock rates is by carrying excessive inventory. They get their comeuppance at the end of the season, when they must clear all of that inventory with markdowns, which hurts profits and can erode a store's brand image. Department stores often use this approach.

If a retailer has enough market power, it can get its suppliers to share some or all of the cost of markdowns. Some department stores have managed to do this. But muscling people with your market power can go both ways. Nike has used its market power to force retailers to place noncancelable orders for shoes several months in advance of the season. Needless to say, these sorts of tactics don't build long-term loyalty.

Smart retailers, in contrast, make supply chain flexibility a cornerstone of their strategy. And most of them find it prudent to use a blend of inexpensive, slow suppliers and fast, expensive ones. Zara, for example, manufactures its most unpredictable items locally, in Spain, Portugal, and Morocco, and produces its more predictable products in Turkey and Asia, where the lead time can be as long as four months.

Destination Maternity, the maternity wear designer and retailer in Philadelphia, excels at this approach. It sells through two subsidiary retail chains—A Pea in the Pod and Motherhood Maternity—as well as through department stores such as Kohl's.

The husband-and-wife team of Dan and Rebecca Matthias founded Destination Maternity. Both Dan and Rebecca trained and worked as engineers before starting the company, and they've used their engineering skills to fine-tune their company's supply chain. As with World and Zara, their lodestar is to design and produce in response to sales, and their lead times for design and sourcing resemble World's and Zara's. Destination Maternity has three categories of suppliers, ranging from quick and costly ones (two-week lead time, produced in Philadelphia) to slow and cheap ones (four-month lead time, produced in China). It achieves an intermediate lead time and cost by sourcing from Latin America. To keep store inventory fresh, it does multiple deliveries per week of fast-selling garments and weekly pickups of products that aren't selling, so they can be transferred to other stores.

Destination Maternity's approach shows not only the benefits of flexibility but also when it pays to invest in the most flexible, responsive supply chain. Maximum flexibility makes sense for high-margin products with unpredictable demand. The high margin makes a high level of product availability profitable, and the unpredictable demand makes this hard to achieve without a flexible supply chain.

If your supply chain isn't as flexible as World's, Zara's, and Destination Maternity's, you're leaving money on the table—lots of it. Product sales are hard to predict. Some items will sell dramatically better than predicted; others worse. Being able to respond quickly to unexpected surges in demand thus can have a huge impact on your profitability. It means that you can buy less initially, knowing you can chase your winners, and it means fewer markdowns at the end of the season. For a retailer, supply chain flexibility cures your two biggest headaches—having too few of the right products and too many of the wrong ones—and thus brings greater profits.

CHAPTER FIVE

Goal Alignment

Reducing Perverse Incentive Misalignment

You can study the latest retailing methods. You can buy the best IT. But if you haven't aligned the incentives of everyone within your company and supply chain, you will not succeed at rocket science retailing.[1]

Consider the impact of incentives within a single retail department: distribution. Distribution and logistics departments' staffers are commonly evaluated on how efficiently they move merchandise through the supply chain. When we worked with a fashion apparel retailer, its distribution manager shared with us a video that he'd created on ways to improve distribution efficiency. It showed that warehouse workers could pick orders more quickly if all stores ordered the same size-mix—regardless of how many smalls, mediums, and larges each really needed. Armed with his video, the distribution chief aimed to persuade store managers to standardize the chain's size-mix even though a basic understanding of the retailer's locations (and the demographics of each) made it obvious that the stores needed individual assortments. We asked the distribution manager about the incongruity: might his efforts result in lost sales because of stockouts or excess merchandise that had to be marked down? He responded that he was evaluated on the distribution center's performance, not on what happened at the stores. That was the store managers' problem.

Perverse incentives can also thwart the smooth operation of the supply chain. In the mid-1990s, we worked with several retailers that were importing or considering importing from India. They grumbled about the long lead times, suggesting that they'd import if they could get goods faster. At the time, many Indian exporters belonged to the *unorganized sector*, a term used in the country to denote small firms that lack the scale to invest in formal systems for supply chain management. We also happened to be doing work at the time with some of them and saw an opportunity to alert them to the benefits of reducing their lead times.

Imagine our surprise when the exporters told us that they not only knew the benefits but also understood how to implement such systems. Long lead times, we realized, sprang not from the exporters' *lack of knowledge* but from the absence of proper *incentives*. They were unwilling to reduce their lead times, not unable to. Carrying fabric and yarn inventory was expensive for them, so they didn't want to do it. The fix—as summarized in a report to the Indian finance minister that a group of us wrote—was to find ways to reduce the cost of working capital to the Indian exporters. This would enable them to carry the inventory that could accelerate production, making their lead times comparable to those of exporters in competing countries like China.

Retailers often have trouble implementing rocket science practices not because their managers and supply chain partners don't know what's right but because bad incentives cause them to behave in ways that undermine the greater good. In these circumstances, the key to improving performance lies in changing the incentives—that is, the metrics and rewards—in the company or supply chain.

How Misaligned Incentives Affect Inventory Levels, Fill Rates, Sales, and Profit in a Supply Chain

To understand how misaligned incentives can affect inventory levels, fill rates, sales, and profit in a supply chain, consider the following fictional example.

A recent college graduate, Anna Sheen, has returned to her hometown of Hamptonshire to start a newspaper called the *Hamptonshire Express*.[2] She publishes and sells it on her own. The marginal cost of printing a copy of the *Express* is 20¢, while each one sells for $1. Anna throws out unsold copies; day-old news, as the saying goes, isn't worth the paper that it's printed on. Daily demand follows the normal distribution, with a mean of 500 papers and a standard deviation of 100. How many newspapers should Anna stock each day?

Table 5-1 shows the optimal stocking values and the resulting fill rates, sales, and profits.[3] Notice that the stocking quantity exceeds the mean daily demand. Anna's gains from selling a newspaper (80¢ per copy) far exceed the cost of overstocking a newspaper (20¢). Hence, she errs on the side of overstocking and obtains high fill rates.

After several years of doing all the work herself, Anna decides to start selling her papers through an agent, Ralph. Their agreement requires Anna to transfer papers to Ralph at 80¢ each. Ralph then sells them for $1 each and handles any unsold newspapers. Demand doesn't change.

Ralph's optimal stocking quantity, as shown in table 5-1, is less than 500 because Ralph's gains from selling an additional copy of a newspaper (20¢) are less than the cost he incurs from having an unsold one (80¢). Consequently, Ralph stocks less than 500 units, resulting in lower fill rates, sales, and profits for the supply chain as a whole.

Notice what hasn't changed between the two scenarios: printing costs, retail demand, and retail price. The lower fill rates, sales, and profits result from the fact that Anna is selling through Ralph. You can trace the loss, in other words, to Ralph's incentives' differing from Anna's.

TABLE 5-1

Comparison of Anna's and Ralph's stocking and selling

	Anna's stocking and selling	Ralph's stocking and selling
Stocking quantity	584	416
Fill rate (% of consumer demand satisfied)	98%	81%
Daily expected sales	488 copies	404 copies
Daily expected profit	$331.40	$282.00

The video rental industry offers a real-world example of this incentive problem. Until the mid-1990s, studios such as Disney sold copies of their videos to retailers like Blockbuster for about $60 each. The retailer, in turn, would rent each videotape for around $3 per rental. Clearly, given the investment ($60) and the rental revenue ($3 per rental), a retail outlet would break even after twenty rentals and would stock, at most, one copy of a movie for every twenty consumers willing to rent it. But this setup left many consumers unhappy because they often had to wait for a long time for "hot" new titles. Retailers and studios also recognized that they were losing revenues from the low levels of inventory in the supply chain. "Out-of-stocks were the single biggest problem in our industry," one video industry executive said.

The marginal cost of producing and stocking an additional tape at a retail store was only $3. So from the perspective of the supply chain as a whole, the break-even volume was one rental. Consequently, everyone should have been willing to stock as much as a videotape for every consumer willing to rent that movie. Changing incentives (how the retailers and the studios got paid) was central to addressing this issue in the supply chain.

Starting in the mid-1990s, many studios and retailers entered into revenue-sharing agreements. Under these deals, studios would sell copies of videotapes to retailers for roughly $3 but also were entitled to a share (usually about 50 percent) of rental revenue.

The impact of these changes was immediate and dramatic. Inventory levels and fill rates shot up and so did sales and customer satisfaction. Not surprisingly, video retailers now offer to waive the rental fee if the new release sought by a customer is not in stock.

Some Principles for Aligning Incentives in Operations

The examples in this chapter draw substantially on what's called principal-agent theory.[4] It is in our judgment extremely useful to think of most incentive problems from the perspective of a principal who is trying to influence an agent's (i.e., another individual's or organization's) behavior. The principal-agent approach, although relatively new to operations and supply chain management, has been applied for many years in businesses such as insurance and financial services and, more recently, in the design of employment contracts and stock options for CEOs.[5] Like most theoretical approaches, principal-agent theory makes some assumptions that do not always translate well to practice. Consequently, in identifying the principles for incentive alignment, we'll draw on our experiences, too.

Principle 1: Incentives Exist to Influence Behavior

To design appropriate incentives, you must first identify the behavior that you want to induce. Principal-agent theory relies on the notion of a rational self-interested "principal" who delegates decision-making authority to an "agent" and seeks to influence the agent's behavior through incentives. The principal *does not* dictate particular decisions or actions but shapes the incentives in such a way that the *agent, while maximizing his welfare, will, to the extent possible, also maximize the principal's welfare*.

Hence, in designing incentives, a principal needs to consider how the incentives will influence the agent's behavior. And in doing that, she also must take into account conduct that she would not like to induce. This problem has arisen in basing incentives for teachers on how well their students perform on standardized tests. Proponents of such incentives argue that they motivate teachers to work harder. Opponents point out that the practice could cause teachers to "teach to the test." In other words, teachers might shift their focus to drilling students only on basic skills such as reading, spelling, and arithmetic and ignore creative thinking and reasoning.

This idea—that incentive designers should consider the behavior that they would (and would not) like to induce—may seem obvious, but managers often forget it. When we were advising one retailer on incentive design, it was obvious that the executives did not have a shared understanding of what they wanted their store managers to do. Some of them wanted the managers to focus on controlling expenses by tightly monitoring labor costs and shoplifting, while others wanted them to focus on increasing sales. Not surprisingly, they couldn't agree on an incentive plan until they'd agreed on goals for the store managers.

Principle 2: Incentive Design Requires Deep Understanding of Operations

Failure to deeply understand operations affects not only incentive design but the design of other tasks, too. Witness the attempts by a large discounter to get its suppliers to introduce *shelf-ready packaging* in its stores. Shelf-ready packaging (also called *retail-ready packaging*) refers to products shipped in containers that store staff can place directly onto the display shelves with minimal unpacking. Done right, shelf-ready packaging simplifies store operations and leads to more efficient replenishment, higher on-shelf availability, and higher sales and profits for the retailer and the manufacturer.

We recently had the opportunity to evaluate some shelf-ready packaging firsthand when we spent half a day shelving bottled drinks at a store operated by a large retailer. The supposedly shelf-ready packaging didn't work. It was too flimsy to support the dozen or so bottled drinks placed on it. We couldn't carry the drinks to the shelves in the packages. Instead, we—like the staffers at the store—ended up removing the bottles, placing the packaging on the shelf, and then replacing the bottles in the package. We believe the problem stemmed from the packaging designers' ignorance of store operations; they'd never actually taken the time to see how the packaging worked—or failed to work—in a store. Had they been more familiar, they would have created packages that could have withstood the weight of bottled drinks. "The drinks manufacturer would have made life much easier in the store and improved on-shelf availability by spending an extra ten cents per case to get better corrugated paper," an executive at another consumer goods manufacturer told us. "We would make the same mistake too," he remarked about his own company.

Principle 3: "Hidden Action" and "Hidden Information" Drive Incentive Misalignment

Principal-agent theory identifies two underlying causes for incentive misalignment. Incentive problems arise either when the actions of an agent cannot be observed (hidden action) or when the agent has information not known by the principal (hidden information). The term *hidden* can be misleading in the previous sentence. By *hidden*, we mean the action or information is uncontractible—that is, the action or information is not observable, verifiable, or enforceable. We describe each of these three terms below. The reader should note that for an action or information to be contractible, it has to be observable, verifiable, *and* enforceable.

If the agent's actions and information could be "unhidden," then the principal could write a contract that covered the actions and information. In the *Hamptonshire Express* example above, had Ralph's stocking quantity been contractible, Anna could have contracted with Ralph to stock 584 newspapers, and eliminated the need to provide Ralph with incentives for stocking newspapers. We assumed in the example that Ralph's stocking quantity was uncontractible because in practice a retailer's stocking quantities are usually uncontractible with the manufacturer because of a practice called *diversion*, where a retailer can divert a portion of its purchase from a manufacturer to another retailer instead of stocking the purchased quantity in its distribution centers and stores. In other words, the retailer's stocking quantity can differ from its purchase quantity. As a consequence of diversion being possible, the retailer's stocking quantity is rendered uncontractible.

Observability. We start by describing contexts where an agent's actions are unobservable to the principal. Subsequently, we also explain how the agent's information can be hard for the principal to observe.

Manufacturers often can't directly observe retailers' efforts to sell their products versus those of their competitors. Take Norwalk Furniture, a maker of custom upholstered goods. It tried to sell its custom pieces through retailers that also sold noncustom ones. Its experiment failed, and executives at Norwalk blamed the retailers' lack of effort, not any problems with its furniture. Its executives concluded that stores were pushing mass production pieces, for which they had inventory on hand, harder. As the adage goes, "A loaded retailer is a loyal retailer."

In this example, Norwalk is the principal, and the retailers are the agents. Hidden action exists because the principal cannot directly monitor whether the agent does what it wants, short of sending spies into stores.

Ensuring adequate sales effort matters most when retailers carry substitutable products from multiple manufacturers. Manufacturers worry that a retailer will push the product on which it earns the best margins; this concern is especially acute if a retailer offers a private label line, like Sam's Choice at Wal-Mart or Kirkland at Costco. Imagine how closely appliance makers such as Whirlpool and Maytag monitor sales of the private label Kenmore brand at Sears.

Manufacturers have taken steps to "unhide" this information through "mystery shoppers," for example. Mystery shoppers could visit a store and, unbeknownst even to the store employees, observe whether salespeople at the store were pushing one brand over another. Sophisticated mystery-shopping companies use advanced technology to track the results of such mystery-shopping audits.

In some cases, it is not the agent's action but the agent's information that is unobservable to the principal. An example from outside of retailing—insurers—offers the clearest illustration of the problem. Imagine that an insurer is planning to sell coverage for heart attacks. It will offer the coverage to all consumers, but not all of them will purchase it. Individual customers know more about their health and histories than the insurer does—do they smoke? Have high blood pressure? Do heart problems run in the family? Thus the ones most likely to have heart attacks (that is, the least potentially profitable ones) are most likely to buy coverage. The insurer, in this situation, suffers from *adverse selection*, leading to a higher incidence of heart attacks in its customer base than in the overall population.

Verifiability. In some cases, actions are observable but not verifiable. In fashion supply chains, for example, experienced buyers or merchandisers at a retail firm can often agree on the quality of a garment. But it is hard to write a contract requiring a designer to develop a product with a certain quality level. Quality, in this case, though observable, isn't measurable and would not be verifiable by a neutral third party such as a court of law. Incentives usually cannot be based on unverifiable actions.

Enforceability. Usually, courts, through contract law, enforce contracts. The law sometimes prevents firms from contracting on certain variables. In many supply chains, for example, manufacturers cannot tell retailers to charge a specific retail price. This renders retail selling price uncontractible.

In developing countries or fragmented industries, contract enforcement can be difficult. In situations in which the legal enforcement mechanism is weak, a firm with a track record of sticking to its agreements can use its reputation as a signal of its intentions. In other words, its reputation can be used to generate trust among channel members.

Solving Incentive Problems

The solutions that we've seen for these problems fall into three categories: contract-based, information-based, and reputation-based. Let's take each one in turn.

Given the principles we just discussed, incentive problems are overcome often by unhiding (i.e., by making contractible) previously hidden action or information. Very effective ways to unhide action or information rely on information technology or on converting episodic interactions into repeat relationships. Equally important, incentives are also aligned by writing better contracts between principals and agents. We start by discussing a contract-based solution, where incentives were aligned by writing a new and better contract. Following that, we discuss an example where costing and information systems were used to reveal hidden information, and ultimately, we examine a situation where relationships were used to align incentives.

Contract-Based Solutions

Here, a retailer might write a new contract that uses existing metrics to reward the desired behavior. At Bryn Mawr Stereo, a chain of twelve consumer electronics stores in suburban Philadelphia, store managers had incentives for generating sales and controlling shoplifting, or, as it's euphemistically known in the industry, *shrink*.[6] The chain rewarded its managers by paying them a percentage of their location's sales. (The percentage ranged from 0.2 percent to 5 percent, depending on the level of sales generated.) In addition, it penalized them for shrink, cutting their compensation by the amount of shrink at their stores. A manager who had $500 in shrink in a particular month would see her pay fall by the same amount. In the mid-1990s, Bryn Mawr was acquired by Tweeter, a similar chain, headquartered in the Boston area. Tweeter chose not to change the name, personnel, or assortment at Bryn Mawr stores, but it changed the store manager incentives dramatically. Unlike at Bryn Mawr, Tweeter paid managers a percentage (up to 20 percent, based on profitability) of "store operating income." Since each dollar of shrink reduced store operating income by a dollar, Tweeter, in effect, cut store managers' pay by a maximum of twenty cents for every dollar of shrink. So the shrink penalty was lower at Tweeter than it had been at Bryn Mawr.

Take a guess at how store manager behavior changed as a consequence of the change in incentives. Before the acquisition, store managers obsessed over shrink, even to the point of suppressing sales. In the words of a Tweeter executive, Bryn Mawr stores exhibited a "sales prevention environment." Managers kept small impulse purchases like batteries and tapes and frequently stolen items like the Sony Walkman locked up. They also paid more attention to receiving and logging shipments than to serving customers. They'd typically leave the retail floor, putting less experienced sales assistants in charge of counseling customers and making sales, so they could go to the back room to receive merchandise. Sometimes, they'd even close their store if an assistant was not available. The atmosphere at the stores, according to the Tweeter executive, was defensive, with Bryn Mawr treating salespeople like clerks, not like what they really were: the sources of its profits.

After the Tweeter acquisition, behavior changed promptly. Managers became more entrepreneurial, focusing on generating sales, not on deterring shoplifting. Figure 5-1 compares monthly sales before and after the acquisition at each Bryn Mawr store. The figure shows sales before the acquisition in the darker bars and sales after the acquisition in the lighter bars. Notice that most stores showed increases in sales, sometimes dramatic ones.

Juxtapose mentally the picture on sales with figure 5-2, which shows the change in shrink before and after the acquisition. The darker bars show shrink before the acquisition, and the lighter bars show shrink after the acquisition. Notice that every store showed substantial increases in shrink, which is measured in negative dollars. (Notice, too, that some stores before the acquisition had more inventory than expected. Thus

FIGURE 5-1
___

Average monthly sales at Bryn Mawr stores before and after the acquisition by Tweeter

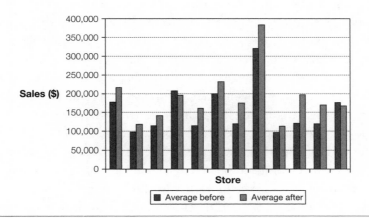

FIGURE 5-2
___

Average monthly shrink at Bryn Mawr stores before and after the acquisition by Tweeter

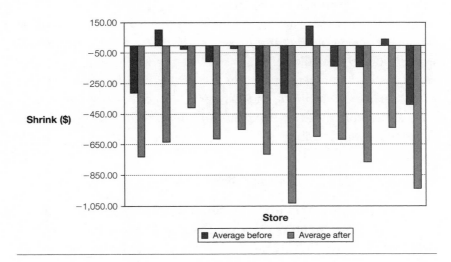

they had "positive" shrink values. One retail executive even remarked to us tongue in cheek that he would have expected Bryn Mawr store managers to grab small electronic devices (e.g., the Sony Walkman) from a shopper and put them in the store's inventory. A more likely cause of the positive shrink was that erroneous excess inventory shipped from the warehouse was not acknowledged by the store. We controlled statistically for variation in such conditions as the level of inventory and the economic growth in the region. We found that the change in incentives contributed to a 9.94 percent increase in sales and an additional $8,834 in shrink. After subtracting the additional theft losses, the stores derived an additional profit equivalent to 2.5 percent of sales.

The natural experiment offered by the Bryn Mawr–Tweeter transition shows the big impact that a retailer can have on its sales and profits by addressing bad incentives. It also highlights the importance of getting the balance among different components of incentives right. Tweeter achieved the change in performance at Bryn Mawr primarily by changing the relative importance of sales and shrink in store manager compensation. At first glance, you might think that Tweeter should have rewarded managers who controlled shrink and increased sales. But Tweeter's experience suggests that an employee who has to accomplish conflicting tasks within a limited time will respond to obvious rewards, even if doing so means sacrificing sales and profit.

Tweeter executives told us that they noticed the excessive attention to shrink and insufficient effort to increasing sales even in their first visits to Bryn Mawr's stores. Oddly, Bryn Mawr's executives—all of whom were experienced and capable—did not see this opportunity, even though they could've just as easily seized it. The change in store manager conduct and the resulting rise in sales occurred within a year of the change in incentives, and Tweeter achieved those results without substantial store manager turnover. All but one of the store managers remained, postacquisition.

Information-Based Solutions

If hidden actions and information are sources of incentive misalignment, then the solution is unhiding them and writing new contracts based on the revelations. Recent advances in information technology have eased both the tracking and the assessment of previously hidden information.

In the early 1990s, for example, consumer goods manufacturers like Campbell Soup and Barilla, a pasta maker, found that orders from distributors fluctuated wildly from week to week.[7] These manufacturers typically offered periodic discounts on their products to distributors. Not surprisingly, distributors wanted to "buy forward" during these promotions. On top of this, the manufacturers' salespeople—who were rewarded for increases in sales to the distributors—encouraged the practice. Barilla and Campbell Soup found that they could reduce demand fluctuation considerably by changing both their discounting practices and the ways in which they evaluated and compensated their sales staffs. Both companies altered promotions so that distributors and salespeople received commissions based not on distributors' purchases (which encouraged buying forward) but on distributors' sales. Campbell's and Barilla eliminated the incentives to buy forward and instead compensated salespeople and distributors based on the amount of product that moved to retailers.

At times, actions in the supply chain aren't hidden, but the incentive misalignment stems from the unforeseen *consequences* of otherwise sensible actions. To understand this distinction, consider the relationship between Owens and Minor (O&M), a distributor of medical supplies, and the hospitals that it provisioned.[8] As in the relationships between most hospitals and their medical supplies distributors, O&M and its customers entered into "cost-plus" contracts. Under these contracts, O&M charged a hospital a price that was a set percentage, usually 7–9 percent, over its cost of purchasing a good. That percentage applied across the board and didn't vary based on the cost of handling a particular item or on the services demanded by the hospital relating to that item. Distributors like O&M thus wanted to ship small high-value items, such as cardiovascular sutures, that yielded fat margins. Prices for these items were high, and they cost relatively little to handle and ship because of their puny size. A distributor operating at 7 percent margins would have received $56 for handling an $800 box of sutures but only $2.10 for a $30 box of diapers even though the latter was more expensive to handle, store, and transport. Needless to say, distributors wanted to supply more sutures than diapers.

But hospitals, which weren't locked into a single supplier, preferred to buy items such as sutures directly from manufacturers. They chose to buy bulky, inexpensive products, such as diapers, from distributors. They also tried to squeeze as many additional services, like expedited deliveries, as possible from their distributors. Distributors, for their part, tried to avoid providing such services for fear of eroding their margins.

These cost-plus contracts resulted in unhappiness all around. Many distributors were hurting financially in the mid-1990s. They faced constant pressure to reduce personnel costs since that was one of the few ways in which they could improve profitability. From 1984 through 1994, O&M managed to cut its staff costs from 12.5 percent to 6.8 percent of sales. But these improvements stalled out, and labor costs started rising again in 1995.

Hospitals weren't happy, either. Distributors didn't offer the services that they wanted. Many of them thus set up costly internal departments to handle logistics functions that would've been better performed by distributors.

Aiming to improve the situation, O&M executives decided to identify their company's cost drivers and break down company profitability by customer. Not surprisingly, the amount of add-on services received by a customer largely determined whether a relationship produced profits. Lots of additional services meant lower profits. Other relevant factors were the numbers of purchase orders per month, lines per purchase order, and deliveries per week, as well as the method of ordering and the inventory carrying cost. As often emerges in this sort of analysis, many customers turned out to be unprofitable.

O&M executives realized that to return their firm to profitability, they needed to alter the adversarial relationship that they'd stumbled into with their customers. They thus developed a concept that they termed *activity-based pricing*. Under it, they developed a menu of services and a specific fee for each service. A hospital that wanted expedited delivery would pay a higher price.

In response to the changes, a few hospitals dropped O&M, but the majority liked the new approach. It let them obtain services that they craved. Within six years of its launch, activity-based pricing accounted for $1.35 billion of O&M's roughly $4.2 billion in annual sales.

Trust- or Reputation-Based Solutions

Trust- or reputation-based solutions reduce incentive misalignment by exploiting the fact that information that is hidden in one-time dealings often gets revealed by repeated interactions. Over the course of relationships, companies want to preserve their reputations for good conduct.

Reputation- or trust-based solutions matter mightily in developing countries, where legal contracts are hard to enforce. Think about the apparel industry. Manufacturers in the developing world often worry that customers in the developed world might renege on their orders or seek to reject shipments on frivolous grounds if they see lower-than-predicted demand for a product. Similarly, developed-world firms often fret over the possibility of a developing-world supplier engaging in unethical practices, such as using child labor, or dropping an order previously committed to when offered a better price by another customer.

Companies thus have used reputation- and trust-based solutions in two ways. Some firms, including Sport Obermeyer, a skiwear manufacturer in Aspen, Colorado, have developed long-term relationships with a single supplier. In other cases, intermediaries like Hong Kong–based Li & Fung, which works with many manufacturers and buyers to coordinate their supply chains, track everyone's conduct.[9] Li & Fung sees itself as a coordinator of the supply chain; the company typically takes orders from customers (for example, branded manufacturers in the United States) and identifies factories that can produce the required product and suppliers that can provide raw materials at the required price, time, and quality. Li & Fung then monitors everyone in the supply chain—the customer, the factory, and each supplier—to ensure that they perform their assigned tasks at the promised time. In the process of coordinating the supply chain and having repeated interactions with many firms in the supply chain, Li & Fung also aligns incentives by tracking each firm's reputation and rewarding good behavior. A given manufacturer and customer might deal with each other only once, but Li & Fung will do business with each of them repeatedly. The manufacturer and buyer may not worry about the cost to their reputations from burning each other, but they will care about their reputations with Li & Fung.

There are, of course, industries in which businesspeople behave as if they'll never see each other again but, in fact, have repeated interactions. Take the automotive industry. There, companies like Toyota and Honda have earned reputations among suppliers for fair, though tough and demanding behavior, while competitors like Ford and General Motors have built ones for unreasonableness. An article by Jeffrey Liker of the University of Michigan and Thomas Choi of the University of Arizona quotes executives at suppliers who describe Ford and General Motors as "extremely confrontational" and having "unleashed a reign of terror."[10] One of them said, "You can't trust anyone in [GM and Ford]." And the CEO of an industrial fasteners supplier noted, "[American] automakers have us work on drawings, ask other suppliers to bid on them, and give the job to the lowest bidder. Honda never does that."

Why do smart executives at the Big Three—some of whom we trained in our classes—fail to recognize that adversarial relationships with suppliers undermine innovation at their firms? And why is this sort of conduct also common at other otherwise well-run companies?

We believe that the answer lies in the failure to recognize the value of reputation in repeated interactions. Accounting systems track measurable costs relating to production and transportation but, by their nature, cannot track the intangible cost of damaging a firm's reputation for fair play. Thus incentive systems—which must rely on the information tracked in the accounting systems—motivate buyers to behave as if they have a one-time relationship with their suppliers, when in reality they are playing in a repeated game.

Conclusion—Some Guiding Principles

Equations, algorithms, and accounting systems don't solve incentive problems. You need insight into people's roles and motivations, whether they are sales associates or CEOs. Managers who tackle these problems have to understand multiple functional areas, including marketing, manufacturing, logistics, and finance.

Accept the Premise That Misaligned Incentives Can Compromise Supply Chain Performance

Alcoholics Anonymous famously counsels people that the first step in solving a drinking problem is acknowledging that you have one. So it is, too, with misaligned incentives in the supply chain. Managers are at times surprised to hear that their supply chains are underperforming because of bad incentives.

But once they accept that premise, they quickly see the sources of the problem within their supply chains. In fact, they usually start jumping to potential solutions right away. But we usually caution managers to hold off on implementing a solution until they have identified the root cause of the misalignment in the following step.

Trace Goal Incongruence to Hidden Action or Hidden Information

Identifying the root of the misalignment enables a discussion of whether the action or information can be unhidden or whether the agent making the decision can be induced to act in the principal's interest through appropriate incentives even if the action or information remains hidden.

In our work with companies, we ask managers to identify decisions that would have turned out differently if the decision maker had the whole supply chain's interests, instead of just his or her own, in mind.

We also ask them to identify the behavior that they would like to induce among the agents. Sometimes, an executive team doesn't have a shared understanding of the desired conduct. In these situations, we ask them to zero in on that first. This is a vital step—how can you design incentives if you are unclear on the behavior that you would like to induce with the incentives?

We then ask why these decision makers acted as they did. Some folks blame improper training. Others point to inadequate tools for decision support. But in many cases, people agree that the problem can be traced to mismatched goals—the theme of this chapter.

Overcoming Goal Incongruence

To line up everyone's goals, you employ the contract-based, information-based, or trust- and reputation-based solutions that we explored earlier in this chapter.

When we began consulting on these kinds of problems, we used to suggest that companies first try contract-based solutions because they're often easy to implement. But the longer we do this, the more convinced we are that information-based and trust-based solutions often work better. Advances in computer technology have eased the implementation headaches and reduced the cost of information-based solutions. These days, thanks to the Internet and mobile telephony, you can quite easily make sales data available throughout the supply chain and thus can ensure that everyone is operating with the same goals and metrics in mind.

Sometimes, managers find trust-based solutions more appealing because they feel less awkward talking with supply chain partners about working more cooperatively than telling them that they intend to monitor them more closely.

Two questions often arise when managers try to implement these solutions. One is which firm in the supply chain should initiate the move toward better goal alignment. Clearly, a dominant firm such as Wal-Mart or Toyota can force others to follow its lead. But exceptions exist. In the late 1980s, Kanthal, a midsize Swedish supplier of heating wires, said that it would charge a penalty every time General Electric changed specifications without warning. GE agreed to the change, and incentives fell into alignment as a result.[11]

The second question is how to nudge a supply chain partner to restructure its internal incentives. A few years ago, one of our former students launched a start-up in the Boston area that placed kiosks, for dispensing its products, in retail outlets not owned by the start-up. Our student and his staff understood the importance of motivating retailers to place the kiosks and offered them suitable incentives for getting them to do so. A retail chain, for example, might be offered a contracted amount for each kiosk placed in a store. Unfortunately, store managers, not their bosses at headquarters, decided *where exactly* to put the kiosks within their locations. Our former student had failed to specify kiosk location in the contract, and store managers did not derive additional income from placing the kiosk in a more attractive spot. The start-up, of course, wanted them in high-traffic areas, but often the managers—who had no motivation to provide prime locations—located them in low-traffic areas. "We found our kiosks near the men's room," our student lamented. Unfortunately, it was too late by the time he recognized the mistake. The start-up would have liked to rewrite its contract with retailers to include an explicit reward for store managers but ran out of cash and closed before it could do so.

As our student learned, rocket science retailing won't work without appropriate incentives for everyone involved in the manufacture, distribution, and sale of a good. Cutting-edge decision tools and technologies depend on people for their implementation. And people are stubborn and myopic. They pick the path that's easiest and most profitable for them—not out of spite but simply because we all have a blinkered view of the world. Given the opportunity, they'll try to advance their self-interest. A rocket science retailer thus must ensure that their interests line up with the greater good of the supply chain. Well-designed incentives are a necessary condition for rocket science retailing to work.

CHAPTER SIX

Store-Level Execution

Increasing Sales Through Better Availability of Products and Store Associates

We've all shopped, and we know that we can have a wide range of experiences, from exasperation to delight, in a store. How we evaluate our shopping experience depends on many things, including what we are shopping for. Most people would use different criteria to evaluate the weekly slog of shopping for groceries than they do for the occasional purchase of a diamond ring or a Rolex watch. But all store visits have several things in common. The customer arrives with a desire to buy something. She may seek a specific item, or she may have a need but not know the best way to satisfy it. Or maybe she's just browsing, in the hopes that something will excite her enough to buy. She may find what she wants and then pick up additional items on the way to the checkout line. Or she may end up exiting empty-handed. She may need help, and whether she finds it may determine whether she has a good experience. She may like the aesthetics of the store, or she may hate them.

Certainly, different things matter to different people. But a retailer must know what matters most to most of its customers. What are the vital few factors that will have the biggest impact on whether a potential customer turns right at the end of her driveway and heads to your store or turns left and heads to the competitor's location? And if the customer comes to your store, what makes her buy a lot, a little, or nothing at all?

Retailers need to know what matters to their customers so they can focus their energy and resources on it. Sam Walton, founder of Wal-Mart, believed that hospitality mattered. So he hired official greeters at his stores, and when he visited locations, he encouraged associates to take a pledge: "I want you to promise that, whenever you come within 10 feet of a customer, you will look him in the eye, greet him, and ask him if you can help him." This concept persists today as Wal-Mart's "10-foot rule."[1]

Another retailer requires its checkout personnel to greet customers by their last name if they present a credit or loyalty card. It enforces this policy with mystery shoppers. Do store associates increase customer satisfaction and sales by greeting customers? Answering questions like this is vitally important for a retailer, but also challenging, so let's now consider a method for determining how the myriad of activities that occur within the four walls of a store impact sales and customer satisfaction.

What Most Impacts Sales and Satisfaction?

Over the last decade, we have worked with six leading retailers to help them determine which of the many things that happen within their stores most raise sales and satisfaction.[2] Our partners in this effort have been three former students of ours—Nicole DeHoratius, now at the University of Portland; Jayanth Krishnan, now at the International Monetary Fund; and Zeynep Ton, now at Harvard Business School—and our Wharton School faculty colleague Serguei Netessine. The six retailers asked to remain anonymous, but they represent these segments: department stores, books, fast food, groceries, office products, and home furnishings and small appliances.

All of them track sales by store and by day, and collect data on a wide range of variables that might affect sales and satisfaction. Four survey their customers. Four also send mystery shoppers into their stores to assess performance on everything from in-stock levels to the friendliness of store associates.

To understand their store challenges, we had extensive discussions with their executives as well as executives at other retailers. We assembled data for each one on sales, as well as a host of factors that might influence sales, and mined this data to discern the primary drivers of their sales and customer satisfaction. We'll use our analysis of the home furnishings and small appliances retailer to illustrate the process.[3] We analyzed monthly data, stretching for seventeen months, on store sales and potential sales drivers for each of about five hundred locations. The information available to us included gross store sales for each month and the results of customer-satisfaction surveys.

An offer to join in the survey was printed on the bottom of customer receipts—if they participated, they were entered into a lottery to win a significant cash prize. Customers called an 800 number and answered automated questions using their phones' keypads. The surveys included an overarching question—"On a 10-point scale, how satisfied were you with your store visit?"—as well as a series of more specific ones. (For yes/no questions, the monthly variable recorded for that store was the percentage who answered yes. For questions requiring a 10-point rating, the monthly variable recorded was the average score.) These were the other questions:

- Were you greeted?

- Was assistance provided if needed?

- Rate the knowledge of any store associates you interacted with on a 10-point scale.

- Did you find everything you were looking for?

- Were any items out of reach?

- Were you able to find prices OK?

- Were the aisles free of debris?

- Was checkout quick and easy?

We also incorporated managerial metrics such as in-stock rate—that is, the percentage of items that the corporate computer shows have positive inventory at the end of the month—planned payroll, actual payroll, and the number of terminations.

Making sense of all of this data required sophisticated statistical analysis, but the conceptual approach is intuitive. You just ask yourself, "If sales in a store are higher than you would have expected, given its past average sales, adjusted for seasonality, what might have caused that?"

While conceptually simple, the approach does have pitfalls. Determining the impact of payroll on sales is a good example. Most retailers, including the ones we analyzed, set a store's payroll budget for next month as a fixed percentage of expected store sales for next month. So if both sales and payroll are relatively high in a month, it's hard to know whether the increased store labor drove increased sales, or a forecast by the retailer of high sales caused it to increase staffing. To illustrate, consider an extreme case in which a retailer can perfectly predict next month's sales in each store, and it sets payroll to 10 percent of forecast sales. Then sales would be perfectly correlated with payroll, but this would be caused by sales driving payroll, not payroll driving sales. Consequently, it would tell you nothing about the impact on sales of a change in staffing levels.

If you therefore wanted to understand the impact of payroll on sales, you might instead do an experiment. You might raise payroll by 10 percent in fifty stores and lower it by 10 percent in another fifty stores and then see what happened. If you saw increased sales in the stores where you added payroll and decreased sales where you reduced payroll (again, adjusting for seasonality), then you could conclude that the payroll level had spurred additional sales.

Retailers inadvertently conduct experiments like this all the time because actual payroll deviates from planned payroll somewhat randomly. Actual payroll can be less than planned because of lack of availability of people. In a given month, a retailer may be unable to hire as many new associates at some stores as it would like. (Because of the high turnover of store associates—typically around 100 percent per year—stores need to constantly hire to maintain staffing.) Or perhaps the retailer can't get its part-timers to commit to work as many hours as it needs them to. Whatever the reason, if lack of labor results in less payroll being used in a month than was planned, the store may be able to bank those hours for use in a future month. That results in actual payroll exceeding planned payroll for some months in the future. Thus you see the random ups and downs.

In exactly this way, the retailer we were studying was performing a natural experiment to measure the impact of payroll on sales. What were the results? With more than five hundred stores and seventeen months of data for each store, we had more than six thousand store–month observations. In some months, actual payroll exceeded planned payroll. In other months, it was below planned payroll. We sorted the store–month data by the ratio of actual payroll to planned payroll and grouped the outputs into quintiles. In the first group, actual payroll averaged 14 percent below planned payroll, and in the fifth group, it averaged nearly 50 percent above planned payroll. For the other three groups, it ranged between these limits. The key question was what happened to sales: was it depressed when payroll was low and elevated when it was high? Figure 6-1 provides the answer. It shows the amount

FIGURE 6-1

Store staffing has a big impact on sales

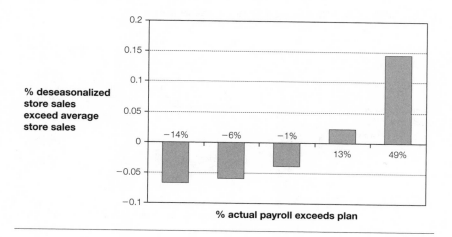

% deseasonalized store sales exceed average store sales

% actual payroll exceeds plan

by which a store's deseasonalized sales exceeded its average sales for each quintile. As is obvious, actual sales soared relative to average sales in months when actual payroll was above planned payroll.

More employees in a store can improve all of the key execution metrics. More staff at the registers reduces checkout times. More people checking the shelves and moving goods from the back room increases the number of customers who find what they were looking for. And more folks offering help on the floor raises the chances of customers' getting assistance when they need it.

So it's no surprise that increasing payroll would increase sales and satisfaction. But later in this chapter, we'll also show that it's a great deal for the retailer because the incremental gross margin earned on the additional sales dwarfs the extra cost.

In our study, payroll was the single biggest driver of sales. The next biggest drivers were customers' average rating, on a 10-point scale, of store associates' knowledge and the percentage who answered yes to the question "Did you find everything you were looking for?" Figures 6-2 and 6-3 show the sales impact of these factors.[4]

High-performance retailers compare sales in a set of stores that have been open at least a year with sales in the same stores in the same period a year earlier. This metric is called *comparable store sales* (*comp sales* for short) and is closely watched by Wall Street as an

FIGURE 6-2

Knowledgeable store associates increase sales

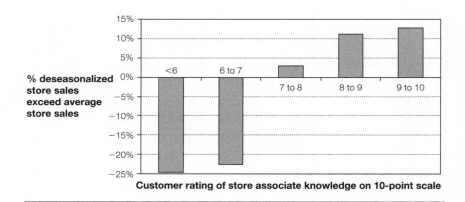

% deseasonalized store sales exceed average store sales

Customer rating of store associate knowledge on 10-point scale

indicator of customer acceptance. Retailers love to see increases in comp sales of 5 percent or more, though they often see negative comp sales. The sales increases in figures 6-1 to 6-3 are for a consistent set of stores and hence show what comp sales could have been with better execution. The data suggests that getting store execution right can produce double-digit rises in comp sales. A favorite retailer trick for jump-starting comp sales is to remodel a store. But that's a one-time stimulus. Imagine how much more powerful it would be for customers to consistently find what they came for with the help of knowledgeable store staff.

We've described a process for mining customer survey data to identify what matters most to your customers and shown that, for one retailer, the answer was knowledgeable store associates and enough of the right kinds of inventory. Another retailer, applying the same method, might find different answers, so we'd urge you to do the surveys needed to identify your customers' priorities. For example, when Staples examined their customer satisfaction survey results they found the four things their customers most valued were (1) fast checkout, (2) in-stock on the basics, (3) easy to find what you want, and (4) courteous and helpful associates.

While these four factors are not identical to the top-three list for the retailer we've just described, they're similar. They, too, involve store

FIGURE 6-3

When customers find what they want, sales rise

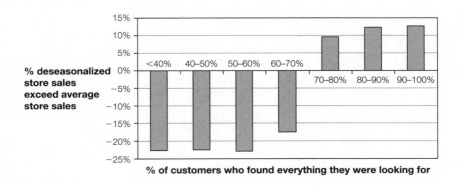

% of customers who found everything they were looking for

associates and finding products. That makes sense. After all, the key components of a retail store are products and people, and we've found that, at most retailers, customers rate these factors as critical to their shopping experience. Therefore, we'll devote the rest of this chapter to improving the quantity and quality of your store associates and achieving better in-stock rates for the customer.

Putting People First

Figure 6-1, which we discussed earlier, shows that store staffing levels matter mightily. Recall that the figure is based on extensive data on sales and potential sales spanning seventeen months and five hundred stores. As part of our analysis, we measured the impact of payroll on sales and found that for an average store in an average month, the sales increase per dollar of additional payroll added was $9.52.[5] This retailer earned gross margins of about 40 percent, which meant that spending an additional dollar on payroll would produce incremental gross margin of 40 percent of $9.52, or $3.81.

Labor Leveragers Versus Cost Minimizers

Spending a dollar to earn $3.81 is a great deal, so an obvious question is why this retailer wasn't employing more people.

We gleaned insight into this question when we spent a day touring stores with a group of grocery CEOs. One store that we visited belonged to a regional operator that had been acquired a couple of years earlier by a large national chain. Several of the CEOs had seen the store before the acquisition and remarked on the differences. Staffing had fallen, the employees looked dispirited, and the few customers in the store didn't look happy, either. Our group conjectured that the acquirer had aggressively cut costs by reducing head count and wages, leading to a minimum number of minimum wage employees in the store. And members of the group speculated that while this may have improved short-term profits, it had obviously done long-term damage to customer satisfaction and sales.

Thinking we had found philosophical allies, over dinner that night we told of the retailer that we'd studied that appeared to understaff its stores, and added that we'd measured the sales impact of more payroll and it turned out to be nearly $10 for each additional dollar spent.

To our surprise, the group's reaction was cool, even negative. One of the CEOs emphasized that labor cost was something to be minimized, not increased, and commented, "I spend my days saying no to a long line of people suggesting ways to spend money, including adding store staff. I don't need a couple of Ivy League professors with their fancy statistical analysis giving them more ammunition!"

This conversation underscored for us that most retailers view labor as a cost, not an asset. Our payroll results were specific to a particular retailer—another firm might see a different result—but this conversation and others like it convinced us that the tendency is for retailers to understaff their stores. And that's understandable. Decisions about staffing trade off a known present cost—paychecks written to employees—against an unknown future benefit, namely, the incremental sales that would result from better staffing. Not surprisingly, the short-term cost is going to be weighted higher than the unknown future benefit.

What's more, store labor is an easy cost to cut quickly, because many store employees work part-time and turn over frequently. In this situation, it's tempting to make your end-of-quarter numbers by shaving a few hours off each store's payroll, arguing that the negative impact will probably be minimal. Unfortunately, this lower staffing level tends to become the baseline for the next quarter's budget. After doing this repeatedly, many retailers find themselves with just a handful of minimum wage associates in each of their stores.

A retailer in this situation probably faces a downward spiral: cost-cutting efforts, aimed at plumping the bottom line, end up sapping the top line because of poor customer service. Given that store labor is the second-biggest cost for most retailers, after the cost of goods sold, we'll concede that wantonly adding staff is equally risky. Add too much or add jobs in the wrong place or time, and your results can be equally bad. But if you use the analytic methods that we're advocating, you can tailor the size of your workforce to your needs.

Rightsizing Your Store Staffs

As mentioned above, we found that for an *average* store at one retailer, the sales increase per dollar of additional payroll was $9.52. However, the particular numbers varied considerably among all of the five hundred stores, ranging from $3.91 to $27.78.[6] Clearly, adding a dollar of payroll to a store to earn a 40 percent margin on a $3.91 sales lift is a marginal call—you'd have to worry about possible estimation error on the $3.91 estimate. But a 40 percent margin on a $27.78 sales increase is more than $11 of incremental profit for $1 of incremental expense. In other words, a great deal—with an ample margin for error.

Figure 6-4 is a histogram showing how the sales rises varied across stores. We pondered what could cause so much variation. Imagine a curve that shows how sales changes as payroll for a store increases. What would you expect this curve to look like? Logically, revenue should increase as store labor is increased, but we would expect diminishing returns.

Figure 6-5 shows revenue as a function of store staffing level for one store in our data set that had considerable variation in staffing levels, and you can see the diminishing returns in the impact of payroll on

FIGURE 6-4

Sales lift per incremental $1 of payroll varied greatly across stores

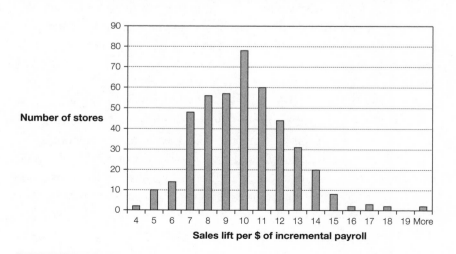

Number of stores

Sales lift per $ of incremental payroll

sales. This makes sense. If you have two associates working in a store and add a third, you might not be surprised to see a 50 percent improvement in results, but you'd never expect a tenfold increase by going from two to twenty store associates. This same pattern will hold for any aspect of store performance. Reducing the wait time at checkout from ten minutes to one minute should significantly increase customer satisfaction. But reducing it from one minute to six seconds would have much less impact. As a retailer works on fixing a problem, eventually it reaches the point of satisfying the customer, and additional improvements provide no more gain.

Figure 6-5 also makes it easy to see why the sales lift from adding payroll would differ by store. For the store depicted in figure 6-5, payroll varied considerably, ranging from around $13,000 per month to over $21,000 per month.[7] But most stores had a relatively constant payroll. If this store's payroll had hovered around $13,000, where the sales–payroll response curve is steep, then the sales lift from incremental payroll would be high. But if its payroll were in the $17,000 to $21,000 range, where the curve is flat, the incremental payroll would have no impact. We found this to be the case when we examined differences in impact of payroll on sales across stores. The stores with a relatively low level of staffing relative to sales had the highest sales lift

FIGURE 6-5

Sales versus associate payroll at one store shows diminishing returns

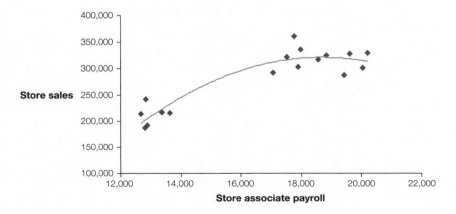

from incremental payroll, and those that were adequately staffed relative to sales showed a lower lift.

Figure 6-5 suggests a natural way to think about how to set a store's staffing level. As you increase staffing, you get less and less sales return for each incremental dollar spent. If payroll is currently at $16,000 and you raise it to $17,000, your sales will increase from about $290,000 to $312,000. At a 40 percent gross margin, the profit on the $22,000 sales bump is $8,800, far exceeding the $1,000 incremental cost. Increasing payroll still further, to $18,000, raises sales by $8,000, to $320,000, and generates another $3,200 in gross margin—still profitable, but less so. Raising payroll above $18,000 appears to produce little gain and would not be profitable, so about $18,000 would be an optimal level, according to figure 6-5.

Note, too, that the sales–labor curve in figure 6-5 is based on the current store layout and level of training. You could shift this curve upward by enhancing training and improving the store layout to make it easier for customers to find what they want.

We've also presented this analysis at a store–month level, but it's best done hour by hour for each department within a store. A recent *Wall Street Journal* article described how several retailers, including Wal-Mart and Payless ShoeSource, are planning labor by the hour and making one of their hiring criteria the willingness of people to work flexible hours and be available when they're most needed.[8]

Best Buy provides an example of best practices by a retailer that views store labor as an asset.[9] Best Buy's journey to store labor excellence began by conducting, for a different purpose, an activity-based-costing measurement of the time it took to perform store activities. It used the analysis to tabulate the time required for store associates to perform their regular duties as well as those related to special one-off corporate programs, and to compare that with the available time. The company's analysts discovered that the required time was about double the available time. In response, store managers were choosing their favorite 50 percent of their assigned activities to perform, resulting in random execution of the special corporate programs. As Best Buy's executives considered this situation, they also noticed that they had fifty people managing the $1 billion annual ad budget, while two managed the $10 billion payroll budget. This had to change, and it did.

Best Buy significantly increased the time and attention paid to labor management.

Let's consider how Best Buy set staffing levels. A store is an amalgam of a factory and a sales office. "Factory" tasks include receiving product deliveries, moving product from the back room to shelves as needed, putting items moved by a customer back where they belong on the shelf, and clearing debris from the aisles. Sales office tasks include managing product location and adjacencies to drive add-on purchases, and all interactions with customers, such as greeting them, asking whether they need help, and, when requested, providing advice to enable them to make a purchase decision and to find the products they have decided to buy. Store associates are thus involved in both taking care of the store (factory functions) and taking care of customers (sales functions). But by taking care of the store, employees are indirectly taking care of the customer by ensuring that fixtures are well stocked, the store is neat and tidy, and checkout is fast and pleasant.

To set staffing levels for factory tasks like unloading delivery trucks, Best Buy used a technique employed by industrial engineers to determine the time required to perform various duties. This gave the company a standard time, which could be multiplied by the number of trucks to be unloaded on a given day to determine the staffing required.

This approach doesn't work for sales. There is no standard time to sell something. To a point, the more time you spend with a customer, the greater your chances of making a sale. So to set staffing levels for the sales function, Best Buy conducts experiments, varying the staffing levels in different stores and observing how sales change. On the basis of these experiments, it can create curves like the one in figure 6-5 and can set payroll, as we described above, to a level that maximizes gross margin, net of payroll cost.

Best Buy also invests heavily in training. One of its most successful innovations has been the use of the Internet to enable store employees to share knowledge. This started with installation of car audio systems, which is complicated because of the variety of car-radio combinations and risky because it involves drilling holes near sensitive areas such as gas tanks. Best Buy set up a Web site on which store employees who had figured out how to deal with challenging car-radio combinations could write instructions for their colleagues at other stores. Soon, the company allowed employees who had read an installation guide to rate its usefulness. And eventually, Best Buy decided to base employee bonuses on the number of readers and the quality ratings of these radio installation guides. Use of the Web site then took off. It has since spread beyond radios to many other areas of store operations.

As Best Buy strove to leverage its store labor, its main competitor, now-defunct Circuit City, was rushing to slash store labor costs. Circuit City announced on March 28, 2007, that it had cut 3,400 store sales-people who were paid "well above the market-based salary range for their role."[10] The *Baltimore Sun* reported that these workers made fifty-one cents more per hour than what Circuit City regarded as the average market wage. The associates cut tended to be the most experienced and knowledgeable, so Circuit City ended up reducing the average knowledge level of its personnel as it was struggling to survive.

This is as close to a controlled experiment as one could hope for in the business world: Best Buy worked to improve its employees, while Circuit City simultaneously slashed staff and pushed knowledge out the door. What were the results?

An answer can be found in a study that interviewed customers to compare the two chains' customer service.[11] One customer's comment captures well the main finding: "They [Circuit City] often don't have what I want. Best Buy just seems a little better. The salespeople actually know what they're doing." The financial impact of this has been vivid. For the first quarter of 2007, Best Buy reported an 18.5 percent profit increase, significantly beating analysts' estimates.[12] In contrast, on September 20, 2007, six months after it cut its most experienced associates, Circuit City reported a comparable-store sales decline of 7.9 percent and a loss for the quarter, and finally closed its doors completely in March 2009.[13] Can there be a more vivid link between top-line results and the quantity and quality of store associates?

The Circuit City–Best Buy comparison is dramatic, but also presents a puzzle. The managers of Circuit City were smart, hard-working, well-intentioned folks. Many of them came from Best Buy. So the question is, "Why do smart people sometimes do apparently dumb things?"

Paul Gaffney, former chief information officer and head of supply chain of Staples, argues that retailer executives fall into two categories: (1) those who see the need to invest for future gain via increased revenue and (2) those who tend to take revenue as a given and focus on expense reduction.[14] Accordingly, Gaffney believes that retailers can fail in two ways: (1) they can invest too liberally and overexpand; or (2) overly zealous cost cutting can lead to a downward spiral of the top line forever, as happened with Circuit City. How can you walk the tightrope between over- and underinvestment? One way is to conduct experiments to measure the benefits of potential expenditures, as Best Buy does as it strives to rightsize its workforce.

Experimentation vexes most retailers because they lack the analytic sophistication to control for factors that can confound their results. (That's why the experiment methodology described in chapter 3 can be useful.) But Staples' efforts over the last five years to improve its store execution offer important lessons.[15] The company's executives believe that the right level of labor investment makes a difference, but even more important, in their view, is what you do with that labor. Customers want store associates who are courteous and helpful. Staples found it can't train courteousness, so it hires for this and for a willingness to help.

Staples provides aids that enable its store associates to excel in these areas. It first identified functions and products, such as selling technology goods like expensive printers, where customers needed the most help. Then it provided the tools that its staffers needed. For selling technology, this took the form of a Web site that compared features of various products and the relative importance of those features given what the customer wanted to do. Staples then tested this and other ways of delivering product information in the stores and found that many customers preferred old-fashioned brochures over the Internet, so this has become the main means of providing product information. Interestingly, only in the last ten years has it become practical to print large volumes of timely information in the stores. People tend to think of IT advances as silicon-age stuff like RFID, but even economical color printing can have an impact.

The cheapest way to increase the quantity of store labor is to reduce the work to be done. Staffers spend most of their time catering to customers and taking care of the store. If the time required to take care of the store can be reduced, that frees up more time for customers.

The simplest way to reduce workload is to stop doing tasks that don't add value. A pet food retailer, for example, used to change its promotional displays weekly. Then it realized that the average customer visits once a month, so a monthly rotation of promotional materials was enough. Kohl's department store employs a staff of industrial engineers to simplify its store processes.

Staples did a number of things to better deploy its associates. It restricted jobs like receiving goods to nonpeak hours. It also reengineered tasks, removing work that didn't add value to the customers' experiences. It now has a smaller number of specialists doing operational tasks like accounting reporting.

In the tension between caring for the store versus caring for customers, the former can get overweighted because most store managers are operations oriented. Talk with them, and you'll commonly hear sentiments like "I can't have my associates spending time with customers. They have jobs to do." But you can influence their orientation by the questions you ask during your store visits. If you quiz them about shrink reduction and unprocessed receipts, you'll elicit a focus on operations. But if you inquire about customer contacts and sales per associate, you'll see their focus switch to customers and helping them find what they want.

But sometimes placing highest priority on taking care of the store is appropriate. Zeynep Ton, one of our former doctoral students and currently a professor at Harvard Business School, worked with the Borders book chain to measure the relative importance of the time store associates spend on production functions to take care of the store, such as restocking and organizing the shelves, and the time they spend on customer service, talking to and helping customers.[16] She identifies metrics to measure the effectiveness of each type of activity at Borders. Customer service is measured by mystery shoppers who visit the store monthly and complete a fifty-question survey about their interactions with store associates. Two metrics are used to measure how well the store performs production activities. First, a store-conditions score is given quarterly based on an inspection of a wide range of store conditions by a senior manager. Second, the percentage of books a store is asked by corporate to return to vendors that it actually returns is important in its own right and also an indicator of how well the store executes.

Professor Ton finds that increasing the amount of store labor improves both conformance and service quality, but only the improvement in conformance quality is associated with an increase in profitability. She argues that this makes sense because of the self-service nature of the Borders format. A customer is used to looking for a book on their own, but is not very happy if they can't find that book because it's in the back room.

In collaboration with Professor Rob Huckman of Harvard Business School, Professor Ton also measured the impact of employee turnover on store performance.[17] They find that, on average, more turnover leads to a reduction in store profitability and customer service scores, but stores that rate highly on the two execution metrics described above see no reduction in profitability due to turnover, while stores that execute poorly see a big reduction. This makes sense—if there is a good operating routine and culture of discipline in a store, then it's easier for a new employee to get up to speed.

The Keys to Customers Finding What They Are Looking For

We saw earlier in this chapter that customers finding what they came to buy was a key sales driver. Here we'll discuss some ideas retailers can use to increase the chances customers will find what they are looking for.

Things Go Wrong in a Store

Products face a perilous journey from delivery to the back room of a store to their exit at the front door in the hands of a customer. In chapters 2 and 3, we discussed mathematical methods for creating optimal assortments and inventory levels. But mishaps in the store can undercut, even destroy, even a highly optimized plan. Your distribution center may deliver the wrong products. Your staffers may misrecord the deliveries or forget to shelve goods. And once products make it to the floor, customers move, damage, or even swipe them.

All of these problems show up as a discrepancy between what customers see when they visit and what the home office's computer says is on the shelves. Several studies that investigated store-level inventory records found that one retailer (see figure 6-6) had errors in 65 percent of its recorded store-SKU inventory levels, with an average error equal to 35 percent of inventory level.[18] Many of its SKUs were really stocked out, though the computer recorded inventory on the shelves. Likewise, a survey at the Borders book chain found that in 19 percent of the instances in which a customer requested a specific book from a sales associate and the Borders computer system said a book was in stock, it could not be found in the store. Of course this does not imply 19 percent lost sales since most customers did not enter the store seeking a specific book, but rather made a selection from the available assortment in the category in which they had an interest. We have heard similar statistics from retailers that have made store-level inventory data available over the Internet so customers can check availability before coming. They find that roughly 20 percent of the time, when the computer says an item is in stock, it cannot be found hours later when the customer arrives. Sure, someone could've bought these items in the interim. But most retailers believed that these instances were rare given the sales rates of the particular items.

FIGURE 6-6

This retailer found that 65 percent of its store-SKU inventory records were wrong

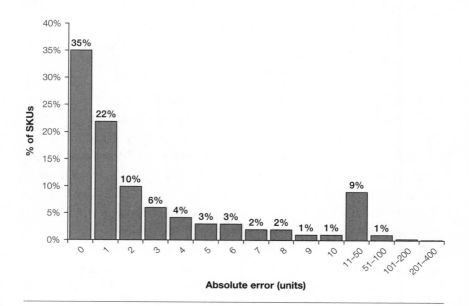

Absolute error (units)

Figure 6-7 shows the graph presented previously in chapter 3 to depict the results of testing the replenishment algorithm developed by 4R Systems and described in chapter 3. As discussed previously, figure 6-7 shows that use of this algorithm significantly reduced lost margin due to stockouts and cut inventory carrying cost. Over the full nine months, the information in the graphic moves in the right direction, with the retailer improving its performance. But keep in mind that we were seeing these results week by week. So imagine how we felt in mid-March. Costs had been heading steadily down since the new algorithm had been introduced, but suddenly in mid-February, they shot up. If that rate of increase continued, the retailer's costs would have soon risen beyond where they were when the test began. We found ourselves wondering whether we'd been lucky during the first ten weeks of the test.

Then we learned that during three weeks beginning in mid-February, the retailer had taken its annual physical inventory in this department,

FIGURE 6-7

In mid-March, cost was going up, not down

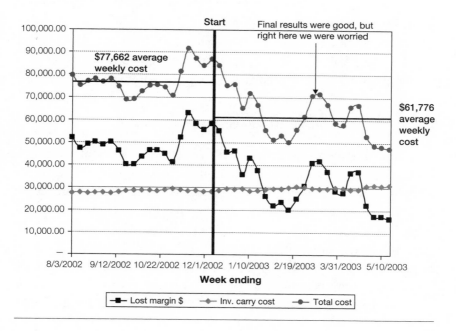

counting every SKU in every store. It found many instances where the computer showed positive on-hand inventory, but no product could be found on the shelf. In all of these cases, it reset the computer-recorded inventory to zero. All of these newly found stockouts contributed to the lost margin estimate, causing the line representing lost margin to climb from $20,000 to $42,000 during the audit. Lost margin didn't truly soar; rather, these stockouts that had existed for some time were just then discovered, which caused recorded lost margin to more than double.

Once the audit ended, the replenishment algorithm optimized against accurate data and drove cost to an even lower level than where it had been before the audit. We wondered whether our method had really produced a benefit, given the inaccuracy in the data. In the end, we concluded that the undetected stockouts had probably existed for some time before the audit. Thus the true average cost before and after use of the algorithm was higher by the $22,000 of recently detected lost margin, as shown in figure 6-8. And the weekly benefit of inventory optimization remained about $16,000 per week in this department. But once the better data was available, costs could be driven to an even lower level, and this "accurate data gain" shown in the figure is of a similar magnitude as the optimization gain obtained on imperfect data.

Experts often debate the relative importance of optimization versus data accuracy. We think that this debate is misguided. You'll make your business better—and your customers happier—if you strive for both.

What Causes Inventory Discrepancies?

A store's contents necessarily equal the deliveries that enter through the back door, minus what leaves through the front door. If a customer can't find an item that the computer says is in the store, there can be only three reasons: (1) errors in recording receipts; (2) errors in recording sales (or rather, in recording exiting products, which can also result from theft); or (3) the item is actually in the store, but not where it is visible to the customer (e.g., it is in the back room). Sometimes, you'll see a combination of causes. If a customer, for example, returns a medium for a small and the salesperson simply makes the exchange

FIGURE 6-8

Taking physical inventory identified hidden stockouts

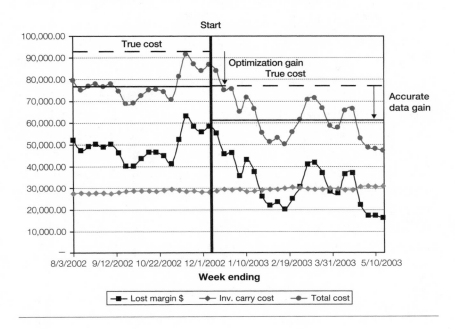

without recording a return and a sale, then you'll have both a receipt error and a sale error.

The Borders survey which found that in 19 percent of the instances in which a customer requested a specific book from a sales associate and the Borders computer system said a book was in stock but it could not be found in the store provides an example of the third problem— items that end up in places where customers can't find them. This firm found that a common cause of its problem was books lost in the back room.[19] Two copies of a book would arrive at a store, and an associate would shelve one and store the other in the back room. When the shelf copy sold, whoever had placed the extra in the back room would have forgotten about it (or had left the chain, since, like most retailers, this outfit had more than 100 percent annual employee turnover), so the shelf was not restocked. Because the book wasn't on the shelf, no more sales could occur, and the computerized replenishment algorithm, seeing no sales and one available copy, ordered no more. Thus sales of this title at this location would stagnate until an audit discovered the problem.

Kevin Freeland, chief operating officer for Advance Auto Parts, related a similar experience from when he was senior vice president of inventory management at Best Buy. Seeking to understand the causes of stockouts, he hired an audit firm, which found that for 30 percent of the stocked-out items, the computer showed positive inventory. His team then did root cause analysis on these stockouts. What did they find?

Most goods that Best Buy sells are in rectangular boxes that stack neatly in the back room. But a few items have odd shapes, such as surge protectors, which hang on pegs at the checkout aisle. These irregularly shaped items caused most of the undetected stockouts. If more surge protectors were shipped to a store than would fit on the display pegs, store staffers often tossed the extras into a box in the back room and often forgot them. Just as with the books, the computers, seeing no sales and inventory on hand, would ship no more units to the store.

Learning from the Best

Which companies stand out to you as having succeeded because of outstanding execution?[20]

We hope that Toyota and the Toyota Production System sits at the top of your list. The Toyota Production System has proved over the last half century to be a crushingly dominant system for efficiently producing affordable, high-quality cars and, thanks to its Prius hybrid, also an innovator. The Prius wasn't the first gas-electric hybrid to hit the market, but it's been the most successful, by far.

Using an auto company as a model for retail management might seem odd, but consider the similarity of the two operations. Store-level execution is about having the right product in the right place at the right time, and, for a big chain, the sheer number of stores and SKUs adds massive complexity. Now what about an auto plant? A typical one makes a car per minute, or nearly one thousand cars in a two-shift day. The assembly line will have about six hundred workstations at which a worker or a robot installs one or more parts, so the plant must have the right parts in the right place at the right time about a million times a day. That's a lot of things that have to go right within a complex environment.

Given that stores and auto plants face similar challenges, let's consider the elements of the Toyota Production System and how they might be adapted to a store.[21]

Make problems instantly self-evident and create pressure for their resolution. *Just-in-time (JIT)* production and delivery of parts is one way that Toyota accomplishes this. When people first hear of JIT, they usually think that it aims to cut the cost of carrying inventory. In fact, one of its big efficiency gains springs from removing inventory that causes confusion and hides what is really happening.

For example, consider the experience of an auto plant we worked with that implemented JIT delivery of steering columns. Soon after, it saw the defect rate on steering columns increase significantly, which led to the plant management berating the supplier in a meeting. One of the plant manager's direct reports then sheepishly explained that the defect rate had not actually increased. Rather, the two-week supply of steering columns the plant had carried prior to JIT had given workers in the plant time to fix defects in steering columns. So inventory had been hiding from the plant manager's eyes the true defect rate, as well as the man-hours spent by his employees, who thought they were being diligent in fixing the defects.

Provide tools for identifying and solving problems. Toyota's shop-floor employees use *statistical process control charts*, made famous by Edwards Deming, the father of the quality movement in management, to track metrics critical to quality.[22] They investigate when they see a metric deviate from expectations. Any process metric fluctuates randomly to some extent. Thus Toyota has a method for determining when a deviation is too large.

Engage people in problem solving. *Quality circles* in which workers meet to discuss and resolve problems are the best-known way of engaging staff in problem solving. Employees have tons of street smarts that can help a plant run better. Allowing them to apply that knowledge makes their jobs more satisfying than the traditional "check your brain at the door" approach ever could. You might wonder why we don't see more of this. A possible reason is that involving employees in this way makes life harder for managers. While employees have tons of good ideas, they have tens of tons of bad ones, too. Distinguishing between the two without dimming employee enthusiasm takes time and tact.

Applying the Toyota Production System to a Retail Store

As you read through our description of Toyota's approach, you probably already identified ways in which you could apply it to reducing stockouts at your stores. But fully integrating the Toyota Way into retailing will take hard thinking over time by the entire retail industry. Below are our thoughts on how to begin that process.

Make problems instantly self-evident and create pressure for their resolution. The underlying principle of JIT is that while inventory is needed to provide product availability, too much inventory sows confusion. We saw this in both the Best Buy and the Borders examples. When a store received more inventory than would fit on the floor, it was kept in the back room, where it frequently got lost.

Two of our former students, Nicole DeHoratius and Zeynep Ton, mentioned previously in this chapter, worked with one of us to study the impact of inventory levels on data accuracy and store execution.[23] The paper "Inventory Record Inaccuracy: An Empirical Analysis" studies the retailer referenced in figure 6-6 and finds that more inventory results in more errors in store-SKU inventory records. The paper "The Effect of Product Variety and Inventory Levels on Retail Sales: A Longitudinal Study" examines the impact of inventory levels on sales and on the incidence of "phantom products," products that are in the store but not in a place where customers can find them—for example, lost in the back room. The authors find that more inventory increases phantom products, which reduces sales, but this reduction in sales is greatly outweighed by the direct positive impact that more inventory and product variety have on sales. An implication of this finding is that given the current store processes, it's better for overall results to tolerate a little chaos in the store via more phantom products, although the obvious question the paper raises is whether some change in store operations could reduce the phantom products caused by more inventory and variety. JIT is just such an improved process.

JIT can help retailers improve store execution. At Best Buy, once Kevin Freeland discovered the cause of phantom stockouts, he implemented a rule of shipping no more irregularly shaped items to a store than would fit in its display place. Borders adopted similar principles, including a policy called "Door to floor in 24." New stock had to be placed on the shelves within twenty-four hours. Bob DiRomualdo, former CEO of the Borders Group, expressed this principle in a graph he drew (see figure 6-9) for students while visiting one of our classes.[24]

The ultimate in application of JIT to a store would be to ditch the back room altogether. We've asked several groups of retail executives to consider how this might work. The common response is that it would solve a lot of problems. But then they offer up some reasons why it can't be done. They point out that case-pack quantities don't fit on store shelves or that a typical day's supply of product doesn't fit on the shelf. But when we press them, it often becomes apparent that they could remove these obstacles through process changes such as changing the case-pack sizes and making more frequent deliveries. In the auto industry, implementing JIT required smaller production batches, which required reengineering to reduce the time required to set up for production of a given model.

FIGURE 6-9

Less is more: Too much inventory increases stockouts

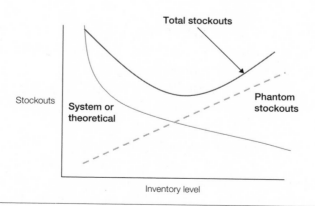

Can you do this at the store level? Absolutely. We know two companies that have managed to.

Brantano is a fast-growing shoe seller based in Belgium, and it's rapidly becoming Europe's leading shoe retailer. Jan Louagie, the chain's buying director, described its approach to supply chain management at a conference of the Consortium for Operational Excellence in Retailing held at the Harvard Business School. Brantano has tried to avoid the mistakes of other retailers. It stocks exactly one pair of each style-color-size shoe in each store. All of its stock sits on the selling floor; the stores have no back rooms. At the end of the day, an employee identifies which SKUs have sold, and reorders. This is easy to do because the shelves have space for only one pair of each SKU, making stockouts obvious. The redelivery arrives the next morning, before opening.

Several retailers at the conference challenged this system as unworkable because carrying just one of each SKU per store would lead to an unacceptable level of stockouts and thus lost sales. But Louagie argued that he could get product from his distribution center to a store faster than other retailers could get it from their back rooms. Besides, the sales rate per SKU for shoes is sufficiently low to make the lost sales negligible compared with the improved process control due to the transparency of Brantano's system.

Destination Maternity, the retailer of maternity apparel introduced in chapter 4, also stresses tight control of its inventory and frequent resupply. It makes deliveries to its stores two to seven times per week and retrieves any excess stock for return to its distribution center once a week.

Each day, before a Destination Maternity store manager can open her cash register, she verifies the count on a randomly chosen SKU number. Of course, getting the count right on just one SKU doesn't ensure inventory accuracy, but the exercise instills in the store manager an ethic of error avoidance.

Provide tools for identifying and solving problems. Figure 6-10 provides an example of how the idea of a statistical process control chart might be adapted to reducing stockouts. Frank Jansen, director of retail R&D at Albert Heijn, the Dutch food chain, provided the information for the

FIGURE 6-10

One store's sales of a bread SKU reveals stockouts

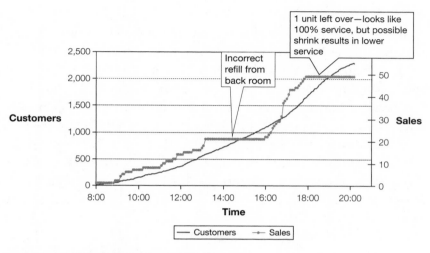

Source: Frank J. Jansen, managing director, R&D, Albert Heijn.

chart. (Albert Heijn's parent is Ahold, one of the world's largest food retailers.) The graphic shows cumulative customer traffic together with sales of a bread SKU in one store on one day. Flat regions on the sales curve correspond to times when none sold. The intervals from 13:00 to 16:00 and from 17:30 to 20:00 are long enough to suggest that stockouts prevented sales in these periods. Albert Heijn investigated and found that store-level stockouts had occurred, for the reasons shown in the figure.

This is exactly the idea of statistical process control (SPC)—investigate for problems when the value of a key metric, in this case the length of a period of zero sales, falls outside of reasonable limits. But what are reasonable limits? Notice that no sales also occurred from 10:15 to 11:00. Given that sales vary minute by minute, we might wonder whether those forty-five minutes of zero sales were due to a stockout or simply that no customers during this period wanted the product. In other words, how long does a period of zero sales need to be before we investigate for a problem? SPC provides a way to answer this question by specifying a method for setting control limits for a process parameter, such as a key dimension of a part being produced, such that under normal operation, the likelihood of observing a value outside of the control limits is at most one in a thousand. Thus if we see a value outside the control limits, we can be 99.9 percent sure something is amiss.

We can apply this concept to the data in figure 6-10 by using something called the *Poisson distribution*, which is a formula, discovered in 1838 by Siméon-Denis Poisson, for calculating the probability of a specified number of events (such as arrival of customers wanting to buy bread) in a fixed interval, provided that these events happen at a fixed known rate. Looking at the data in figure 6-10, we can see that twenty sales occurred from 8:00 to 13:00 and another twenty-nine from 16:00 to about 18:00, so that's forty-nine sales in seven hours, or seven per hour on average. At this rate, the Poisson distribution would assign a probability of 0.0009 to zero sales in a one-hour period, almost exactly one out of one thousand. So following SPC, we would not check for problems in the forty-five-minute period from 10:15 to 11:00 (or any of the shorter periods of zero sales), but Albert Heijn's investigation and discovery of problems in the two longer periods was consistent with SPC principles.

A simpler variation of sales-based control is what some retailers call a *zero balance walk*—that is, having employees walk the store periodically to check for stockouts. The reasoning is that while a physical audit of inventory is challenging, it's easy to count zero. If an employee finds a stockout, he investigates, including verifying computer inventory record accuracy, and remedies it.[25]

Engage your people in problem solving. Zara, the Spanish clothing retailer, also introduced in chapter 4, exemplifies the effective engagement of store personnel to enhance performance. You'll recall that, at Zara, when a customer fails to buy an item that she has been considering, a store associate will ask what she didn't like about it. Is it the color or the silhouette, or was the size wrong? Store managers collect this frontline intelligence at the end of the day and feed it to country managers and, through them, to category managers at the headquarters. There, it augments the market picture created by traditional POS data. POS data captures only what customers bought, not why they didn't buy. This is the void Zara aims to fill.

Conclusion

The dominant retailers of the future will be those that can harness the talent of their store associates to improve the speed and accuracy of execution and thus delight their customers by always having the right product in the right place at the right time. One way of doing that is borrowing Toyota's techniques. If that happens, it would be fitting payback: one of the original inspirations for the Toyota Production System was a supermarket. As described in a company history, "[Taiichi] Ohno went to the United States to visit automobile plants, but his most important U.S. discovery was the supermarket . . . Ohno admired the way the supermarkets supplied merchandise in a simple, efficient, and timely manner. In later years, Ohno often described his production system in terms of the American supermarket."[26] We hope that retailing will so perfect the art of store execution as to once again become a beacon that other companies in other industries look to, as Toyota did in the 1950s, for wisdom on execution and human resource management.[27]

CHAPTER SEVEN

Technological Risk

How Retailers Should Assess and Manage Emerging Technologies

Evaluating emerging technologies accurately is hard for everyone, even seasoned technologists. Thomas J. Watson Sr., for example, is rumored to have estimated a "world market for five computers." Retailers, not being technologists, have even more difficulty, and they routinely make mistakes. That's hardly surprising. After all, most people in retailing entered the business through operations or merchandising, not the IT department. Before they were executives, they were distribution managers and buyers, not programmers.

In this chapter, we identify some typical errors in assessing and investing in new technologies and provide advice for overcoming them. Our purpose isn't to review every emerging technology in retailing. Changes come too fast for that; doing so would render this chapter obsolete the day it appeared. Rather, we want to give you a framework for analysis, a way of thinking about which technologies make sense for your company and when you should adopt them.

To make the discussion more concrete, we'll examine radio frequency identification (RFID), arguably the most innovative technology in retailing today. With RFID, a user applies a tag to a product (or to an animal or even a person) so that the product can be identified by reading the tag remotely using radio waves. RFID holds great promise—it could change retailing as radically as the cash register did. But for now, it also entails great risks: the technology and standards associated with it are still evolving, and countries haven't even agreed on which frequencies to assign to its radio transmissions.

RFID: An Emerging Technology

You've probably already used RFID without even realizing it.[1] A familiar application, with over 6 million users in the United States, is the Exxon Mobil Speedpass. Each Speedpass, contained in key fobs given to Exxon Mobil customers, contains an RFID tag that's unique to a customer. Thus that customer doesn't need to scan her credit card or pay cash when she fills her gas tank. Instead, an electronic reader located nearby identifies the customer and charges her account. Another common RFID application, introduced in the 1980s, is the system for automated toll payments in use on many major highways in the United States. If you have an E-ZPass or a FAST LANE tag, you've used RFID. You've also used an RFID application if you've run the Boston Marathon. RFID tags attached to runners' shoes track their progress along the race course.

Systems like these have three main components: RFID tags, unique serial numbers on each tag, and a software and hardware infrastructure capable of processing data collected from the tags.

The RFID tag itself consists of three simple parts: the chip that holds information about the object to which the tag is attached, the antenna that transmits to a reader using radio waves, and a case for the chip and antenna that can be attached to a physical object.

Tags come in *passive* and *active* varieties; some application authors have also used a classification called *semipassive* for a category that combines the features of both. Passive tags do not have their own batteries.

Instead, electromagnetic waves emitted by the reader activate them. Consequently, they can only be read over shorter distances, usually three to seven meters. Active tags have their own batteries and can have a range of up to thirty meters. Passive tags also have limited memory capacity—about 2 kilobits (kb) of read-only memory, compared with the 32 kb or more of read/write memory in active tags. Despite these limitations, most applications have used passive tags because they're cheaper. They currently cost anywhere from 10¢ to $1 each, while active tags start at $5 and can range as high as $100. Active tags suffer from two other weaknesses. Their tag batteries can wear out or malfunction, resulting in signal loss and catastrophic failure in some applications. And because their signals travel farther, they are more likely to encounter interference. Semipassive tags have small batteries that are partially recharged every time the tag enters the electromagnetic field of the reader. They can operate with simpler batteries than active tags even though, like active tags, they have 32 kb of read/write memory.

The second component of an RFID system is the serial number within the tag. The easiest way to understand the importance of the serial number is to look at bar codes, which are precursors to the *electronic product code* (EPC) in RFID tags. The twelve-digit bar code, or Universal Product Code (UPC), is ubiquitous in consumer goods. The first eleven digits of a typical twelve-digit UPC bar code identify the company and the product. The company prefix can vary between six and ten digits. The rest of the eleven digits (i.e., those not identifying the company) identify products at the company. The twelfth digit verifies the accuracy of the read. Figure 7-1 represents a typical UPC.

FIGURE 7-1

A twelve-digit UPC bar code

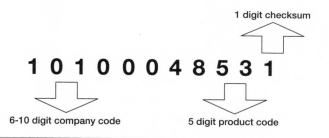

1 digit checksum

1 0 1 0 0 0 4 8 5 3 1

6-10 digit company code   5 digit product code

The EPC, in contrast, is large enough to identify not just the specific product but the individual unit; it can distinguish between two different units of the SKU.

The EPC scheme has four parts. The first, the *version number*, contains information on the length and structure of the code being used. The second and third parts, as in the UPC, identify the manufacturer and the product. The last one identifies the individual unit; the EPC has sufficient digits to identify roughly 60 billion individual units.

RFID tags can store and communicate more data than EPC tags can. Active tags can even transmit environmental information, such as the temperature in the area around the tag. Table 7-1 summarizes the differences between RFID/EPC and UPC tags.

Considerable infrastructure needs to exist for RFID technology to operate. Tags are useless without a network of readers, and you need a

TABLE 7-1

Differences between RFID/EPC and UPC tags

RFID/EPC	UPC (bar codes)
• Not an established technology; standards still evolving.	• Stable, open standard that has existed for 30-plus years.
• Can read several items at the same time. Does not require direct "line of sight" between reader and tag.	• Reads one item at a time. Direct line of sight between reader and code required.
• Can identify discrete items.	• Conventional bar codes can only identify SKUs.[a]
• Subject to interference and other problems. Read rates can be low especially near metal and water.	• High accuracy when read.
• Hard to counterfeit.	• No barrier to counterfeiting.
• Could capture data in new locations (e.g., on the door from a retailer's back room to the selling floor) even without human actions to scan the item.	• Subject to human errors.
• Tag price is key cost driver.	• Inexpensive labels.

Source: Adapted from Eric M. Johnson, untitled slide presentation, 2005.

a. However, the new 2-D bar coding can also identify discrete items.

lot of readers because they have limited fields in which they can detect tags. Readers remain expensive, though manufacturers are trying to reduce the cost to less than $200 per unit. Given the high cost, companies try to reduce the number of readers needed by using additional antennas to expand the range of a reader.

Widespread deployment of RFID tags will require frequency standards, which are still developing. The frequency available for passive tags in the United States is the band between 902 and 928 MHz; most passive tags operate at around 915 MHz. That frequency band is not available worldwide. In Europe, the bandwidth is between 865.7 and 867.6 MHz. Many emerging markets, which play a crucial role in the supply chains for many products, have yet to allocate frequencies. The lack of a universally available frequency poses a barrier to the widespread adoption of RFID. Companies have come together to create such a standard, and it's called Electronic Product Code Information Services, or EPCIS. EPCIS is at its early stages, and adoption so far has been slow.

RFID Applications Outside of Retailing

RFID has its roots in World War II, when the military started to use radar to provide warnings of approaching planes. Radar could not distinguish between friend or foe—on a radar screen all planes looked the same. The British Royal Air Force figured out a way to use RFID technology to address this problem by developing an "identify friend or foe" transponder.

Some of the most compelling emerging applications of RFID are situations in which failing to track an object can be equally catastrophic. Consider the pharmaceutical industry, where counterfeit drugs represent a problem with lethal implications. With RFID, you can track each unit of a drug from the factory floor to the pharmacy shelf. The authenticity of a bottle of aspirin can be determined by tracing its origins. This track-and-trace ability also helps in law enforcement. If a thief is caught with a drug, the contraband's path through the supply chain can be determined, offering clues to where it was stolen from.

Potential Applications in Retailing

In retailing, too, the potential of RFID—at the pallet, case, or even item level—is huge. When fully deployed at the item level, RFID will enable retailers to track individual units even if their tags are not directly in the line of sight of a reader. Consider how checkout might change with individually tagged goods. A retailer could install readers close to a store's exit, eliminating the need for checkout counters. Shoppers would simply walk their shopping carts, containing their RFID-tagged purchases, past a reader. It would scan all the items in the carts, and the store's computer would tally each shopper's bill and print out or e-mail a receipt.

Item-level tagging would also facilitate product recalls, a critical help in sectors like food, medicine, and even toys, where hazardous products can harm and even kill. Witness the 2008 outbreak of salmonella linked to Mexican jalapeño peppers, and the 2007 recall of lead-painted Thomas & Friends wooden train sets. If a batch of goods had a defect, then the manufacturer could identify all items in that batch for recall quite easily using RFID applications. Visualize, for example, what could happen if a manufacturer discovered that the items produced at a particular factory on a specific date in the past were contaminated. Without RFID or some other form of item-level tagging, the manufacturer would be unable to distinguish items from the contaminated batch, and would have to recall all previously produced items. Clearly, restricting the recall to only contaminated batches would reduce the cost and time associated with the recall. Suitable RFID applications can also enable manufacturers to locate these contaminated items; manufacturers, for example, could figure out that the batch was at store X or warehouse Y, and hence withdraw these items before they could harm people.

RFID also can help retailers streamline their handling of inventory. As noted in chapter 6, misplaced goods within stores vex many retailers and may account for as much as a quarter of stockouts at the store level.[2] Book and music superstore Borders found that consumers couldn't find one in six books that were listed as in its stock.[3] With RFID tags on each book, a clerk could point a shopper seeking any of the close to 200,000 titles available at a typical superstore, not simply to the section where the book should sit, but to its exact location, even if someone had accidentally shelved it in the wrong section.

METRO Group, of Germany, has been experimenting with ways in which technologies like RFID can improve shoppers' in-store experiences.[4] In September 2002, METRO created a technology-enhanced grocery in Rheinberg, Germany. There, shoppers could use small computers known as *personal shopping assistants*, which they would borrow at the store's entrance. Akin to PDAs, these handheld devices helped them find products and provided in-depth information on goods, including such details as nutritional values and features. Information terminals scattered around the store also offered recipes, wine recommendations, and suggestions on healthy eating. Customers loved the innovations. A third of them reported using the technology, and most users called themselves highly satisfied. Just as important, the number of customers and sales at the location increased significantly. The store also provided METRO with considerable publicity. Fashion model Claudia Schiffer, a Rheinberg native, was invited to be the first customer, and METRO's experiment garnered favorable mentions in the media.

Once standards emerge, RFID should facilitate information flow among various firms in a supply chain. Companies in a chain will be able to share information as it emerges. A supplier, for example, might use RFID to monitor when its shipments reach Wal-Mart or even to track their movement within the retailer's stores. Thus Procter & Gamble might know whether a pallet of Tide had been forgotten in a back room or a storage area.

Similarly, RFID could enable vendors to improve promotions by ensuring that store staffers place display quantities and materials in a store promptly. According to some studies, half of all promotional displays at consumer goods retailers are either not put up or put up late.[5]

Pilot Studies Applying RFID in Retailing

Besides METRO, several retailers have tried to quantify the benefits of RFID. These experiments have focused on short-term benefits, not on overhauling supply chains. Mostly, they've examined the use of RFID tags on cases and pallets, though Swiss retailer Charles Vogele has tried item-level tagging.

Wal-Mart did an experiment at twenty-four stores to examine the impact of RFID on stockouts.[6] At twelve of these stores, it tagged 4,554 unique products at the case level. It equipped the test stores with RFID readers at various back-room locations, such as receiving doors, sales floor doors, and box crushers. Thanks to RFID, the test stores could track whether cases had been delivered to the store and taken to the sales floor. By combining this information with point-of-sale data, a store could generate an automatic pick list of items in the back room that needed to be taken to the sales floor. The experiment sought to identify the extent to which these automatic pick lists could reduce stockouts.

In a control group of comparable stores without RFID, pick lists had to be generated manually. An employee often had to inspect the shelves for stockouts or near stockouts and log them in to a handheld device. Alternatively, the staffer could inspect merchandise in the back room and scan items that seemed appropriate for moving to the sales floor. These methods, besides being laborious, invited errors.

In the test stores, stockouts decreased from 474 to 352 among the items studied. In other words, they went from 10.4 percent to 7.7 percent, a reduction of 2.7 percentage points, or 26 percent of the original 10.4 percent. Stockouts fell by 5 percent in the control stores. Thus, after controlling for improvements not due to RFID, you'd conclude that the technology accounted for a 21 percent reduction in stockouts. Other studies of RFID in retailing have also concluded that the technology can reduce stockouts substantially, though the estimated reductions have varied considerably among the studies.

What might be the change in sales due to stockouts declining by 2.7 percentage points? It could be smaller than 2.7 percentage points, or it could be larger. It would be smaller if consumers were willing to substitute other items when their favorite products sold out. Likewise, it could be smaller if stockouts were measured late in the day, after many customers already had shopped. (In its study, Wal-Mart scanned stockouts between 2 and 10 p.m.) Stockouts might have been lower earlier in the day, when most people were doing their shopping.

In contrast, the sales increase could be higher than 2.7 percentage points if the stockouts hit popular items with higher-than-average sales rates or if the retailer lost sales on "complimentary items" when consumers encountered stockouts. Housewares sellers, for example, often lose sales of matching pillow covers when they sell out of a particular set of sheets. Most retailers that we have consulted assume that the resulting sales increase will be a fraction, usually 25 percent to 50 percent, of the reduction in stockouts.[7] That would lead us to conclude that sales could rise by 0.675 percent to 1.35 percent (or roughly 1 percent) because of RFID adoption.

A 1 percent increase in sales at Wal-Mart would increase the company's gross margins by roughly $791 million.[8] Of course, this increase needs to be compared with the added cost associated with tags, readers, software, and training, which would also be substantial for a company as large as Wal-Mart.

In the case cited above, METRO's analysis accounted for cost savings as well as for the reduction in stockouts. It examined labor savings and found that some manual steps could be eliminated because RFID enabled the automated scanning of shipments and receipts. It also found that other processes could be streamlined.

METRO drilled down to the impact of pallet-level and case-level tagging, and quantified separately the benefits to the manufacturer and to METRO. With pallet-level tagging, all the benefits identified by METRO stemmed from labor savings. METRO estimated that its annual savings would be 15.7 €-cents (euro cents) per pallet and that the manufacturer's would be 50 €-cents per pallet, for a total supply chain savings of 65.7 €-cents per pallet. The average METRO store received thirty pallets per week, and the company had roughly 2,300 stores at the time of the analysis, so the total savings for the supply chain amounted to slightly more than €2 million per year, or 0.004 percent of METRO's sales. METRO's own savings amounted to roughly 0.001 percent of its sales.

With case-level tagging, the benefits were larger. The manufacturer saw a roughly 7 €-cents in savings per case, while METRO got roughly 8.9 €-cents per case. When all of this is taken together—and considering that each pallet has roughly seventy cases, on average—the annual savings to the supply chain totaled roughly €40 million, or 0.07 percent of sales.

Do the quantified benefits identified at Wal-Mart and METRO make a compelling case for investing in RFID? According to the metrics above, it's not even close.

Consider that METRO's projected savings from tagging cases (15.9 €-cents each) roughly matched the cost of a passive RFID tag at the time of the experiment. And this analysis does not include the expenses associated with the installation of readers and the creation of software for capturing and analyzing the data from the tags. On top of that, the costs of training and process redesign would probably exceed the cost of hardware and software combined.

Does the lack of a compelling financial return from RFID mean that retailers should shun the technology? Not necessarily. RFID's costs should fall over time, and innovative applications, giving greater benefits, should emerge. So why not wait until then to invest? As you'll see in the next section, a small early investment can enable you to learn about a technology and better understand the benefits that it might provide for your unique operations. You might view a small bet today as buying an option that will position your company to make a larger, smarter investment in the future, when the financial case becomes compelling.

Managing Emerging Technologies: Lessons from RFID and Other Technologies

How should managers evaluate and invest in new technologies such as RFID? What lessons can they derive from past examples of innovative technologies? Three major guidelines emerge from our observations of RFID and technologies such as flexible manufacturing systems (FMS) and the Internet.

1. In evaluating new technologies, understanding the key details helps a lot.

2. To derive the full benefits from a technology, you must integrate the technology with your firm's operations, which usually requires changing operations to take advantage of the technology.

3. In evaluating the economics of a new technology, managers should factor in the declining cost of the technology and the uncertainty in benefits associated with it.

Understanding the Key Details

Managers are often insufficiently aware of how emerging technologies like RFID work. Many people who talk up RFID's potential haven't even taken time to understand the different types of tags—that is, passive versus active ones—or the evolution of global standards for frequencies. Retailers often use the term *RFID* loosely, assuming that the capabilities of active tags will be available at the prices projected for passive ones.

Adopting a new technology without understanding its details usually ends in disaster. Consider managers' love-hate relationship with *optimization*. This technology, which improves decision making with computers and mathematical algorithms, can be extremely powerful. Deployed appropriately, it can dramatically improve operational performance, and thus it is widely used today in a number of applications, such as factory scheduling, airline yield management, and transportation planning. But managers often fail to understand that optimization does not apply universally. It must be customized in each operating context. Even subtle differences in assumptions and parameters can affect whether an algorithm can address a particular problem.

During the past few decades, operating managers have periodically become enamored of optimization. Their naive enthusiasm has often led to poorly conceived attempts to buy their way into optimization without paying attention to the fit between the technology and their desired application. Not only do these attempts fail to improve decision making, they often result in operational fiascos. A European retailer recently installed a commercial software package for optimized replenishment of inventory to its stores. The software failed to take into account the fluctuating workload at stores and consequently often shipped items to stores when they did not have store labor available to receive the merchandise. Frustration resulted, and store managers pretty soon were overriding most of the system's recommendations. In many such incorrect applications, managers get disillusioned with optimization even though the problem wasn't caused by the technology itself but rather by an ill-considered and mishandled application. An appropriately designed program (that took into account workload at the store) would have likely improved the retailer's operations substantially.

Many managers have difficulty understanding the subtleties of tailoring technology to the complexities of a particular enterprise. Technology specialists often understand technical details but not the nuances of a firm's business. Operating managers, in contrast, see their business and operational needs but misunderstand the requirements and capabilities of the technology. One chief information officer told us that his chief challenge was finding people within his company who understood both. He's right. Indentifying these folks and assigning them to the evaluation and management of new technologies might be the most important task for a company that's evaluating a new technology.

Integrating the Technology with Operations

The importance of changing operations to best exploit technology is shown by the adoption in the United States of new kinds of manufacturing technologies in the 1980s.[9] This was a period when U.S. companies faced strong new competition from foreign firms, especially those in Japan. As a result, many U.S. manufacturers were rushing to increase their efficiency by embracing such new technologies as computer-aided design and engineering, flexible manufacturing systems, and robotics. As is often the case with new approaches, proponents promised "to improve everything: cost, quality, flexibility, delivery, speed, design—everything."[10] But many managers had difficulty reaping these advantages because they had not tailored their processes to the new technologies.

When talk turns to new technology, people typically imagine computers and software. But a more tangible technology, like a helicopter, better illustrates the promise and perils that new approaches can bring.

If you buy a helicopter and merely use it instead of your car in your daily commute to work, then maybe you can turn a thirty-minute commute into a twenty-minute commute. And you might not see any time savings, given that a helicopter is a tad harder to park than a car. But a helicopter can facilitate major changes in your lifestyle. You can live in some remote place, visit faraway clients more easily, and get a new perspective on the lay of the land. If you don't do these things—or don't find some other beneficial uses for your machine—you've wasted the small fortune you've paid for the copter and your pilot. "In short, you shouldn't buy a helicopter unless you're committed to getting the most out of it. You have to organize for it."[11]

Or let's go back even farther in history, to the early twentieth century, when trucks began to replace horse-drawn buggies. An advertisement for the International Commercial Truck, circa 1910, on display at Maine's Owls Head Transportation Museum provides this warning:

> That the motor truck is an excellent substitute for the horse has been proven in every instance where business men have given it a fair trial. But the man who uses his motor truck simply as a substitute for horses neglects to make the most of his opportunities. The horse is not a machine—five to six hours actual work—fifteen to twenty miles—is its maximum day's work. A motor truck can be used twenty-four hours a day if necessary, and it will travel the last hour and the hundredth mile just as fast as the first.
>
> Business men who are using the motor truck in place of horse and wagon equipment with the greatest success are men who have given this problem careful study. In most instances, it was necessary to change the plan of routing—delays which were necessary to give the horses rest were eliminated—plans were laid to keep the truck busy the entire day with as few delays as possible.[12]

New technologies, whether trucks a hundred years ago or RFID tags today, require leaders with an "integrative imagination." These managers can identify the most effective ways to employ a technology within their firms and can modify their operations to take maximum advantage of the technology.

When considering the adoption of a new technology, you must also understand that it often takes years before that technology gets fully integrated with operations. Often, the technology goes through three phases: substitution, scale, and structure. Initially, it substitutes for an existing way of operating. Eventually, it reaches scale. And finally, as the technology matures, the firm makes structural changes to accommodate it.[13]

The evolution of business-to-business (B2B) e-commerce demonstrates this evolution. In its early days, B2B replaced old ways of making orders and processing payments, like the phone and the fax machine. At this stage, the Internet offered limited advantages, mainly lower transaction costs.

During the scale-up stage, the Internet enabled firms to reach out to many more buyers and sellers and to cut out brokers with whom they'd previously had to share their revenue. Thus, for example, traditional travel agents began to disappear, as they lost their usefulness due to airline Web sites and online travel bookers such as Travelocity and Expedia. Today, most of us search for flights online and buy our airline tickets there. Airlines accordingly have reduced travel agents' commissions over time.

The biggest changes occur in the structural stage. This is where entirely new business processes emerge to suit the technology. In the airline industry, for example, companies can offer unsold seats to consumers at a discount just days, even hours, before a flight is scheduled to depart. Similarly, Amazon provides customer reviews of products that would have been too expensive to pull off without the Internet.

Factoring In Cost and Benefits

The price of RFID tags and readers has dropped over time and should continue to fall over the next few years. This, in the minds of many analysts, is the simplest way to justify investing in RFID. In other words, the benefits of adoption eventually will exceed the costs as the technology becomes cheaper. It is tough to argue with the logic. Analysts, after all, are projecting a five-cent price for passive tags.

Despite the likelihood that costs will drop, considerable uncertainty remains about how precisely RFID will evolve—about such topics as how companies will integrate the technology into their operations and which applications will work best. Managers must accept this uncertainty.

At times, operating managers, especially those unaccustomed to making decisions facing considerable uncertainty, attempt to eliminate the uncertainty through better forecasting, or simply ignore it. They'd be better served if instead they would "prepare for, and adapt to, what the organization does not know, so as to benefit from the desired possibilities that can arise."[14]

Metrics used in the capital-budgeting process to evaluate new technological investments can compound the management bias against longer-range and higher-risk research programs.[15] Managers thus need to consider carefully the appropriate metric to evaluate different types of projects.

R&D programs in large companies differ substantially in associated uncertainty and the attendant level of investment. At one extreme, "knowledge building" moves involve considerable uncertainty but require little cash. The appropriate approach—and one followed by many managers—is to view these as a cost of doing business. At the other end of the spectrum, are "business investments," where the uncertainty is low but the dollars large. Return on investment (ROI) or some other capital-budgeting approach makes sense in evaluating such projects.

In between these extremes lies the category of R&D projects that require a hefty financial bet but also carry a lot of uncertainty. This category encompasses applied research, exploratory development, and, at times, feasibility demonstration. With these projects, neither the ROI nor the "cost of doing business" approach works.

Managers considering these sorts of projects must understand that what they're doing, in effect, is working toward the creation of an option. As with a call option in finance, you commit relatively modest resources today to provide an opportunity to make a profitable investment at a later date.

In practice, this means that you'll be staging your investment. You'll follow your current investment (call it X) with a bigger investment (Y) at a later time, but by then, the uncertainty surrounding the new technology will have diminished. If you decide not to make the second investment (Y), you'll lose only your first investment (X), which is analogous to the exercise price on a call option. Managers often mistakenly assume that once they begin the process, they must invest Y and lose all of the money in both investment rounds if the technology does not pan out.

We can illustrate the difference between treating RFID as an investment or as a call option by revisiting the METRO market example, described earlier in the chapter. Imagine that METRO is assessing whether it should invest in RFID at the case level. As of the moment that METRO is making its decision, the benefits from implementing RFID at the case level barely exceed the cost of the tags. To achieve a positive ROI, METRO would have to identify new benefits, or the cost of tags, readers, and related technology would have to drop substantially.

Without the call-option approach, a manager at METRO might not recommend case-level RFID. After all, the projected benefits are low, the risk is high, and several years might pass before METRO realized benefits.

But a manager taking a strategic-option approach might view this differently. She might ask herself what relatively small investments METRO could make today to help it learn more about the technology so it can make informed decisions in the future. Just as important, she'd consider ways in which the company might structure its activities so that it could identify new opportunities for applying RFID as they emerged. Using the call-option approach, the manager would recognize the value of creating several projects to explore various aspects of the technology, as opposed to placing a single big bet on just one application.

A temptation for any manager when faced with significant cost and uncertainty is to simply wait. You know this line of thinking. It says that waiting will allow time for the technology to improve and for its costs to fall. Then you can adopt it later without any of the difficulties associated with experimentation. To put this in terms of the call option, the manager might wonder whether she really needs to buy an option today to be able to make an investment tomorrow. Can't she count on some other retailer to make the required investment?

But waiting carries risks of its own. As we have pointed out before, tailoring new technologies to *your* operations requires customization of hardware and software and some changes to your processes. These sorts of changes take time. By making early experimental investments, you gain a head start over competitors. What's more, retailers that make early investments often have a chance to influence the development of a technology and the evolution of its standards. With RFID, for example, early adopters like Wal-Mart and METRO may be able to influence the allocations of frequencies. Finally, consumers and even investors at times identify an early experimenter as a technological leader. This phenomenon is best illustrated in the battle among the big book retailers—Borders, Barnes & Noble, and Amazon.[16] Borders was historically a pioneer among retailers in the application of technology. As early as the 1990s, Borders' CEO Robert DiRomualdo, in Borders' annual report, had discussed distributing computer floppy disks that customers could use to order books from home. However, during the Internet boom in the late 1990s, Borders was slow to capitalize on Web-based commerce and allowed Amazon and Barnes & Noble to set up and publicize Web sites before it did. The company argued that it was unclear how the technology would evolve and how it could sell books profitably on the Internet. Consumers and even investors perceived Borders as a laggard and penalized its stock. (Borders' stock price fell from over $30 on January 1, 1998, to roughly $16 two years later. By comparison, the Dow Jones Index rose roughly 50 percent during the period, the NASDAQ index rose by roughly 150 percent, and Amazon saw its stock price go from roughly $5 to over $70.) Once Borders did launch its Web site, it had difficulty attracting consumers relative to its speedier rivals. Equally important, investors—who had rallied behind Amazon and Barnes & Noble—were not enthusiastic about Borders' foray into Internet retailing, even when the company belatedly launched the Internet site.

Conclusion

Rocket science retailing relies crucially on information technology.[17] IT will continue its pace of rapid evolution in the next few decades, and cutting-edge retailers will have to stay abreast of these changes and find ways to evaluate emerging technologies like RFID and apply them to their operations.

RFID, in particular, will alter the nature of retailing as surely as the cash register and desktop computers did. As of this writing, it's expensive, and its applications are limited. The current benefits don't seem to justify the costs, when viewed on a strict ROI basis.

Regardless, retailers should continue to invest in it. It will get cheaper, and its benefits will grow. Thus managers evaluating investments in RFID should frame the expense in terms of a call option on the technology. Think of your RFID investments as tickets purchased today to play a game that will happen tomorrow. When the game begins, you may not be able to play effectively unless you've already bought a ticket.

RFID is the rare sort of technology to which the overused term *revolutionary* applies. Typically, in its early stages, this kind of technology suffers from poorly defined standards, unreliable performance, uncertain benefits, and high costs. Managers are understandably reluctant to invest. But they should heed the lesson of Borders' late entry into e-commerce. Sometimes, a series of staged early investments offer critical opportunities to learn and to tweak a technology for your needs. The failure to seize that opportunity can handicap you over the longer term.

CHAPTER EIGHT

Companywide Implementation

Managerial Issues Affecting Implementation

Recently, we were asked to conduct an executive program at a leading multinational manufacturer of branded goods with operations in dozens of countries. The company was concerned about the availability of its products, and, consequently, the program would focus partly on analytical approaches that the company could use to improve its supply chain. In preparing for the course, we asked one of the executives whether the approaches we were proposing were new to this manufacturer. "Everything you plan to cover has been tried at some time somewhere in our company, but we fail to follow these approaches consistently and across our entire organization," he responded. "That is our problem!"

When it comes to rocket science retailing, the *missionary*—a term we use to refer to a manager but that can also apply to an external consultant—can be more important than the rocket scientist.[1] In this chapter, we address the missionary's perspective and show, with case studies from inside and outside retailing, how some missionaries have taken their companies to the Promised Land.

Rocket science retailing entails having the capabilities to generate good data, analyze it to extract insights, incorporate these insights into decisions, and align incentives so the organization can move ahead. Progress in implementing rocket science retailing can be made on each of these dimensions.

The Challenges in Implementing and Sustaining Rocket Science Retailing

Elements of rocket science retailing have been adopted by almost every company that we have studied. Today, most retailers collect point-of-sale data electronically and use that information to forecast demand and plan their inventory and operations. Information technology has changed the industry substantially and will continue to do so. High-tech retailing is here to stay.

Even so, we believe that these techniques have had less impact than they could have had. Plenty of retailers are not very adept at using the vast amounts of data that they collect. For one, retail data—especially inventory data—is often not of very high quality. As discussed in chapter 6, inventory data is often inaccurate (that is, the store's physical inventory of a particular product is less or more than the quantity the computer system indicates is available). Such inventory record inaccuracy can often compromise demand forecasts as well. Consider a product that is stocked out at a store but the "system" inventory (i.e., what the computer says is available at the store) is positive. This product will show zero sales, of course, because the product is stocked out. A naive computer algorithm (that failed to account for inventory inaccuracy) would wrongly conclude that demand for the product was zero because the product did not sell when it was in stock.

Moreover, most retailers lack the ability to respond quickly to signals that they can glean from analyzing even sound data. On top of that, they fail to adopt analytical techniques that have been shown to work in their own pilot programs.

This raises a question: why are some retailers so elephantine when it comes to adopting cutting-edge practices? Are they overly cautious? Ignorant? Aware but incapable? In our research, we have studied many such slow movers. Managers have shared the following explanations for the sluggishness.

It's Hard to Change People's Behavior

Rocket science retailing requires people to change their thinking and behavior, and doing that is always challenging and time consuming. Managers often underestimate the changes needed when adopting a new technology. Consider, for example, the experience of a consumer electronics retailer that had invested millions of dollars in purchasing and installing a software package for forecasting and inventory planning. About a year after the installation, company experts were overriding more than 80 percent of the software's recommendations. (Incidentally, the software was intended to support the decisions of those same experts.) The company had done a good job of installing the software, but it had failed to convince its staffers that they should trust the results more often or to investigate why the software was generating forecasts and stocking quantities that needed to be changed so often. Thus the company's attempts to make its forecasting and planning processes more analytical failed. This retailer, like many others, focused its effort on the technical aspects of improving forecasting and inventory planning while underinvesting in the managerial aspects pertaining to changing people's behavior and mind-set. An alternate approach—that would have probably been more beneficial—would be to gradually build confidence among the staffers through pilots and a phase where the staffers' overrides of the system's recommendations, and the ensuing impact on forecast errors and inventory levels, were tracked. Over time, such steps would have led to a better algorithm and greater confidence among the human experts, who would now have been free to direct their effort to more challenging tasks.

A History of Exaggerated Benefit Promises Has Created Skepticism

Many managers and employees are jaded when it comes to new analytical approaches, having heard pitches in the past from software vendors and consultants that promised more than they delivered. At many companies, skepticism trumps even a well-documented pilot or proven results at another retailer.

New Skills Are Needed

Retailers may not have the right people to sustain the rocket science effort. Traditionally, retailers have emphasized product and industry knowledge over analytical skill when hiring. Thus their employees tend to rely on their instincts and judgment over data and analysis in making decisions. At times, organizational culture even explicitly discourages analysis. In an extreme case, a former executive at a large fashion retailer told us how a CEO, upon seeing her crunching numbers to forecast demand, grabbed the sheaf of papers on her desk and flung it across the room. As she tells the tale, the CEO was concerned that his organization would become overly dependent on the analysis and lose its feel for its market. Not surprisingly, analytical techniques still are shunned at this retailer.

Broad Organizational Changes May Be Required

Some executives complain that using rocket science techniques will require substantial changes in other parts of their companies. They say that they do not have good operational execution in their stores or distribution centers. "How do we apply analytical techniques when our data quality is so poor?" some of them have asked us. At retailers with long response times for replenishing products, we've heard arguments that the inability to respond to early sales data removes the primary benefit of being able to discern trends from it. Ironically, at one of these retailers (where merchants questioned the value of early sales data because their supply chain could not react soon enough), the logistics department argued to us that reducing lead times was not very useful because their merchants did not have the capability to discern trends and optimize purchase quantity from early sales data. This seemed like a question of which function—merchandising or logistics—was going to give in first.

Cross-Functional Collaboration Is Required

A senior executive, upon reading a draft of our chapter, noted that many of the suggestions in the book would require cross-functional projects. For example, improving supply chain responsiveness would require close collaboration among buyers and the supply chain and would possibly involve changes in the factory as well. Similarly, improving store execution would require coordination among store managers and human resources. Retailers are often reluctant to launch such cross-functional projects, presumably because such projects can be tough to implement. This executive noted that "the tendency in most retailers is to work on tactical, functional improvements." Moreover, he noted that "the effort spent on a collection of these [tactical, functional] projects often eliminates organizational capacity for the kinds of broader changes" needed for rocket science retailing.

Analytics May Take the "Fun" Out of Retailing

Finally, some executives have even noted that rocket science retailing, with its emphasis on process discipline, data analysis, and mathematical approaches, could take the fun out of retailing. One executive at a fashion firm noted that people joined his company because they loved the catwalk, not because they loved crunching numbers.

Notwithstanding these doubts, complaints, and obstacles, many retailers have adopted at least some rocket science practices, and some of them have sustained large rocket science projects effectively. In other words, we've seen considerable variation in the rate of adoption. In fact, the most interesting question might be how some firms manage to implement rocket science when so many others seem to stumble with it. This chapter offers insights that we have gleaned from the successful cases that we have observed and participated in.

Tactical Implementations of Rocket Science Retailing

Here, we'll consider small-scale "tactical" implementations, which didn't require big cultural or structural changes. Often, the managers leading these efforts didn't have the authority to change organizational structure and culture. Given the politics of their companies, perceived changes to structure and culture could have undermined their implementation. These managers often told us that they sought to stay "under the radar." For them, tactical approaches might not have been the best option. They might have been the *only* option. But sometimes, small tactical shifts presage more profound changes in a firm. They can help an organization determine whether rocket science retailing will be worth the investment that would be required to implement deeper structural and cultural changes.

Our study of and involvement in successful tactical implementations has led us to the four principles described below.

Recognize That There Are Multiple Customers, and Cater to All of Them

Projects that have successfully introduced analytic approaches have recognized the need to create champions at multiple levels. I2 Technologies, a provider of decision support software, embodied this principle in the late 1990s. I2 recognized that it needed to sell its software not only to "C-level executives" (who usually had the budgetary authority to approve purchases) but also to the staffers who would regularly use the software. The company's attention to creating champions lower down in companies was and is relatively rare.

I2 created and sold a product to serve schedulers in factories. Schedulers at most factories determine which tasks should be performed by specific machines and operators at various points in time. Their decisions in large part determine not only the factory's capacity utilization and inventory levels but also the level of service offered to specific customers. Yet in many factories, senior managers were unaware of the centrality of schedulers. I2's founder, Sanjiv Sidhu, related to us one of the first sales calls that he and cofounder Ken Sharma made at The Timken Company, a steelmaker. Sharma asked the executive they were meeting with what it would take to get a $10 million investment at Timken. The manager had responded that it would take a meeting of the company's board of directors. Sharma then pointed out that the production schedulers made $10 million investments in inventory *every day* with little oversight from senior management and few tools to support decision making. Not surprisingly, many schedulers felt they did not get much respect from colleagues. I2 recognized the schedulers' key role and understood that they could be crucial allies when implementing advanced analytic approaches to improve factory planning.

Consequently, when implementing its "factory planner," i2 emphasized the importance of the work done by schedulers and the tools they needed to do their jobs better. Equally important, i2 pushed to increase schedulers' visibility within and outside their organizations. One industry analyst told us, "i2 created rock stars out of these schedulers."[2] Following a successful implementation, i2 would invite the schedulers to make presentations to other companies and at i2's annual conference, Planet, which by the late 1990s was attracting three thousand participants a year. As a consequence of the greater visibility, many schedulers were able to negotiate better wages or switch to other companies. Not surprisingly, the schedulers remained loyal to i2. Planet became an i2 lovefest or, as one analyst characterized it, "Woodstock for middle-aged i2 users." In fact, as a consequence of the loyalty that i2 inspired among them, schedulers often offered suggestions to i2's engineers to identify ways in which the software could be improved.

Why do managers seeking to implement rocket science retailing have to create champions at all levels? As with the United Nations Security Council, multiple stakeholders have effective veto power over rocket science retailing projects because the adoption of rocket science retailing tends to be discretionary. Lower-level staffers can stymie a project even after senior managers have decided to purchase a particular piece of software. It's not uncommon, for example, to see companies where multiple software packages have been purchased and installed but never used. Lower-level staffers cannot necessarily decide whether to *buy* software but they can decide whether to *use* it.

What's more, implementations of rocket science retailing usually require drawing upon knowledge that already exists in the firm (and they almost always perform better if they do). In one of our early projects at a skiwear manufacturer, users pointed out to us the vital role of production minimums in their supply chain. Without incorporating these minimums, our approach would have been useless to the manufacturer. When users get excited about an application, they're more likely to offer up these sorts of nuggets of wisdom. Hence, catering to *all* levels in the company—not just senior executives—turns out to be critical during implementation.

Quantify the Benefits—Using Agreed-upon Assumptions—But Recognize That Precise Quantification Is Often Impossible

Consider our experience at the first two retailers where we worked on improving aspects of operational execution (such as inventory record inaccuracy and misplaced SKUs) in the stores. The two projects started more or less concurrently.

At one retailer, we estimated the annual benefits (in dollars) that could accrue to the company from improving store execution. At the second retailer, where the opportunity was clearly much bigger, we resisted offering an estimate. We instead pointed out to the top managers that the opportunity was clearly huge and that quantifying the benefit was unnecessary. The first retailer launched its project to improve execution soon after our analysis, while the second one failed to take any serious steps for more than a year. The two retailers certainly differed in many ways, and thus you'd expect them to behave differently. Even so, we believe that our failure to quantify the opportunity at the second retailer caused the project to languish. Soon after we quantified the benefits there, it gained traction.

Put simply, you have to quantify the potential benefits of a project if you want it to succeed. I2 Technologies was passionate about quantifying benefits and even hired an independent auditing firm to interview past clients and collect data on performance improvements brought about by its projects.

Recognize, however, that quantifying benefits usually requires making assumptions that can be challenged. The supply chain vice president at a high-end jewelry retailer, in arguing for supply chain improvements, estimated the benefits from reducing stockouts in the company's stores. To perform his analysis, he had to assume that stockouts led to lost sales, and his colleagues challenged him, arguing that consumers at this high-end retailer often substituted another product when faced with a stockout. The manager then redid his analysis, assuming various levels of consumer substitution and showing that the savings still could be substantial.

Why is it important for missionaries to quantify the benefits of rocket science retailing? For one thing, doing so ensures that they get recognition for their efforts. Often, once the benefits of rocket science retailing are realized, other people—including some who were originally opposed—are likely to want to claim credit for the benefit. As the old saying goes, failure is an orphan, but success has a thousand fathers.

Kevin Freeland, one of the architects of Best Buy's turnaround and a believer in analytical approaches to retailing, advises missionaries to "own a benefit" with senior management.[3] While Freeland worked at Best Buy, the company engaged a consultant to measure the impact of various activities within the firm, such as increasing inventory turns. According to the consultant's analysis, Freeland and his team had generated close to $1 billion in value.

Win Quickly! Quick Wins Matter More Than Big Wins

A few years ago during a case discussion at an executive program, a participant asked us how to identify the projects with the *highest* return on investment. Given the political realities in many organizations, he should've been worrying about how to identify the projects with the *quickest* return on investment. Quick wins create and sustain enthusiasm for change.

Missionaries might consider the following framework in choosing "quick win" projects. You categorize potential projects along two dimensions: the potential benefit and the degree of technical and organizational difficulty. Low-difficulty/high-potential-benefit projects are most desirable but typically hard to find. High-difficulty/low-potential-benefit projects should be avoided. Managers then have a choice between low-difficulty/low-potential-benefit projects or high-difficulty/high-potential-benefit projects. Low-difficulty/low-potential-benefit projects usually offer quicker wins, so managers should start with those before transitioning to the more challenging and rewarding projects (e.g., high-difficulty/high-potential-benefit projects).

Small wins can attract the resources needed for larger projects. Freeland says managers should test and experiment and "fail fast and quietly" so that they can refine their processes and create success stories.

Why do quick wins matter? Every rocket science retailing project that we have witnessed has had its share of naysayers and doubters. Doubters are typically willing to change their minds when they can see evidence of success. However, if that evidence fails to appear relatively quickly, they are likely to become naysayers as well. And naysayers rarely change their minds.

Don't Be Sexy

When seeking a test case, choose the unglamorous tasks that other staffers do not like to do. In most fashion firms, for example, merchants have strong views on style and enjoy choosing cuts and colors for clothing. In contrast, they often find the task of choosing sizes tiresome. Thus missionaries seeking to implement rocket science retailing in this sector should apply their techniques to size optimization first. That way, they'll face less resistance and can more easily score quick wins.

If you start off by messing with style, you're more likely to set off a political squabble. Consequently, you might fail to get your test case, and even if you do get it, coworkers with valuable insider knowledge might not want to help you. On the other hand, if you take an unglamorous task, you may win support because the knowledgeable folks might welcome your help. What's more, these sorts of tasks may not have attracted talented people or substantial resources. Consequently, the potential to generate savings is substantial. As i2 discovered with factory scheduling, you might find low-hanging fruit. Finally, if you fail, not as many people will notice. In Kevin Freeland's words, you'll fail quietly.

Using Structural and Cultural Changes to Implement Rocket Science Retailing

While tactical changes are extremely valuable in implementing rocket science retailing, they have limitations. Without accompanying structural and cultural changes, it is often hard to sustain these tactical efforts. Multiple times we have been involved in developing decision support tools that were shown to be extremely effective in improving performance, but the tools fell into disuse after one or more missionaries left the organization or moved to different roles.

Moreover, tactical changes tend to be incremental, and often a string of such incremental changes turns out to be less optimal for the organization than a holistically conceived large change. You can end up with a hodgepodge of projects that do not work well together. Consider, for example, what happens often on the system side, where it is quite common to see retailers that have a number of small applications (e.g., individual spreadsheet-based tools for forecasting, pricing, or scheduling), with each application intended to improve a particular decision in the organization. Collectively, however, these small applications lead to poor communication and often inconsistent assumptions among the applications. Moreover, many of these applications have poor (or nonexistent) documentation, and changes are not tracked carefully. This can lead to considerable frustration and has at times induced managers to replace all their small applications with an enterprise-wide effort (like installing an enterprise resource planning [ERP] system). Not surprisingly, companies that we have worked with and studied have resorted to substantial structural and cultural changes at the appropriate time.

Structural Changes to Sustain Rocket Science Retailing

Organizational structure plays a vital role in sustaining rocket science retailing. In altering their organizations, retailers have found ways to allocate tasks to people with the appropriate skills and access to appropriate information.

Many retailers, for example, create separate departments for buying and planning within the merchandising function. A buyer and a planner might form a team to make merchandising plans for a specific product category (say, women's swimsuits). Buyers typically handle duties such as spotting the next major trend, identifying the appropriate supplier for a product, and negotiating the best terms with the supplier. They tend to focus on longer-term decisions (for example, for the following season or year). Planners, on the other hand, tend to focus on the short term and make more detailed decisions, such as how many units of a particular SKU to carry at a store. Not surprisingly, buyers tend to rely more on intuition, while planners tend to stress detailed analysis of historical sales data.

The buyer-planner division recognizes that good merchandising requires a combination of big-picture creativity and detailed analysis. And it reflects the understanding that few people are capable of excelling at both.

Retailers also design their organizational structures to reflect the differences between top-down and bottom-up forecasting. Old Navy, a division of Gap, for example, has a company planner, who does a top-down forecast from economic factors and corporate growth goals. Merchandising teams, on the other hand, develop bottom-up forecasts based on their evaluation of individual SKUs. The approaches yield different forecasts, and managers from both groups meet to reconcile them.

Retailers have also sought to inject the top-down perspective through the budgeting process. Footwear seller Nine West, like many chains in the United States, required its "retail directors" (who combined the roles of buyers and planners) to seek to maximize gross margins and sales while operating within a budget.[4] Retail directors had considerable leeway to determine how much of each SKU to carry at each store, but the budget for each director for each season was set cooperatively by that director and a division president. In these meetings, the director brought the bottom-up perspective, and the president offered the top-down view.

Cultural Changes to Sustain Rocket Science Retailing

Sustained improvement in operational execution requires a company to attend to its culture with active support from the CEO and other senior executives.

Our favorite example of this comes not from retailing but from a distributor of electronic components called Arrow Electronics, headquartered in Melville, New York. Soon after Steve Kaufman joined Arrow in 1982, he realized that Arrow's practice of having a distribution center for each sales region was inefficient.[5] A few well-run warehouses could service all the sales regions. But Arrow's sales representatives often needed to know whether parts were available at a distribution center before they took customer orders, so they had to have real-time visibility of on-hand inventory, and the inventory records had to be nearly 100 percent accurate.

Kaufman determined that organizational culture was undermining data accuracy. He decided that he needed to create a culture that cared about maintaining accurate records, so he launched a four-pronged push to change the culture. He modified the physical audit process in the warehouses to focus on operational results, not just financial metrics, and also made the results a subject of discussion at weekly senior staff meetings. He lauded the work of Betty Jane Scheihing, an Arrow employee with a "missionary's passion" for accuracy. He held warehouse-floor workers accountable for the accuracy of their counts. And he took personal actions to sustain the culture that he was working to create. His effort was so thorough and successful that we'll walk you through each step below.

Inventory Accuracy Metrics

When Kaufman joined Arrow, the company operated thirty-seven warehouses, which were physically audited once a year. To underscore the importance of these audits, Kaufman made their results a feature of his Tuesday morning staff meetings. He usually discussed results from a particular audit on the next Tuesday. During the meeting, Kaufman would highlight discrepancies between the company's records and the auditors' counts.

Each audit team reported the percentage of bins with miscounts of more than a specified tolerance, usually ten pieces or $10, whichever was less. Bins outside the tolerance were called "dings." If a warehouse had less than 2 percent dings, Kaufman rated its performance on inventory record accuracy as good. If it had between 2 percent and 5 percent dings, it needed "tuning up." If it had more than 5 percent dings, it had a "serious problem" and needed a team from the corporate office to come in and suggest improvements. And if a warehouse had more than 10 percent dings, Kaufman deemed it "out of control" and transferred or terminated the manager.

The key takeaway in Kaufman's approach was not the specific rules for accuracy that he created. More important was the quickness and clarity of his communication. He and his management team examined the results of audits promptly, shared their view of acceptable performance, and made clear the consequences of falling short. Just as critical, Kaufman did not state his goals in financial terms alone: a warehouse could have been classified as a "serious problem" or "out of control" even if it had the appropriate value of inventory in dollars but many inaccurate inventory records.

Identify and Empower Champions

Kaufman also got lucky. Someone who shared his zeal for accuracy had arrived even earlier than he had. Betty Jane Scheihing came to Arrow as an inventory clerk in 1968 after graduating from Philadelphia Bible College. Back then, the company stored its inventory information in a manual Cardex system. Such was Scheihing's passion for ensuring accuracy that she wore the title of "Cardex Girl" with pride. Scheihing retired in 2004 as senior vice president of global operations and human resources, making her one of the most senior officers at the company. Throughout her career, she remained an accuracy maven.

Once he arrived, Kaufman not only publicly cheered Scheihing's efforts, he also ensured that she had the backing she needed from him and saw to it that her ideas were implemented. Scheihing, for example, insisted that salespeople and sales managers not be allowed to interfere in the operations of the warehouse and that even their presence could compromise inventory accuracy. Salespeople—typically to meet a client's urgent request—would be tempted to remove a few units of a product from the warehouse without going through the necessary and associated paperwork. Consequently, the company redesigned processes to bar sales staff from distribution centers. Scheihing also believed that all movement of products within the warehouse should not only be tracked but also directed by the company's inventory control systems. Thus a salesperson could not generate a pick ticket, even for a big customer with an urgent need, without entering an order into the system. Finally, Scheihing believed that managers who failed to maintain accurate data should be fired. She once shut down a warehouse in Texas because inventory record accuracy was too low.

Setting a Personal Example

As is often the case with successful leaders, Kaufman's actions spoke louder than his words. He made frequent trips to distribution centers. At a center, he would meet with the operating manager and review the results of the last count. He even would personally check the inventory accuracy for a common part number every time he visited a warehouse anywhere in the world. He also wrote frequent e-mails to employees emphasizing the importance of accurate inventory. Staffers with primary responsibility for this metric often received e-mails multiple times a year, praising their accuracy levels or urging improvements. The message, Kaufman believed, was clear: "Inventory record accuracy is so important even the chairman attends to it."

Empowering the Shop Floor

Arrow gave relatively low-level warehouse operators the responsibility for finding and correcting errors. This approach was relatively rare outside of the company. Every firm Arrow had acquired over the prior twenty years (more than sixty) had followed the more traditional approach of assuming that warehouse personnel could not be trusted with this responsibility, and thus had not provided them with the ability to make changes to records in the inventory management systems. Instead, the prior owners, Scheihing said, "assumed that only college-educated corporate office managers or finance and accounting types could be trusted with this responsibility." In one company, all new hires in the management-training program rotated through the department that did inventory adjustments, on the assumption that their analytical and financial skills uniquely qualified them for this role.

Scheihing believed that this approach failed on several counts. One, the work itself—that is, fixing physical count errors—required attention to detail but wasn't difficult. Two, the people closest to the errors had the best chance of spotting, correcting, and fixing them and the underlying causes. They also had the greatest motivation since the errors slowed their work. Three, managers and corporate-office staff would never be enthusiastic or consistently motivated by what they saw as grunt work, nor would they give it the needed priority and focus. Four, the people closest to the work would take pride in keeping their own houses in order rather than being treated as human extensions of the conveyors.

Whenever Arrow acquired a company, it disbanded the headquarters group doing inventory adjustments and trained the warehouse workers to do it. In every case, this improved accuracy as shown by the cycle count statistics.

Conclusion

In describing lessons from successful implementations of rocket science retailing or, in the case of Arrow, similar principles in a different context, we identified four principles for missionaries to follow. One, you must recognize that you have multiple customers and appeal to all of them. Two, you have to quantify the projected and realized benefits from the changes you make. *Show* people the money! Three, you should seek quick wins even though you may be tempted to chase the big ones. And finally, you should start by focusing on unglamorous tasks, to minimize resistance and maximize your chances of discovering low-hanging fruit.

Tactical changes must be accompanied by structural and cultural changes, which is where senior executives can play a substantial role. A CEO or another high-ranking manager can commit her firm to important metrics, identify and support champions, and empower frontline employees. Just as important, she can send a loud message to the organization through her actions. Seeing the CEO on the warehouse floor checking the number of shirts in a bin says more than a hundred e-mails ever will.

Conclusion

The Way Forward

September 2008, when Lehman Brothers declared bankruptcy, marked the beginning of the worst economic crisis many of us have seen in our lifetimes. Panic on Wall Street quickly spread throughout the rest of the economy, including into retailing. Same-store sales crashed, and that, coupled with difficulty in obtaining credit, drove many retailers into bankruptcy or to its brink. Even healthy companies had to make deep cuts, finding ways to shore up operations while preserving their brands and store experiences. As our friend Jim Halpin, former CEO of CompUSA and a veteran of many turnarounds, told us, "The secret in managing through a crisis is to survive the short term without doing things that will destroy your long term."

As we have discussed the crisis with colleagues in academia and retailing, a common view has emerged: yes, the economy will recover, but the postcrisis world will be different in significant ways. We will reach what many are calling a "new normal."

In this conclusion, we'll provide suggestions of what the new normal may be like and how retailers may need to adjust their strategies as a result. But even in a new environment, the ideas of this book should remain useful. They're especially helpful, even vital, in the troubled economic conditions that are likely to persist in the near future.

Rocket science retailing may be easier to implement today than it was when the economy was booming, and stock and house prices were rising. Difficult times make people more willing to change. Talent is more available now, too. Recruits are willing to work for less money than in the past, and well-trained "quants" and smart young MBAs, who formerly might have targeted jobs on Wall Street, are more open to different kinds of careers. On top of that, your company probably has slack capacity that you can devote to implementing the ideas described in this book.

With limited opportunity for top-line growth, operational improvements may be your surest source of profits.

The "New Normal"

On the basis of our reflections and conversations with executives and academics, we're comfortable making three predictions for the new normal.

1. *The economy will grow more slowly*. Much of the growth of the last decade or so was fueled by leverage, which is unlikely to return to the same degree. Consumers are deleveraging, and this will probably continue to suppress their spending. Martin Walker argues that spending will likely fall back to its lower, historical trend.[1] "For several decades after World War II, private consumption measured as a share of gross domestic product had remained within a range of 61 to 63 percent," he says. "But in 1983, [it] began a steady rise, peaking at 70 percent in 2007. Initially, this increase was fueled by the erosion of private savings, which declined from 9 percent of GDP in 1982 to nearly zero in 2005." Often, home equity loans fueled these expenditures, with people tapping the fast-rising value of real estate.

But consumers are no longer spending with such abandon. As of the summer of 2009, the personal savings rate in the United States had risen to almost 6 percent of GDP. Walker points out that even a small reduction in U.S. consumption would shrink the economy substantially. "In cash terms, U.S. consumption in 2007 amounted to $9.7 trillion—70 percent of the $13.8 trillion GDP. At a rate only two percentage points lower, Americans would have spent $300 billion less that year. At a normal rate of 63 percent, they would have spent $1 trillion less."

Several well-known executives have predicted that a changed economy is inevitable. Steve Ballmer of Microsoft has referred to the current climate as "a fundamental economic reset." Jeffrey Immelt of General Electric expects permanent changes in the financial system and tighter credit, and also expects the government to play a more substantial role as a partner, regulator, and financier of business. Hence, he says, "There are going to be elements of the economy that will never be the same, ever. We're going to come out of this in a different world."[2]

Not only will retailers face an economic headwind as they seek to increase sales, they will find it harder than in the past to obtain credit to open new stores. They thus must generate more of their sales growth from existing stores and use their stores, people, and warehouses more efficiently.

2. *Cheap will continue to be chic.* During the recession, customers became more frugal and postponed discretionary purchases. We've found two schools of thought among retailers on how long this behavior will persist. Some argue that consumer frugality is here to stay because the recovery will be slow and the severity of the downturn brought about a permanent change in mind-set, just as the Great Depression did for an earlier generation. Others argue that Americans, naturally optimistic, tend to revert to their old ways and will soon forget the scare they've just had.

   If consumers remain frugal, retailers may want to introduce products that appeal more to cost consciousness. Convenience store chain Cumberland Farms has done precisely this. When

Ari Haseotes took over as the president of the company's 550-store retail division in late 2008, he saw an opportunity to increase its market share for coffee. During the last decade, Cumberland had lost ground to coffee chains such as Starbucks and Dunkin' Donuts. Haseotes launched a new brand of coffee, called Farmhouse Blend, which acknowledged Cumberland's roots in the dairy farm business. Unlike at Starbucks and Dunkin' Donuts, where the smallest cup of coffee could cost $1.50, Cumberland offered any size for 99¢. It also promoted its new blend aggressively, in a series of "free coffee Fridays," soon after launch. Finally, Haseotes got employees excited about the program by offering to get a Mohawk haircut if they increased coffee sales by 50 percent in the first half of the year. In July 2009, he had to head to the barber and make good on his promise: coffee sales grew by over 50 percent, sometimes even hitting 60 percent or higher (all the way up to 80 percent in one week).

We believe that the recession contributed to Cumberland's success. Strapped consumers sought better value and were happy to try a free cup.

3. *Volatility will continue to rule.* Some economists predict that the United States will soon see a period of high inflation, while other equally eminent ones continue to worry about deflation. Many of the country's banks remain weak, and as we write this, about 10 percent of workers are unemployed. These sorts of macroeconomic woes translate to uncertainty for retailers. Consider, for example, recent evidence on sales. Many established retailers are seeing unprecedented drops in revenue. In July 2009, Abercrombie & Fitch reported that its sales had fallen by 28 percent from the prior year, and Neiman Marcus saw a 27 percent drop. JC Penney, Dillard's, American Eagle Outfitters, and Macy's also endured double-digit decreases. Retailers have become accustomed to dealing with uncertainty in their inventory mix. Now they're also likely to see considerable uncertainty in their total sales.

Rocket Science Retailing in the New Normal

How will rocket science retailing be different in the new normal than it was in the past? Equally important, what are the salient aspects of rocket science retailing that need to be reinforced? In the new normal, managers will have to learn to cope not only with *mix uncertainty* but also with *aggregate demand uncertainty*. In addition, managers will have to redouble their effort to improve product availability and operational execution.

Anticipate and React to Fluctuations in Aggregate Demand

With total revenue likely to fluctuate much more than in the past, managers must be ready to take anticipatory action. Consequently, they should improve their ability to forecast aggregate demand. Supply chains during the last few decades have focused on dealing with *mix* uncertainty. In fact, many of us—rightly for the time we were focused on—assumed that firms could forecast their *aggregate* demand well but not their *mix*, and we worked on improving approaches for mix forecasting. Unfortunately, these tools don't translate well to situations with aggregate demand uncertainty.

How well do managers forecast total revenue? You can get a sense of that from looking at investment *analysts'* forecasts. While it is true that managers have information that analysts lack, analysts' estimates and management's guidance on earnings (as opposed to sales) show that the two groups are closely aligned in their thinking. Analysts are often in frequent and close contact with management, even though they're not privy to inside information.

Examining analysts' sales forecasts in 2008 reveals that analysts—and probably managers too—were slow to update their demand forecasts as the economy deteriorated and the financial crisis intensified. Consider the consensus forecast for Abercrombie & Fitch, summarized in figure C-1. Notice that the company ended the year with sales of $3.54 billion.

In March and April 2008, when it was making operational plans (for example, sourcing raw material and planning production), analysts

FIGURE C-1

Analysts' sales forecasts for fiscal year Jan. 31, 2008–Jan. 31, 2009

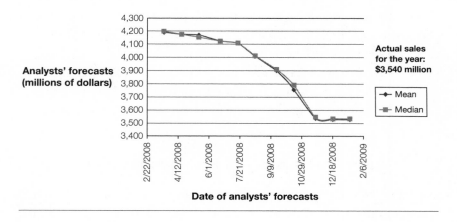

were expecting its annual sales to be roughly $4.2 billion. As late as August 2008, they were still expecting more than $4 billion, and even in October—that is, after Lehman Brothers declared bankruptcy—they were projecting close to $3.8 billion. In other words, they overestimated by roughly $250 million in October, nine months into the year for which they were forecasting. The evidence that we've seen suggests that this performance is typical: analysts and managers have trouble making forecasts in the kind of volatile economy that will probably be part of the new normal.

Pay Attention to Product Availability

Repeated studies in supermarkets and other retailers of fast-moving goods have shown that roughly 8 percent to 10 percent of the SKUs in a store are stocked out at any given time. Stockouts are expensive for retailers for two reasons. First, they lead to lost sales. A 2004 study that surveyed over seventy thousand consumers in twenty-nine countries found that when they did not find the exact item they wanted, nearly one-third went to another store to buy the product, while less than half bought a substitute.[3] Perhaps more significantly, stockouts harm customer goodwill. A study conducted by a multinational consumer-goods maker showed that consumers blame retailers for the stockout a whopping 83 percent of the time, irrespective of who caused it.

Pilot programs at many retailers have shown that stockouts can be reduced with better forecasting, inventory planning, and in-store execution—exactly the techniques described in this book.

Companies often understate sales lost due to stockouts. Our favorite example comes not from retailing but from Hugo Boss Bodywear, a division of Hugo Boss AG.[4] In a test, the bodywear division recently moved 45 of its SKUs from monthly to weekly ordering while leaving the ordering process for 269 SKUs, which served as a control, untouched. The in-stock rate on the 45 weekly SKUs went from 98.24 percent to 99.96 percent. Sales for the 45 SKUs increased by 32 percent, even while sales for the control SKUs *fell* by 10 percent. Why did sales rise by 32 percent rather than 1.72 percent, the difference between 98.24 percent and 99.96 percent? Though the division had historically achieved high in-stock rates *on average*, there were periods when in-stock rates on popular styles dropped to roughly 85 percent. Anticipating periods of low availability, retailers often carried an "insurance brand," which they could order more of during the periods when Boss's products were in short supply. By taking the in-stock rate close to 100 percent, Boss reassured retailers that certain SKUs would never be out of stock. Many retailers responded by dropping the insurance brand from their assortments, causing Boss's sales to skyrocket.

Improve Operational Execution

Steve Kaufman, former CEO of Arrow Electronics, a large distributor of electronic components, often says, "A less than perfect strategy with perfect execution will beat a perfect strategy with less than perfect execution every time." The adage is definitely true in retailing.

Execution can take many forms in retailing. In stores, for example, you must greet customers appropriately, keep inventory accurate, and minimize misplaced product. In any economy, these tasks will remain vital to competitiveness. Improving them requires attending to basics like employee training, appropriate staffing, and store layout. Everyone in retailing knows this, but basics are boring, and it's easy to lose sight of them.

The U.S. automotive industry offers a cautionary tale of the perils of not tending to the basics. The Big Three—General Motors, Ford, and Chrysler—declined and Toyota rose primarily because Toyota, with its push for continuous improvement, focused on operational excellence and produced more reliable, economical cars. Not surprisingly, Toyota's market capitalization during the last few years has exceeded by substantial amounts the market capitalizations of Ford, GM, and Chrysler *combined*—and that was true even before GM filed for bankruptcy and Chrysler was merged with Daimler.

Retailers should learn from the Big Three's mistakes. Toyota couldn't have beaten them without innovative human resource practices that engaged and empowered its line workers to identify ways to improve its production processes. Retailers, too, must recognize that to excel at execution, they must empower their people, including in their stores and distribution centers.

A few years ago, we visited a Toyota factory where we asked the plant manager why Toyota allowed other manufacturers (including competitors) to tour its plants. "Wouldn't they be able to copy the Toyota Production System?" we asked. "Others cannot replicate our performance unless they can replicate what goes on in our people's heads," he said. The more we learned about the Toyota Production System, the more we agreed. Other companies could (and did) easily copy physical attributes of the Toyota Production System, such as andon cords and kanbans. But they couldn't replicate Toyota's approach to people. The challenge with retail execution is similar. Not only do retailers, like manufacturers, have to focus on operational details, they also need to transform their frontline workers into a "community of scientists."

As we discussed earlier in this book, the hardest part of deploying analytics is implementation. It can take a long time and must be done in phases. It's a long journey for most companies. But as the Chinese proverb says, "A journey of a thousand miles begins with a single step." Are you ready to take a step?

APPENDIX

Section A-1: Using the Gamma Function in Excel to Create Table 3-6 and Using This Table to Calculate an Optimal Buy Quantity

Table 3-6 and table A-1 below can be created using Excel. We used the GAMMADIST(d,a,b,true) function in Excel, where d is a demand value, a and b are two parameters that define the Gamma, and *true* indicates that we want the probability that demand will be less than or equal to d. The parameters a and b can be computed from the average and standard deviation using the formulas a = (average / standard deviation)^2 and b = (standard deviation)^2 / average.

For the navy turtleneck with an average of 94.75 and a standard deviation of 7.3272, we get a = (94.75 / 7.3272)^2 = 167.219, and b = (7.3272)^2 / 94.75 = 0.567.

The Gamma distribution is defined for all values, including fractional values, but since demand needs to be an integer, we use the probability for values plus or minus 0.5 of a demand value as the probability of that demand. For example, the probability of .0054 for a demand of 95 is computed as GAMMADIST(95.5,167.218,0.567,true) − GAMMADIST (94.5,167.218,0.567,true).

The cumulative probability in table 3-6 is simply the sum of all probabilities up to and including that demand value.

This shows how to create table 3-6 using Excel. Next we'll explain how to create table A-1 using the table 3-6 Excel model as a basis.

First we show how to find the probability-weighted cost for a particular buy quantity—for example, 95. Enter this in a cell somewhere

TABLE A-1

Finding an optimal buy for the navy turtleneck using a Gamma

Buy quantity	Probability-weighted cost	Buy quantity	Probability-weighted cost
70	$495.01	96	126.18
71	475.01	97	131.54
72	455.02	98	139.03
73	435.05	99	148.52
74	415.08	100	159.87
75	395.15	101	172.92
76	375.25	102	187.47
77	355.42	103	203.36
78	335.69	104	220.40
79	316.11	105	238.43
80	296.72	106	257.29
81	277.62	107	276.83
82	258.90	108	296.93
83	240.68	109	317.48
84	223.10	110	338.39
85	206.33	111	359.57
86	190.54	112	380.97
87	175.93	113	402.53
88	162.70	114	424.22
89	151.04	115	445.99
90	141.14	116	467.84
91	133.19	117	489.73
92	127.31	118	511.65
93	123.61	119	533.60
94	122.18	120	555.57
95	123.04	121	577.54

in the table 3-6 model; create a column next to the "Demand," "Probability," and "Cumulative probability" columns, and enter in this the cost for the trial buy quantity and the demand value, using the fact that the cost of overbuying is $22 and of underbuying $20, for the navy turtleneck. For example, for the trial buy of 95 and a demand of

75, this cost would be (95 − 75) units × \$22 = \$440; for a demand of 105, the cost is (105 − 95) units − \$20 = \$200.

Now in a column next to this, record the product of the cost for each demand value times the probability for that demand value, and sum these products over all rows to get the probability-weighted cost for that trial buy quantity.

This shows how to compute one entry in table A-1—that is, the probability-weighted cost for a particular buy quantity. We could laboriously create table A-1 by changing the trial buy quantities one by one, observing the probability-weighted cost, and recording this value in table A-1. Fortunately, the Data Table function in Excel will do this automatically for us.

To use the Data Table function to create table A-1, first enter the possible buy quantities 70 through 121 in an unused portion of the table 3-6 Excel model.

Suppose you entered 70 through 121 in cells F2–F53. Then enter in cell G1 the label of the cell containing the probability-weighted cost for a trial buy quantity, highlight cells F1–G53, go to the Data tab, click the What If icon, then Data Table and when you see the command box, enter the cell containing the trial buy quantity in the 'Column input cell:' box.[1] Then click OK, and Excel will create table A-1 for you, by substituting one by one the values 70 through 121 as trial buy quantities and recording the associated probability-weighted costs in column G next to the buy quantity. Table A-1 shows the expected cost of all buys from 70 to 121. You can see from the table that a buy of 94 minimizes expected cost.[2]

Section A-2: Creating Store Clusters Based on Sales Mix

Table A-2 shows a simplified hypothetical example designed to illustrate how we clustered stores based on sales. The top section in this table shows unit sales of four products in three stores. In the middle, we have computed the percentage that each product's sales constituted of total store sales. And on the bottom, we have computed a *mix difference score* for each pair of stores by summing the absolute differences in product sale percentages for the pair of stores. For example, the sales mix

TABLE A-2

Measuring the difference in sales mix between stores

Store	UNIT SALES OF FOUR SKUs AT THREE STORES			
	A	**B**	**C**	**D**
1	100	400	20	40
2	8	32	160	320
3	200	300	10	30

Store	SALES CONVERTED TO PERCENTAGES			
	A	**B**	**C**	**D**
1	18%	71%	4%	7%
2	2%	6%	31%	61%
3	37%	55%	2%	6%

Store	STORE MIX DIFFERENCE SCORES		
	1	**2**	**3**
1		162	38
2	162		168
3	38	168	

difference between stores 1 and 2 is computed as $|18 - 2| + |71 - 6| + |4 - 31| + |7 - 61| = 162$. Note that the difference score of 35 between stores 1 and 3 is small relative to the differences between 2 and 1 or 2 and 3. Thus we concluded that stores 1 and 3 sold a similar mix of products, while store 2 was an outlier. If we were forming two store clusters, stores 1 and 3 would be in one cluster, and store 2 in the other.

To choose ten test stores from the stores of a chain, you'd use this approach to compute a difference score between every pair of stores, and then employ standard clustering procedures to form ten clusters chosen to minimize the average difference score between stores within a cluster. With more than one thousand stores, a difference score needs to be computed for more than one thousand times one thousand store pairs, so obviously a computer is needed.

You'd then use your sales history database to create a formula that best predicts chain season sales from test sales. You can use a statistical technique called *linear regression*, which is available in Excel and many other statistical analysis packages, to do this. Recall how the retailer we worked with would have predicted its total sales by multiplying each store's test sales by 80. The approach here is similar, in that you multiply each test store's sales by a factor (the coefficient in the regression equation), except now the factor for each store can differ. To illustrate how useful this can be, imagine that you have a store with relatively low sales that is highly predictive of the sales for the chain. It would be an ideal test store, but because its test sales will be relatively low, it needs a bigger factor in a prediction formula.

Section A-3: A Forecast Model Incorporating Price and Inventory

We used the formula shown in figure A-1 and explained here to forecast sales, for a shoe retailer, of a particular style/color sandal (call it sandal j) in a particular week in the season in all stores and sizes. The formula consists of a base forecast of what you expect to sell over the entire season with an average price and enough inventory to avoid stockouts, multiplied by factors for seasonality and price and inventory adjustment. The base forecast, K_j, was simply what we had used before—that is, sales in the first eight weeks of the spring season divided by 0.107. The seasonality factor, $s(t)$, is the percentage of total-season sales we expect to occur in week t. These factors can be computed using sales from the prior year's spring sandal sales and computing the fraction that each week's sales constitute of total season sales. The price factor raises the forecast if sandal j is priced relatively lower than other sandals, and lowers the forecast if it is priced higher. The average ratio of price to cost in week t for all of the retailer's sandals is $p(t)$, and $p_j(t)$ is the ratio of price to cost for sandal j. We compare price–cost ratios rather than raw prices because the various sandals differed in quality, which caused differences in their base price. We reasoned that quality was correlated with cost, and the price–cost ratio would reflect how a sandal was priced relative to its intrinsic quality.

FIGURE A-1

Forecast model incorporating the impact of price and inventory

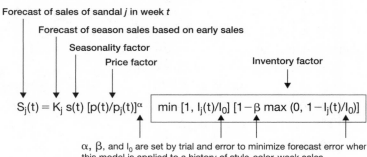

If $p(t)/p_j(t)$ is less than 1 (that is, sandal j's price–cost ratio is high relative to an average sandal in week t) then the price factor $[p(t)/p_j(t)]^\alpha$ is less than 1, and it lowers the forecast. Conversely, if $p(t)/p_j(t)$ is greater than 1 (that is, sandal j's price–cost ratio is low relative to an average sandal in week t) then the price factor raises the forecast.

The inventory factor is 1 if the retailer has enough inventory to avoid stockouts, and less than 1 if its inventory falls below a critical threshold, I_0. $I_j(t)$ is the inventory of sandal j in all stores in week t. We chose the parameters α, β, and I_0 to minimize forecast error when we applied this model to the 1997 history. We found the best value for I_0 was ten pairs per store, which makes sense because when inventory falls below this level, popular sizes are stocked out in many stores, causing lost sales.

Notes

Introduction

1. Unless otherwise indicated, all quotations from retailers are from discussions, interviews, or talks given at a class or conference with the authors.

2. Source: S&P's Industrial Annual Database accessed through Wharton Research Data Services (WRDS).

3. See Marshall L. Fisher, Ananth Raman, and Anna Sheen McClelland, "Rocket Science Retailing Is Almost Here: Are You Ready?" *Harvard Business Review*, July–August 2000, 115–124, for a more extensive description of this study.

Chapter One

1. For a discussion of David Berman's business model and investment approach, see Ananth Raman, Vishal Gaur, and Saravanan Kesavan, "David Berman," Case 605-081 (Boston: Harvard Business School, 2005).

2. Nardelli had worked at General Electric (GE) before taking over as CEO of The Home Depot.

3. A periodic report where Berman discusses his thoughts on retail, focusing on inventories.

4. Raman, Gaur, and Kesavan, "David Berman."

5. Ibid.

6. Saravanan Kesavan, Vishal Gaur, and Ananth Raman, "Incorporating Price and Inventory Endogeneity in Firm-Level Sales Forecasting" (working paper, Harvard Business School, Boston, 2009).

7. "No Mood For Shopping—Part II," *Barron's*, June 12, 2006.

8. See Richard Lai, "Inventory Signals" (doctoral candidate research paper, Harvard Business School, 2006.

9. Inventory turns are calculated by dividing the retailer's annual cost of sales by the average level of inventory at a firm. The calculation for an analogous term, *days of inventory*, is similar; to derive days of inventory, the firm's average inventory level is multiplied by 365 (i.e., the number of days in a year) and then divided by the cost of sales. Some practitioners, including David Berman, have argued to us that days of inventory is more intuitive and hence, more easily accessible to people. We agree but continued using inventory turns because a number of our technical results (e.g., the regression analysis reported later in the chapter) were easier to explain using inventory turns.

10. A detailed discussion of the results in this section can be found in Vishal Gaur, Marshall Fisher, and Ananth Raman, "An Econometric Analysis of Inventory Turnover Performance in Retail Services," *Management Science* 51, no. 2 (2005): 181–194.

11. Using the pooled model, adjusted inventory turns can be calculated from the following equation: $\log(\text{adjusted inventory turns})_{it} = \log(IT)_{it} + 0.2431 \log MU_{it} - 0.2502 \log CI_{it} - 0.143 \log SS_{it}$.

12. Gross margin is calculated as the difference between the sale price and the cost of goods sold, divided by the sale price. It is usually expressed as a percentage.

13. A formal argument for this logic can be found in the *newsboy model* or the *newsvendor model*, which is usually described in most texts on inventory management; e.g., Steven Nahmias, *Production and Operations Analysis*, 5th ed. (Boston: McGraw-Hill Irwin, 2005).

14. Gaur, Fisher, and Raman, "An Econometric Analysis of Inventory Turnover," calculate capital intensity as the ratio of the *gross fixed assets* (i.e., the noninventory assets) to the total assets at a retailer (which comprises inventory and gross fixed assets).

15. We conducted our analysis with multiple forecasts based on past sales data.

16. We were introduced to this example by Vishal Gaur.

17. Vishal Gaur, presentation at the Consortium for Operational Excellence in Retailing, Philadelphia, PA, Wharton School, University of Pennsylvania, June 2006.

18. Vishal Gaur, Nikolay Osadchiy, and Sridhar Seshadri, "Sales Forecasting with Financial Indicators and Experts' Input," Johnson School Research Paper Series No. 06-09, October 23, 2008.

Chapter Two

1. Our discussion of current practice is based on Michael Levy and Barton Weitz, *Retailing Management* (New York: Irwin-McGraw Hill, 2007) and conversations with several retail executives, including Kevin Freeland, chief

_____

Rocket Science Retailing in the New Normal

How will rocket science retailing be different in the new normal than it was in the past? Equally important, what are the salient aspects of rocket science retailing that need to be reinforced? In the new normal, managers will have to learn to cope not only with *mix uncertainty* but also with *aggregate demand uncertainty*. In addition, managers will have to redouble their effort to improve product availability and operational execution.

Anticipate and React to Fluctuations in Aggregate Demand

With total revenue likely to fluctuate much more than in the past, managers must be ready to take anticipatory action. Consequently, they should improve their ability to forecast aggregate demand. Supply chains during the last few decades have focused on dealing with *mix* uncertainty. In fact, many of us—rightly for the time we were focused on—assumed that firms could forecast their *aggregate* demand well but not their *mix*, and we worked on improving approaches for mix forecasting. Unfortunately, these tools don't translate well to situations with aggregate demand uncertainty.

How well do managers forecast total revenue? You can get a sense of that from looking at investment *analysts'* forecasts. While it is true that managers have information that analysts lack, analysts' estimates and management's guidance on earnings (as opposed to sales) show that the two groups are closely aligned in their thinking. Analysts are often in frequent and close contact with management, even though they're not privy to inside information.

Examining analysts' sales forecasts in 2008 reveals that analysts—and probably managers too—were slow to update their demand forecasts as the economy deteriorated and the financial crisis intensified. Consider the consensus forecast for Abercrombie & Fitch, summarized in figure C-1. Notice that the company ended the year with sales of $3.54 billion.

In March and April 2008, when it was making operational plans (for example, sourcing raw material and planning production), analysts

FIGURE C-1

Analysts' sales forecasts for fiscal year Jan. 31, 2008–Jan. 31, 2009

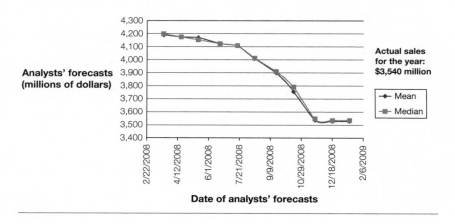

Date of analysts' forecasts

were expecting its annual sales to be roughly $4.2 billion. As late as August 2008, they were still expecting more than $4 billion, and even in October—that is, after Lehman Brothers declared bankruptcy—they were projecting close to $3.8 billion. In other words, they overestimated by roughly $250 million in October, nine months into the year for which they were forecasting. The evidence that we've seen suggests that this performance is typical: analysts and managers have trouble making forecasts in the kind of volatile economy that will probably be part of the new normal.

Pay Attention to Product Availability

Repeated studies in supermarkets and other retailers of fast-moving goods have shown that roughly 8 percent to 10 percent of the SKUs in a store are stocked out at any given time. Stockouts are expensive for retailers for two reasons. First, they lead to lost sales. A 2004 study that surveyed over seventy thousand consumers in twenty-nine countries found that when they did not find the exact item they wanted, nearly one-third went to another store to buy the product, while less than half bought a substitute.[3] Perhaps more significantly, stockouts harm customer goodwill. A study conducted by a multinational consumer-goods

operating officer, Advance Auto Parts; Herb Kleinberger, principal, ARC Business Advisors; and Rob Price, chief marketing officer, CVS.

2. Sometimes the term *merchandise planning* is used for what we are calling strategic assortment planning.

3. This discussion is based on Zeynep Ton and Ananth Raman, "Borders Group, Inc.," Case 9-601-037 (Boston: Harvard Business School, 2003).

4. Subsequent to BJ's, Mr. Halpin was CEO of CompUSA and is currently founder and CEO of River Bend Inc.

5. See Jena McGregor, "At Best Buy, Marketing Goes Micro," *BusinessWeek*, May 15, 2008; Vanessa O'Connell, "Reversing Field, Macy's Goes Local," *Wall Street Journal*, April 21, 2008; Ann Zimmerman, "To Boost Sales, Wal-Mart Drops One-Size-Fits-All Approach," *Wall Street Journal Online*, September 7, 2006; and Ann Zimmerman, "Home Depot Learns to Go Local," *Wall Street Journal*, October 7, 2008, for descriptions of efforts by Best Buy, Macy's, Wal-Mart, and Home Depot to localize their assortments.

6. The material on operational assortment optimization is based on Marshall Fisher and Ramnath Vaidyanathan, "Retail Assortment Optimization: An Attribute Based Approach" (white paper, Wharton School Operations and Information Management, Philadelphia, PA, September 2008; revised May 2009).

7. The total demand estimate column of table 2-6 is an estimate calculated as total sales divided by percent share of demand captured, as described above. The total demand column gives the total of the four brand-size estimates. The two differ for any flavor for which demand estimates were replaced by actual sales.

8. This estimation approach, while relatively simple, has some weaknesses. For one thing, the chain offered all four brand-sizes for two flavors, which made the calculations easier. In most cases, you can't count on this happening. Also, by using only two flavors to estimate shares, you're throwing away lots of data that could be used to improve the accuracy of the estimates. In the butter, cheese, raspberry, vanilla, and honey flavors, this retailer offered both Yummy Cakes and Tiny Tina in the single-serving size, so these sales are undistorted by substitution and could be used with sales in the chocolate and cinnamon categories to more accurately estimate the relative demand shares of Yummy Cakes and Tiny Tina in the single-serving size. All sales data is somewhat influenced by random events (weather, the ever-fluctuating economic news, etc.), so the more data you can bring to bear on estimating a value, the more accurate your estimate is likely to be.

For these reasons, in practice, you'll employ a statistical method called *maximum likelihood estimation*, which uses all of the sales data to find brand-size shares and substitution frequency estimates. You'll apply this technique to sales data for each store to capture store-specific differences in customer preferences. To estimate price on SKUs not currently carried by a retailer, you regress the prices of existing SKUs against their attributes to obtain an attribute-based pricing formula. For additional details, see Fisher and Vaidyanathan, "Retail Assortment Optimization."

9. Canadian Tire Corporation Ltd., Annual Report 2007.

10. The idea of using stockouts as an opportunity to estimate substitution was suggested to us by Kevin Freeland.

Chapter Three

1. The methodology described here was developed in collaboration with one of our former doctoral students, Kumar Rajaram, now a professor at UCLA's Anderson School. Additional details are reported in Marshall Fisher, Kumar Rajaram, and Ananth Raman, "Optimizing Inventory Replenishment of Retail Fashion Products," *Manufacturing & Service Operations Management* 3, no. 3 (2001): 230–241.

2. The committee forecasting process we'll describe here, and its use in estimating the standard deviation of forecasts, was first developed in a project we conducted, together with Janice Hammond of Harvard Business School, at Sport Obermeyer, a fashion skiwear firm. The idea was suggested by Wally Obermeyer when he was president of Sport Obermeyer and working with us on this project. For more details see Marshall Fisher, Janice Hammond, Walter Obermeyer, and Ananth Raman, "Making Supply Meet Demand in an Uncertain World," *Harvard Business Review*, May–June 1994.

3. In using this approach, we are ignoring for simplicity the fact that the 55 percent value also varies from season to season. This approach makes sense if this variation is small, which it is. We used the relationship that the probability that demand in the first fourteen weeks is less than or equal to X equals the probability that total season demand is less than or equal to X / 0.55[1] to first find a continuous distribution, and then converted this to a discrete distribution using the approach described in table A-1.

4. The approach to testing described here was developed in collaboration with one of our former doctoral students, Kumar Rajaram, now a professor at UCLA's Anderson School. Additional details are reported in Marshall Fisher and Kumar Rajaram, "Accurate Testing of Retail Merchandise: Methodology and Application," *Marketing Science* 19, no. 8 (2000): 266–278.

5. Freeland is currently chief operating officer, Advance Auto Parts.

6. To determine that 2.5 was the price elasticity that best fit the data, we made price elasticity a parameter in a cell of an Excel model containing the historical data, and then computed the forecast error measure mean absolute

deviation (MAD) by, for each historical data point, finding the absolute difference between predicted and actual lift and summing across all points. Then we used the Excel function Solver to find the elasticity value that minimized MAD, which turned out to be 2.5. See Stephen Smith and Dale Achabal, "Clearance Pricing and Inventory Policies for Retail Chains," *Management Science,* 1998, for additional details on estimating the sales impact of markdowns.

7. Facing severe competition, Zany Brainy discontinued operation in 2001. Schlesinger is now cofounder and president of Five Below, a leading extreme value retailer to the teen market and beyond.

Chapter Four

1. See Marshall L. Fisher, Ananth Raman, and Anna Sheen McClelland, "Rocket Science Retailing Is Almost Here: Are You Ready?" *Harvard Business Review*, July–August 2000, 115–124.

2. This discussion is based on Marshall Fisher, "National Bicycle Industrial Co" (unpublished case), the Teaching Note for this case, and "Japan's New Personalized Production," *Fortune*, October 22, 1990.

3. A *hansha* (for "sales company") is a distributor more or less peculiar to Japan that is incorporated as an independent company but that is completely captive to a particular manufacturer. National Bicycle used ten hansha that had been established by Matsushita Electric and were run by ex-managers of Matsushita. The hansha carried only Panasonic bicycles that they bought from National Bicycle and resold to retailers in exclusive territories.

4. A servomotor has an output shaft that can be set to a specific angular position based on a signal from a computer. Servos are used in a wide range of applications, from remote-controlled planes to robots.

5. L. Kopczak and H. Lee, "Hewlett-Packard Company DeskJet Printer Supply Chain (A)," Case GS3A (Stanford, CA: Stanford Graduate School of Business, May 2001).

6. Dana Canedy, "McDonald's Burger War Salvo: Is 'Made for You' the Way Folks Want to Have It?" *New York Times*, June 20, 1998.

7. For additional details, see Marshall Fisher et al., "Making Supply Meet Demand in an Uncertain World," *Harvard Business Review*, May–June 1994.

8. G. N. Georgano, *Cars: Early and Vintage, 1886–1930* (London: Grange-Universal, 1985).

9. One might also argue that labor costs have become a smaller portion of total costs and hence maximizing labor efficiency is less crucial.

10. This section is based in part on the cases "Supply Chain Management at World, Ltd.," by Anna Sheen McClelland, Ananth Raman, and Marshall Fisher, Case 9-601-072 (Boston: Harvard Business School, 2001) and "Zara: IT for Fashion," by Andrew McAfee, Vincent Dessain, and Anders Sioman, Case 9-604-081 (Boston: Harvard Business School, 2007). The facts about World are accurate as of the time of the case.

11. For additional details on the Obermeyer forecast process, see Marshall Fisher, Janice Hammond, Walter Obermeyer, and Ananth Raman, "Making Supply Meet Demand in an Uncertain World," *Harvard Business Review*, May–June 1994.

12. Freeland is currently chief operating officer, Advance Auto Parts.

Chapter Five

1. The term rocket science retailing is discussed in the Introduction and is used equivalently in this book with scientific retailing. See also Marshall L. Fisher, Ananth Raman, and Anna Sheen McClelland, "Rocket Science Retailing Is Almost Here: Are You Ready?" *Harvard Business Review*, July–August 2000, 115–124, for a discussion of this concept.

2. For further details, see V. G. Narayanan and Ananth Raman, "Hamptonshire Express," Case 1-698-053 (Boston: Harvard Business School, 2002).

3. Optimal stocking values can be derived from the *newsvendor model*. A derivation of the newsvendor model can be found in most textbooks on inventory theory—e.g., Steven Nahmias, *Production and Operations Analysis*, 5th ed. (Boston: McGraw-Hill Irwin, 2005).

4. Ideas for this section are taken from V. G. Narayanan and Ananth Raman, "Aligning Incentives for Supply Chain Efficiency," Note 600-110 (Boston: Harvard Business School, April 10, 2000).

5. See, for example, Michael C. Jensen and Kevin J. Murphy, "CEO Incentives—It's Not How Much You Pay, But How," *Harvard Business Review*, May–June 1990.

6. Details of the analysis reported in this section can be found in Nicole DeHoratius and Ananth Raman, "Store Manager Incentive Design and Retail Performance: An Exploratory Investigation," *Manufacturing & Service Operations Management* 9, no. 4 (2007). *Shrink* refers to inventory reductions usually associated with theft or merchandise lost from the store.

7. Zeynep Ton and James L. McKenney, "Campbell Soup Company: A Leader in Continuous Replenishment Innovations," Case 608-141 (Boston: Harvard Business School, 2008); and Janice H. Hammond, "Barilla SpA (A-D)," Case 694-046 (Boston: Harvard Business School, 2007).

8. V. G. Narayanan and Lisa Brem, "Owens and Minor, Inc. (A)," Case 100-055 (Boston: Harvard Business School, 2008).

9. Victor Fung and Joan Magretta, "Fast, Global, and Entrepreneurial: Supply Chain Management, Hong Kong Style: An Interview with Victor Fung," *Harvard Business Review*, May 1998.

10. See Jeffrey Liker and Thomas Choi, "Building Deep Supplier Relations," *Harvard Business Review*, December 2004.

11. V. G. Narayanan and Ananth Raman, "Aligning Incentives in Supply Chains," *Harvard Business Review*, November 2004.

Chapter Six

1. See "10-Foot Rule," Wal-Mart Stores, http://walmartstores.com/AboutUs/285.aspx.

2. Results for specific retailers are reported in Nicole DeHoratius and Ananth Raman, "Inventory Record Inaccuracy: An Empirical Analysis," *Management Science* 54, no. 4 (2008): 627–641; Marshall Fisher, Jayanth Krishnan, and Serguei Netessine, "Retail Store Execution: An Empirical Study" (working paper, Wharton School, Operations and Information Management, Philadelphia, PA, January 2007); Marshall Fisher, Jayanth Krishnan, and Serguei Netessine, "A Cross Sectional Study of Retail Store Performance" (working paper, Wharton School, Operations and Information Management, Philadelphia, PA, October 2007); Zeynep Ton and Ananth Raman, "Cross Sectional Analysis of Phantom Products at Retail Stores" (working paper, 2000); Zeynep Ton and Ananth Raman, "The Effect of Product Variety and Inventory Levels on Retail Sales: A Longitudinal Study," *Production and Operations Management Journal* (forthcoming); Zeynep Ton, "The Effect of Labor on Profitability: The Role of Quality" (Harvard Business School working paper, 2009); and Zeynep Ton and Robert S. Huckman, "Managing the Impact of Employee Turnover on Performance: The Role of Process Conformance," *Organization Science* 19, no. 1 (2008): 56–68.

3. The results described for this retailer are based on Fisher, Krishnan, and Netessine, "Retail Store Execution."

4. Fisher, Krishnan, and Netessine, "Retail Store Execution," describes two statistical analyses done to determine the most important driver of sales: one using a technique called *stepwise regression* that adds explanatory variables sequentially in order of importance, and the other using *variable normalization* so that a variable's coefficient represents its importance in explaining sales.

5. The exact methodology used to measure the impact of store labor on sales is described in detail in Fisher, Krishnan, and Netessine, "Retail Store Execution"; but briefly, we had over six thousand observations in our data on store–month sales, planned payroll, and actual payroll, and we were able to analyze this data to measure the impact of payroll on sales.

6. A detailed description of how store-specific payroll sales lifts were computed is given in Fisher, Krishnan, and Netessine, "Retail Store Execution." A store that had high sales variation that correlated with a relatively low payroll variation would have a high sales lift, whereas a store that had high payroll variation but little sales variation would have a low sales lift.

7. Obviously, there will be variation in sales and payroll due to seasonality, but the numbers in figure 6-5 have been deseasonalized.

8. K. Maher, "Wal-Mart Seeks New Flexibility in Worker Shifts," *Wall Street Journal Online*, January 3, 2007.

9. This discussion is based on conversations with Kevin Freeland, chief operating officer, Advance Auto Parts, and former senior vice president of inventory management, Best Buy.

10. As reported in "Short-Circuited: Cutting Jobs as Corporate Strategy," *Knowledge@Wharton*, April 4, 2007.

11. May Wong, "Best Buy Service Trumps Circuit City," Associated Press, April 8, 2007.

12. "Best Buy Reports 18.5% Increase in Profit," *New York Times*, April 5, 2007.

13. RTT News Global Financial Newswires, "Circuit City Slips to Loss in Q2: Sees Continued Weakness in Q3," September 20, 2007.

14. Gaffney is now executive vice president of operations at AAA Northern California, Nevada, and Utah.

15. The discussion on Staples is based on an interview with Paul Gaffney.

16. Ton, "The Effect of Labor on Profitability."

17. Ton and Huckman, "Managing the Impact of Employee Turnover."

18. Nicole DeHoratius and Ananth Raman, "Building on Foundations of Sand?" *ECR Journal* 3, no. 1 (Spring 2003); Ananth Raman, Nicole DeHoratius, and Zeynep Ton, "Execution: The Missing Link in Retail Operations," *California Management Review* 43, no. 3 (Spring 2001); Ananth Raman, Nicole DeHoratius, and Zeynep Ton, "The Achilles Heel of Supply Chain Management," *Harvard Business Review*, May 2001, 136–152; DeHoratius and Raman, "Inventory Record Inaccuracy"; and Ton and Raman, "Cross Sectional Analysis of Phantom Products." For additional information on the status of in-stocks in the grocery industry, see Daniel Corsten and Thomas Gruen, "Stock-outs Cause Walkouts," *Harvard Business Review*, May 2004; and Daniel Corsten and Thomas Gruen, "Desperately Seeking Shelf Availability: An Examination of the Extent, the Causes, and the Efforts to Address Retail Out-of-Stocks," *International Journal of Retail & Distribution Management* 31, no. 12 (2003): 605–617.

19. For additional details, see Ton and Raman, "Cross Sectional Analysis of Phantom Products"; and Ton and Raman, "The Effect of Product Variety and Inventory Levels."

20. This section is based in part on Marshall Fisher, "To You It's a Store; To Me It's a Factory," *ECR Journal—International Commerce Review* 4, no. 2 (Winter 2004).

21. See K. Mishina, "Toyota Motor Manufacturing, U.S.A., Inc.," Case 0-693-019 (Boston: Harvard Business School, 1995) for an excellent description of the Toyota Production System.

22. See W. A. Shewhart, *Economic Control of Quality of Manufactured Product* (New York: D. Van Nostrand Company, Inc., 1931); and W. Edwards Deming, *Out of the Crisis* (Cambridge, MA: MIT Press, 1986).

23. DeHoratius and Raman, "Inventory Record Inaccuracy"; and Ton and Raman, "The Effect of Product Variety and Inventory Levels."

24. DiRomualdo is currently founder, chairman, and chief executive officer of Naples Ventures, LLC.

25. See DeHoratius and Raman, "Inventory Record Inaccuracy," for additional details.

26. See http://www.toyotageorgetown.com/history.asp.

27. See W. J. Salmon, "Retailing in the Age of Execution," *Journal of Retailing* 65, no. 3 (1989): 368–378, for an excellent overview of the importance of execution in retailing.

Chapter Seven

1. The term rocket science retailing is discussed in the Introduction and is used equivalently in this book with scientific retailing. See also Marshall L. Fisher, Ananth Raman, and Anna Sheen McClelland, "Rocket Science Retailing Is Almost Here: Are You Ready?" *Harvard Business Review*, July–August 2000, 115–124, for a discussion of this concept.

2. This section draws from Edmund W. Schuster, Stuart J. Allen, and David L. Brock, *Global RFID: The Value of the EPCglobal Network for Supply Chain Management* (Berlin: Springer-Verlag, 2007).

3. D. Corsten and T. Gruen, "Desperately Seeking Shelf Availability: An Examination of the Extent, the Causes, and the Efforts to Address Retail Out-of-Stocks," *International Journal of Retail & Distribution Management* 31, no. 12 (2003): 605–617.

4. Zeynep Ton and Ananth Raman, "Borders Group, Inc.," Case 9-601-037 (Boston: Harvard Business School, 2007).

5. Zeynep Ton, Vincent Dessain, and Monika Stachowiak-Joulain, "RFID at the METRO Group," Case 606-053 (Boston: Harvard Business School, 2005).

6. Brian Harris and James Tenser, "Retail Execution: The Buck Starts Here," *Progressive Grocer*, May 1, 2008.

7. Bill C. Hardgrave, Matthew Waller, and Robert Miller, "Does RFID Reduce Out-of-Stocks? A Preliminary Analysis" (Fayetteville, AK: Information

Technology Research Institute, Sam M. Walton College of Business, University of Arkansas), http://itrc.uark.edu.

8. As an example, note that METRO (from the "RFID at the METRO Group" case) reasoned that reducing out-of-stocks by 2% would cause sales to increase by 0.5%.

9. Based on 23% gross margins and annual sales of $344 billion.

10. Robert Hayes and Ramachandran Jaikumar, "Manufacturing's Crisis: New Technologies, Obsolete Organizations," *Harvard Business Review*, September 1988.

11. Ibid.

12. Ibid.

13. Advertisement for International Commercial Truck, circa 1910, on display in Maine's Owl's Head Transportation Museum.

14. Hau Lee, "Peering Through a Glass Darkly," *ECR Journal: International Commerce Review*, Spring 2007, articulated this phenomenon first.

15. Alan MacCormack, "Managing Innovation in an Uncertain World: Module 1: Innovation and Uncertainty," Module Note 5-606-125 (Boston: Harvard Business School, 2006).

16. Graham R. Mitchell and William F. Hamilton, "Managing R&D as a Strategic Option," *Research-Technology Management* (May–June 1988), reprinted March–April 2007.

17. Zeynep Ton and Ananth Raman, "Borders Group, Inc."

Chapter Eight

1. The term rocket science retailing is discussed in the Introduction and is used equivalently in this book with scientific retailing. See also Marshall L. Fisher, Ananth Raman, and Anna Sheen McClelland, "Rocket Science Retailing Is Almost Here: Are You Ready?" *Harvard Business Review*, July–August 2000, 115–124, for a discussion of this concept.

2. Jim Shepherd, AMR Research.

3. Freeland is currently chief operating officer, Advance Auto Parts.

4. See Ananth Raman and Colin Welch, "Merchandising at Nine West Retail Stores," Case 698-098 (Boston: Harvard Business School, 1998).

5. Kaufman joined Arrow as corporate EVP and president of Electronics Distribution Division in August 1982, was named corporate president in May 1985, named CEO in September 1986, named chairman in May 1992, stepped down as CEO July 2000 (remaining chairman), was interim CEO June 1–September 15, 2002, and retired fully from the company on September 15, 2002.

Conclusion

1. From Martin Walker, "The New Normal, *Wilson Quarterly* 33, no. 3 (Summer 2009).

2. Martin Walker, "The New Normal," *Wilson Quarterly* 33, no. 3 (Summer 2009): 63–66.

3. Daniel Corsten and Thomas Gruen, "Stock-outs Cause Walkouts," *Harvard Business Review*, May 2004.

4. Cite Hugo Boss case or paper.

Appendix

1. This instruction is for Microsoft Excel 2007. If you have a different version, you may need to consult the help command for how to construct a data table.

2. We created tables 3-6 and A-1 using demand values ranging from 0 to 222, but only show demand from 70 to 121 in table 3-6, since other demand values have negligible probability.

Index

A Pea in the Pod, 129
Abercrombie & Fitch, 16, 219–220
activity-based pricing, 144
adjusted inventory turns (AIT),
    19, 24, 26
adverse selection, 138
Amazon, 197
American Pacific Enterprises (APE),
    125
apparel industry
    assortment planning
        strategies, 31–32
    challenge of buyers understanding
        customers, 2
    failure to use the data they have, 4
    incentives that inhibit profitability,
        131–132
    lead time differences example,
        106–107
    product assortment deliberations
        (see product launch decisions)
    reliance on trust with
        suppliers, 145
Arrow Electronics
    empowering a champion, 212
    empowering the shop floor,
        213–214

inventory issues at distribution
    centers, 210–211
new focus on inventory accuracy
    metrics, 211–212
senior management's example
    setting, 213
assortment planning
    assortment allocation examples
        (see snack cake assortment
        planning; tire assortment
        planning)
    complexities of SKU choices,
        33–34
    conjoint analysis, 58–59
    data needed to forecast sales,
        30–31
    estimation steps, 58–59
    forecasting assumptions, 37
    forecasting based on attributes,
        36–37
    levels of, 29
    localizing assortments, 35–36,
        54–57
    logic behind carrying slow-moving
        SKUs, 34–35
    marginal return on incremental
        resources, 32–33

assortment planning (*continued*)
  modeling steps, 57–58
  operational level of planning,
    33–37
  optimization steps, 59–60
  stockouts and, 59
  strategic level of planning, 30–33
  value in using a complex model,
    50–51
automotive industry, 222. *See also*
  Toyota Production System

Ballmer, Steve, 217
Barilla, 143
Barnes & Noble, 197
Bed Bath & Beyond, 35–36
Berman, David, 9–10, 14–15, 25
Best Buy
  analysts' focus on sales, 16
  assortment planning, 29, 30–31,
    33–34
  causes of stockouts, 172
  inventory turns, 18
  partnering with suppliers,
    122–123
  staffing levels setting practices,
    162–164
  switch to sales-capture rate, 92–93
Block, Greg, 125
Bombay, 10
Borders
  assortment planning, 32
  late-adoption repercussions, 197
  localizing of assortments, 36
  metrics used to evaluate store
    performance, 166
  phantom products and stockouts
    problems, 171, 175
Brantano, 176
Bryn Mawr Stereo, 139–142

Campbell's, 143
capital intensity, 19–20
Choi, Thomas, 146
Chrysler, 222
Circuit City, 18, 164
collaborative planning, forecasting,
  and replenishment (CPFR),
  105–106
comparable store sales, 156–157
Consumer Outlook Survey, 3
contract-based solutions to incentive
  problems, 139–142
Costco Wholesale Corporation, 19
Cumberland Farms, 217–218

decouple point, 114–115
DeHoratius, Nicole, 152, 174
Dell, 115–116
Deming, Edwards, 173
Destination Maternity, 106, 129, 176
Díaz, Miguel, 121
DiRomualdo, Bob, 175, 197
discounted cash flow model, 11–13

earns retailers, 19
"Econometric Analysis of Inventory
  Turnover Performance in Retail
  Sales," 20
"Effect of Product Variety and
  Inventory Levels on Retail
  Sales," 174
electronic product code (EPC),
  183–184
Electronic Product Code Information
  Services (EPCIS), 185
employee turnover and store
  performance, 167
enforceability as a contractible
  element, 138–139

fashion apparel. *See* apparel industry
Fisher, Jerome, 1
Fisher, Marshall, 20
Ford, 146, 222
Ford, Henry, 117
forecasting sales
  approaches used, 62–63
  assumptions, 37
  balancing forecasts, flexibility, and
    inventory, 127–129
  based on attributes, 36–37
  CPFR process, 105–106
  data needed, 30–31
  improving accuracy of (*see* launch
    forecast accuracy)
  for a new product (*see* product
    launch decisions)
  profits reclaimed by more accurate
    forecasts and better inventory,
    3–4
  retailers' unwillingness to invest in
    accurate forecasting, 125–126
  top-down versus bottom-up
    forecasting, 210
  at World, 121–122
4R Systems, 95
Freeland, Kevin, 92–93, 122,
  172, 207

Gaffney, Paul, 164
gamma distribution, 72–75, 223–225
Gap, 18
Gaur, Vishal, 19, 26
General Motors, 146, 222
greedy rule, 46–48
grocery industry
  assortment planning, 59–60
  availability of data, 35
  buyers' inability to be correct, 2
  CPFR process, 105–106

labor expenses versus cost
    minimizers, 158
  logic behind carrying slow-moving
    SKUs, 34
  RFID applications, 187
gross margin, 19

Halpin, Jim, 34, 215
Harris Teeter, 24–25
Heijn, Albert, 176
Hewlett-Packard, 116, 122
Hitachi Global Storage Technologies,
  116
Home Depot, 14–15
Honda, 146
Huckman, Rob, 167

I2 Technologies, 204–205, 206
Immelt, Jeffrey, 217
implementing retail strategies
  challenge of skepticism about
    promised improvements, 201
  cultural changes example
    (*see* Arrow Electronics)
  failure to focus on changing
    people's behavior when imple-
    menting new systems, 201
  failure to hire for analytical
    skill, 202
  failure to leverage the available
    information, 200
  getting over the tedium of
    analytics, 203
  hesitancy to use cross-functional
    collaboration, 202–203
  limits of tactical changes, 209
  possibility that broad
    organizational changes may be
    required, 202

implementing retail strategies
(*continued*)
principles for tactical implementation (*see* tactical implementation
of retail strategies)
structural changes that may be
needed, 209–210
top-down versus bottom-up
forecasting, 210
incentives for goal alignment
acknowledging existence of
misaligned incentives, 147
bad incentives' impact on sales and
profits, 142
consequences of failure to recognize the value of reputation, 146
contract-based solutions to
incentive problems, 139–142
distribution and supply chain
incentives that inhibit
profitability, 131–132
hidden incentives in cost-plus
contracts, 143–144
identifying the root of a
misalignment, 147
information-based solutions to
incentive problems, 142–144
metrics use to reward desired
behavior, 139–142
misaligned incentives hurting
business example, 134
misalignment from unforeseen
consequences of actions,
143–144
overcoming goal incongruence,
148–149
principal-agent theory
(*see* principal-agent theory)
principles of, 147–149
profit loss due to differing
incentives, 133

trust- or reputation-based
solutions to incentive
problems, 145–146
Inditex, 118
information-based solutions to
incentive problems, 142–144
information technology. *See*
technology and retailing
inventory
information used to predict stock
price, 11–14
levels affect on retail valuation,
16–17
relationship to a firm's valuation,
14–15
stock valuations based on
inventory management, 10
turns (*see* inventory turns)
understating of the relationship
between inventory and sales, 15
inventory control best practices,
173–174
"Inventory Record Inaccuracy," 174
inventory turns
analyst's focus on, 25–27
data analysis, 20–22
defined, 17–18
metrics for, 19–20
pooled model results, 22–23
time trends and benchmarks, 23–25

Jansen, Frank, 176
Jos. A. Bank, 16–17
just-in-time (JIT) manufacturing,
173, 174, 175

Kanthal, 148
Kaufman, Steve, 211, 221
Kesavan, Saravanan, 15

Kohl's, 166
Krishnan, Jayanth, 152
Kroger Company, 18
Kurt Salmon Associates (KSA), 3

launch forecast accuracy
    problems from clustering based on
        attributes, 87–88
    problems with using "average"
        stores as a predictor, 86–88
    referencing products from prior
        seasons, 85
    test sales data use, 85–88,
        225–227
    updating forecasts based on early
        sales, 88–90, 227–228
law of large numbers (averages), 50
Li & Fung, 145–146
Liker, Jeffrey, 146
L.L.Bean, 29
Louagie, Jan, 176

MAD (mean absolute deviation), 65
marginal productivity, 33
marginal profitability analysis,
    75–76
marginal return on incremental
    resources, 32–33
markdowns
    in calculation of cost of forecast
        errors, 67–72
    and consolidation used to clear out
        inventory, 97
    in determination of optimal buy
        quantity, 75
    inventory levels and, 14, 16
    optimization, 97–100
    optimization using price testing,
        100–103

order point determination and, 93
    position in product lifecycle
        planning, 63
    rise in quantity of, 2–3
    taking into account to reduce
        forecast error, 89
markup, 19, 24
Matthias, Dan and Rebecca, 129
McDonald's, 116
mean absolute deviation (MAD), 65
Men's Wearhouse, 16, 17
METRO Group, 187, 189
mystery shoppers, 138

Nardelli, Bob, 14
National Bicycle
    accommodation of variation in
        demand, 112
    cost of customization, 116–117
    customization process, 109–110
    decouple point, 114–115
    lead time components,
        108–109
    mass production supply chain,
        107–108
    offering of product versions, 112
    process for setting the custom lead
        time, 113
    reductions in lead times,
        112–113
    sales losses due to inventory
        management, 109
    small quantity production
        efficiencies, 111
National Retail Federation, 2
Nechleba, Jiri, 95
Netessine, Serguei, 152
Nike, 128
Nine West, 210
Norwalk Furniture, 137–138

observability as a contractible element, 137–138
Ohno, Taiichi, 179
Old Navy, 210
opportunity cost, 67
optimization technology, 191–192
order point, 92
Ortega, Amancio, 118
Owens and Minor (O&M), 143

personal shopping assistants, 187
PetSmart, 166
phantom products and stockouts, 174–175
Poisson distribution, 178
pooled model for inventory, 22–23
price testing, 100–103
principal-agent theory
    enforceability as a contractible element, 138–139
    observability as a contractible element, 137–138
    principle that incentive design requires an understanding of operations, 136
    principle that incentives exist to influence behavior, 135
    principle that there are underlying causes for incentive misalignment, 136–139
    uncontractible defined, 137
    verifiability as a contractible element, 138
Prius, 172
product launch decisions
    actual versus forecast demand calculations, 65–66
    cost of forecast errors, 66–70
    cutting the cost of errors, 70

    determining an initial buy amount, 78–81
    early sales used to improve accuracy, 76–77
    financial evaluation of different strategies, 67–70
    finding an optimal hedge, 70–72
    forecast deliberations, 64–65
    gamma distribution used to find optimal buy quantities, 72–75, 223–225
    marginal profitability analysis to find optimal buy quantities, 75–76
    order lead time considerations, 63–64
    replenishment decisions (*see* stockouts)
    revising data based on reduced lead time, 82, 83
    summary, 84–85
    updated forecasts used for a second buy decision, 81–82
product lifecycle planning
    categories of, 63
    forecasting sales, 62–63
    launch forecast accuracy improvement (*see* launch forecast accuracy)
    life stages of a product, 62
    markdown optimization, 97–100
    markdown optimization using price testing, 100–103
    markdowns and consolidation used to clear out inventory, 97
    new product launch decisions (*see* product launch decisions)
    summary, 103
Project Gemini (Best Buy), 122

radio frequency identification.
   See RFID
RadioShack Corporation, 18, 19
Raman, Ananth, 20, 174
relative sales per title (RST), 32
reputation-based solutions to
   incentive problems, 145–146
retailing
   adopting an investor's perspective
      (*see* retail valuation)
   aggregate demand uncertainty
      versus mix uncertainty,
      219–220
   assessing inventory levels
      (*see* inventory turns)
   buyers' inability to be correct,
      1–2
   complexities of buying decisions,
      4–6
   current state of the sector, 1
   discrepancy between what
      retailers stock and what
      customers want, 2
   excess inventory problem for
      retailers, 2–3
   fixed costs issues, 3
   lifecycle of, 7
   operational execution improve-
      ment focus, 221–222
   predictions for in light of current
      economic crisis, 216–218
   product availability attention
      importance, 220–221
   profits reclaimed by more
      accurate forecasts and better
      inventory, 3–4
   strategies implementation (*see*
      implementing retail strategies)
   technological risk in (*see*
      technology and retailing)
retail-ready packaging, 136

retail valuation
   inventory information used to
      predict stock price, 11–14
   inventory levels affect on, 16–17
   inventory levels' relationship to a
      firm's valuation, 14–15
   inventory turns (*see* inventory
      turns)
   steps for managers to take, 27
   stock valuations based on
      inventory management, 10
   understating of the relationship
      between inventory and sales, 15
RFID (radio frequency identification)
   applications inside retailing,
      186–187
   applications outside retailing,
      182, 185
   cost and frequency availability
      issues, 184–185
   current limits to compelling
      financial returns, 190
   indications of a decrease in
      stockouts with use, 188–189
   passive versus active tags, 182–183
   pilot studies in retailing, 187–190
   recommendations for, 197–198
   serial numbers and, 183–184
   viewed as an investment or as a call
      option, 196
RST (relative sales per title), 32
Ruddick Corporation, 24–25

sales-capture rate, 92–93
sales surprise, 20
Saucony, 9
Scheihing, Betty Jane, 211, 212
Senk, Glen, 31
service level, 18
Sharma, Ken, 204–205

shelf-ready packaging, 136
shrink, 139
Sidhu, Sanjiv, 204–205
snack cake assortment planning
  benefits of localization, 54–55
  computing estimates of demand,
    43, 44, 45
  estimating demand for flavors not
    offered, 39–40
  estimating likelihood of
    substitution, 40–42
  finding an optimal assortment,
    46–48
  sales data, 38, 39
Sport Obermeyer, 116, 145
staffing levels impact on sales
  achieving balance between over-
    and under-investment, 165
  cheapest ways to increase quantity
    of store labor, 165–166
  considerations for setting staffing
    levels, 162
  diminishing returns from increased
    staffing, 160–161
  example process at Best Buy,
    163–164
  identifying metrics for
    evaluating store performance,
    166–167
  labor expenses versus cost
    minimizers, 158–159
  link between revenue results and
    staff quantity and quality, 164
  payroll and, 154–156
  providing training to improve the
    customers' experience, 165
  sales increases per dollar of payroll,
    160, 161–162
Staples, 165, 166
statistical process control charts, 173,
  176–178

stockouts
  applying Toyota Production
    System to a retail store (*see*
    Toyota Production System)
  assortment planning and, 59
  best practices for inventory
    control, 173–174
  causes of at Best Buy, 172
  causes of inventory discrepancies,
    170–172
  challenge of accurately tracking
    inventory, 167–170
  customers' response to, 93
  determining an optimal order
    point, 93–95
  finding the trade-off between
    carrying costs and lost sales,
    91–93
  phantom products and, 171, 175
  reducing with the right assortment
    (*see* assortment planning)
  stocking related to sales, 156
  system application results example,
    95–97
  tracking with RFID, 188–189
store-level execution
  applying Toyota Production
    System to a retail store
    (*see* Toyota Production System)
  associates' knowledge related to
    customer satisfaction, 156
  best practices for inventory
    control, 173–174
  causes of inventory discrepancies,
    170–172
  challenge of accurately tracking
    inventory, 167–170
  managerial metrics' impact on
    sales, 154
  staffing levels and (*see* staffing
    levels impact on sales)

stocking's relation to sales, 156
survey questions asked of
customers, 153–154, 157
sunk cost, 97
suppliers
contractible elements of the
relationship, 137–139
goal alignment through incentives
(*see* incentives for goal alignment)
partnering with for better
inventory control, 122–123
reliance on trust with, 145
supply chain flexibility
balancing forecasts, flexibility, and
inventory, 127–129
company examples (*see*
World; Zara)
cost of flexibility, 116–117
CPFR, 105–106
decouple point used to enable,
115–116
Destination Maternity's process,
106, 129
inflexible chain example (*see*
National Bicycle)
lead time differences example,
106–107
lead-time mapping, 122–123
need for trust in the chain, 124–125
partnering with suppliers, 122–123
push and pull boundary, 114–115
tendency to accept savings over
flexibility, 123–124
unwillingness to invest in accurate
forecasting, 125–126

tactical implementation of retail
strategies
achieve buy-in from users at all
levels, 204–205
aim for quick wins, 207–208
quantify the benefits, 206–207
start with a mundane task, 208
technology and retailing
factoring costs and benefits of
implementation, 194–195
importance of integrating technology with operations, 192–194
late-adopter risks, 196–197
optimization complications,
191–192
recommendations, 197–198
reliance on for inventory
management, 19–20
requirement to understand key
details, 191–192
retailers' failure to use the data they
have, 4
RFID (*see* RFID)
stages of technology integration, 194
treating adoption as an investment
or as a call option, 195–196
"10-foot rule" at Wal-Mart, 152
Terai, Hidezo, 119
Timken Company, 204–205
tire assortment planning
benefits of localization, 54–57
brand-warranty combinations, 49
estimating substitution frequency, 49
finding the optimal assortment,
51–53, 54
resulting revenue increase, 57
Ton, Zeynep, 152, 166, 174
Toyota, 146, 222
Toyota Production System, 172
engagement of people in problem
solving, 178
managing inventory to reduce
"phantom products," 174–176
statistical process control charts
used to track inventory, 176–178

trust- or reputation-based solutions
to incentive problems, 145–146
turns retailers, 19
Tweeter, 140–141

Universal Product Code (UPC), 183
Urban Outfitters, 31

Vaidyanathan, Ramnath, 36
verifiability as a contractible
element, 138
video rental industry, 134

Walker, Martin, 216
Wal-Mart
customer service and, 152
focus on inventory turns, 25
pilot study of RFID technology
use, 188–189
Walton, Sam, 152
wealth effect, 26
Weiss, Michael, 2
World
company background, 117
empowerment through design
teams, 119–120
forecasting and inventory
planning, 121–122

integration of design,
merchandising, and production, 122
lead times, 106
production steps allowing
flexibility, 118
program of having suppliers hold
fabric, 125
sales and nonsales data
collection, 120
success from flexibility, 126

Zara
company background, 118
customer engagement practices,
178
empowerment through design
teams, 119–120
integration of design,
merchandising, and
production, 122
lead times, 106
production steps allowing
flexibility, 118
response to market signals, 121
sales and nonsales data
collection, 120
success from flexibility,
126–127
zero balance walk, 178

About the Authors

Marshall Fisher is the UPS Professor of Operations and Information Management at the Wharton School of the University of Pennsylvania and Co-Director of the Fishman-Davidson Center for Service and Operations Management. His research, teaching, and consulting focus on retail and global supply chain management. He is a member of the Harvard Business School Visiting Committee and the National Academy of Engineering, and is a Fellow of the Institute for Operations Research and the Management Sciences, the Production and Operations Management Society, and the Manufacturing and Service Operations Management Society. In 2004, his paper "The Lagrangian Relaxation Method for Solving Integer Programming Problems," published in *Management Science* in 1981, was voted by the Institute for Operations Research and Management Science as one of the ten most influential papers published in that journal's fifty-year history.

Ananth Raman is the UPS Foundation Professor of Business Logistics at the Harvard Business School. His research focuses on supply chain management, retail operations, and the investor's perspective on operations. In addition to his scholarly papers, he has authored over twenty case studies based on real-world operational issues and student notes, which are taught extensively in courses at Harvard and other business schools. He has created and taught numerous courses to MBA students and executives, and serves as an adviser to a number of CEOs.

Professors Fisher and Raman co-direct the Consortium for Operational Excellence in Retailing, a research group that involves academics from numerous universities and leading retailers worldwide, and are cofounders of 4R Systems, Inc., a software and consulting firm that manages inventories for large retailers.